Curriculum

THE TEACHER'S INITIATIVE

Third Edition

John D. McNeil
University of California, Los Angeles

Merrill
Prentice Hall

Upper Saddle River, New Jersey
Columbus, Ohio

Library of Congress Cataloging-in-Publication Data

McNeil, John D.
    Curriculum: the teacher's initiative / John D. McNeil.—3rd ed.
      p. cm.
    Includes bibliographical references and indexes.
    ISBN 0-13-093804-1
    1. Education—United States—Curricula. 2. Curriculum planning—United States.
  I. Title.
  LB1570 .M386 2003
  375′.001—dc21

                                         2002141578

Vice President and Publisher: Jeffery W. Johnston
Executive Editor: Debra A. Stollenwerk
Editorial Assistant: Mary Morrill
Associate Editor: Jessica Crouch
Production Editor: Linda Hillis Bayma
Copyeditor: Laura E. Larson
Design Coordinator: Diane C. Lorenzo
Cover Designer: Debra Warrenfeltz
Cover Image: Artville
Production Manager: Laura Messerly
Director of Marketing: Ann Castel Davis
Marketing Manager: Krista Groshong
Marketing Coordinator: Tyra Cooper

This book was set in Zapf Elliptical by BookMasters, Inc. It was printed and bound by R.R. Donnelley & Sons Company. The cover was printed by Phoenix Color Corp.

Pearson Education Ltd.
Pearson Education Australia Pty. Limited
Pearson Education Singapore Pte. Ltd.
Pearson Education North Asia Ltd.
Pearson Education Canada, Ltd.
Pearson Educación de Mexico, S.A. de C.V.
Pearson Education—Japan
Pearson Education Malaysia Pte. Ltd.
Pearson Education, *Upper Saddle River, New Jersey*

10 9 8 7 6 5 4 3 2 1
ISBN: 0–13–093804–1

Preface

This book is for teachers—beginning, experienced, and teachers of teachers. It is designed to engage readers in understanding curriculum, reflecting on it, and carrying out their own role in its making. The text goes far in reconciling the gap between curriculum as a laid-out body of content and curriculum as enacted by teachers and students. Constructivist pedagogy is a central element throughout the text.

New to This Edition

Unlike former editions, this revised edition gives much attention to the political and social forces impacting the teacher's role—the accountability movement, the profitization of education, changed views of learning, and the influence of technology. Emphasis is given to the need for balancing personal preferences, institutional credibilities, moral and professional responsibilities, and the critical dimensions of curriculum making. The historical antecedents to curriculum issues and practices remain embedded in the text.

Web-based activities are also a new feature of this edition. These featured activities allow the reader to interact with the text, providing additional web-based resources for the reader who wants to pursue a topic in greater depth or to clarify and elaborate on a topic of special interest.

Organization

Curriculum: The Teacher's Initiative, Third Edition, consists of 12 chapters arranged in six parts. Part 1 presents the context of curriculum making, including the efforts of federal, state, and local authorities to control the curriculum. Examples of how teachers can seek and create opportunities for curriculum making both beyond and within official parameters are described.

Part 2 focuses on learners as most important in deciding what should be taught as well as how learning best occurs. This part features teachers who give voice to students by putting students at the center of curriculum and drawing on knowledge of human development and activity theories of learning.

Part 3 emphasizes the importance of relating curriculum to world and local situations. This part highlights teachers whose curricula improve the quality of life in different social contexts. A distinction is made between those who adapt to changed circumstances and those who initiate changes.

Part 4 offers perspectives on the subject matters taught in schools. This part is designed to stimulate readers' thinking about beliefs regarding particular school subjects, to identify what is central in a given field, and to recognize how knowledge is socially determined rather than eternally fixed. Curriculum standards and efforts at ending "wars" in math, reading, and other areas are described. Part 4 shows many ways teachers have interpreted the academic fields and transformed them to meet changed social needs and influences.

Part 5 is for teachers designing plans for instruction and arranging learning opportunities consistent with constructivism and social reconstruction. Assessment from these viewpoints is treated as well.

Part 6 addresses questions about the selection and use of curriculum materials—technologies and texts. The content of this part consists of information for both teachers who will perform as autonomous consumers and those who will develop curriculum materials. It serves both cases by showing how teachers adapt materials to their particular teaching situations and enrich existing materials.

Viewpoint

There are two worlds of curriculum. One is the rhetorical world in which members of commissions, boards of education, heads of government, and others give their answers to what should be taught and how. The rhetorical world also includes business leaders, politicians, and academics with single-minded views about what teachers should do. Curriculum reform, policy statements, goals, frameworks, mandates, standards, and other features of school restructuring are associated with this world. The other curriculum world is the experiential world in which the teacher and students enact curriculum and pursue their goals, constructing knowledge and meanings in the process. This book deals directly with both worlds—the rhetorical world of curriculum revealing the special interests underlying efforts to control the curriculum and the experiential world in which students and teachers decide what to learn and how.

Curriculum: The Teacher's Initiative falls in the genre for texts of possibility. It describes the curriculum work of more than 50 teachers to illustrate what is possible when teachers undertake curricular initiatives in the interest of human betterment. Examples from both present and distant elementary and secondary school teachers and their curricula are included, not as examples to be copied but as sources for stimulating fresh thinking about the curriculum initiatives the reader may want to take.

It is a "readerly" text in that it tries to convey a message about the influence of constructivist pedagogy upon curriculum. It is a "writerly" text in that it expects readers to rewrite parts, giving their own interpretations, finding omissions and contradictions, and, more important, giving their own ideas on how they would initiate curriculum with their students.

Acknowledgments

I appreciate very much the guidance given in developing and producing the book by the editors at Merrill/Prentice Hall, particularly Debra A. Stollenwerk, executive editor; Jessica Crouch, associate editor; Linda Hillis Bayma, production editor; and Laura E. Larson, copyeditor. The great assistance of Mary Ellen McNeil in all aspects of writing and producing the text is also gratefully acknowledged.

I would also like to express my appreciation to the reviewers of this book: Harriet Arnold, University of the Pacific; Benita Cahalane, Mississippi State University; Janice Jackson, Boston College; Jann James, Taylor Road Academy; and Andrea Maxie, California State University, Los Angeles.

Discover the Companion Website Accompanying This Book

The Prentice Hall Companion Website:
A Virtual Learning Environment

Technology is a constantly growing and changing aspect of our field that is creating a need for content and resources. To address this emerging need, Prentice Hall has developed an online learning environment for students and professors alike—Companion Websites—to support our textbooks.

In creating a Companion Website, our goal is to build on and enhance what the textbook already offers. For this reason, the content for each user-friendly website is organized by topic and provides the professor and student with a variety of meaningful resources. Common features of a Companion Website include:

For the Professor—

Every Companion Website integrates **Syllabus Manager**™, an online syllabus creation and management utility.

- **Syllabus Manager**™ provides you, the instructor, with an easy, step-by-step process to create and revise syllabi, with direct links into Companion Website and other online content without having to learn HTML.

- Students may log on to your syllabus during any study session. All they need to know is the web address for the Companion Website and the password you've assigned to your syllabus.

- After you have created a syllabus using **Syllabus Manager**™, students may enter the syllabus for their course section from any point in the Companion Website.

- Clicking on a date, the student is shown the list of activities for the assignment. The activities for each assignment are linked directly to actual content, saving time for students.

- Adding assignments consists of clicking on the desired due date, then filling in the details of the assignment—name of the assignment, instructions, and whether it is a one-time or repeating assignment.

- In addition, links to other activities can be created easily. If the activity is online, a URL can be entered in the space provided, and it will be linked automatically in the final syllabus.

- Your completed syllabus is hosted on our servers, allowing convenient updates from any computer on the Internet. Changes you make to your syllabus are immediately available to your students at their next logon.

For the Student—

- **Topic Overviews**—outline key concepts in topic areas

- **Web Links**—a wide range of websites that provide useful and current information related to each topic area

- **Lesson Plans**—links to lesson plans for appropriate topic areas

- **Projects on the Web**—links to projects and activities on the web for appropriate topic areas

- **Education Resources**—links to schools, online journals, government sites, departments of education, professional organizations, regional information, and more

- **Electronic Bluebook**—send homework or essays directly to your instructor's email with this paperless form

- **Message Board**—serves as a virtual bulletin board to post—or respond to—questions or comments to/from a national audience

- **Chat**—real-time chat with anyone who is using the text anywhere in the country—ideal for discussion and study groups, class projects, etc.

To take advantage of these and other resources, please visit the *Curriculum: The Teacher's Initiative,* Third Edition, Companion Website at

www.prenhall.com/mcneil

Brief Contents

Contents

PART 2
Giving Voice to Students   37

PART 3
Labyrinth of Curriculum Relevance   89

PART 5
Creating Curriculum in the Classroom   187

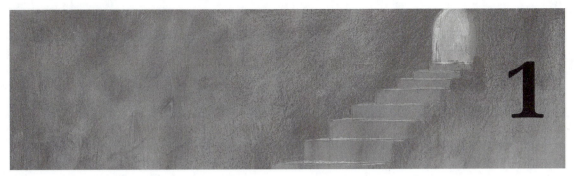

1

The Contexts of Curriculum Making

Part 1 begins with curriculum in the context of the school as an institution, describing the interests that teachers confront when they and their students create curriculum. The second chapter deals with the whirlwind of political and economic forces of reform that buffets teachers and students and threatens to sweep away curriculum—an idea that became a thing.

CHAPTER **1**

WHO MAKES CURRICULUM? ROLES AND LEVELS OF DECISION MAKING

Merl: Teachers make curriculum? Ridiculous! Students, frameworks, courses of study, and textbooks determine what is to be taught, learned, and tested.

Sara: Well, I make curriculum by giving my students opportunities to envision the possible lives they want to live and the people they want to be.

One can infer that Merl is a realist. He knows that in the United States today policymakers at all levels—national, state, and school district—are prescribing particular goals, content, and programs in response to economic, social, and political interests. Or perhaps Merl is an insecure teacher who doesn't want the responsibility for making decisions about what and how to teach. He might see his role as similar to the military instructor who is given a training manual and expected to follow its instructional procedures with little deviation. Merl is unlikely to individualize his curriculum for particular learners or the local community.

And Sara? It's clear she believes, as did the philosopher Jean-Jacques Rousseau, that "a child is not a vessel to be filled, but a flame to be ignited." In her curriculum we would expect to find less transmission of knowledge and more emphasis on the learner seeking knowledge of personal worth and extending what is taught through application and creativity. She is likely to be concerned with the development of the "whole person," not just achievement in a subject or skill. Indeed, her curriculum would take into account a wide expanse of time, connecting the learner's past and present to a distant future. In assessing the question "What do you teach?" Sara probably would reply, "I don't know; I haven't met my students yet."

Merl and Sara are entering an ongoing conversation about the role of teachers in curriculum making. As reported by Shoemaker (2001), Harold Rugg, an influential curriculum developer, said nearly 75 years ago, "The day is past in which a single individual—be he professor, teacher, administrator, psychologist, sociologist, or researcher of what ever brand—can encompass all of these [curriculummaking] tasks singlehanded" (p. 21). In his construction of curriculum, Rugg placed teachers alongside the curriculum expert but not in place of the expert.

Companion
Website

Donna Moffett had given up her career as a legal secretary to teach first graders in one of New York's most woebegone schools but without any training in teaching or curriculum. The *New York Times* published an account of Ms. Moffett's first year of teaching that brought many responses from readers. The account is a good illustration of a nurturing curriculum. If you want to read about Ms. Moffett's sentimental journey as well as her experiences with relating to colleagues in the school and her efforts to comply with the school's standards—back to basics curriculum—go to *www.prenhall.com/mcneil* and click on Moffett. After reading the piece, decide whether Ms. Moffett is a good teacher with promise and whether her curriculum is one that you would want your child to experience.

In reading this account, we learn of Ms. Moffett's concern of why she couldn't teach Daysha how to sound out words, why she didn't try harder to stop the absenteeism of those who lagged academically, and why her carefully planned lesson fell apart. We also learn that she accomplished some amazing things, such as helping a girl who used to cry for her mother, throw temper tantrums, and run out of the classroom but later said, "I'm not afraid to be here anymore."

He drew from the best minds in all fields and from the thinking of teachers and students.

Certainly the idea of influencing students in a profound way is daunting, yet many teachers, like Mary Baratta-Lorton, are curriculum innovators because they listen to their students and create materials of value to their own classroom and often find their way to the classrooms of others. Baratta-Lorton knew she could develop better curriculum materials for the teaching of math in her kindergarten than the materials that the school district had delivered for her use. And she did, authoring one of the most successful curricula for kindergarten (Baratta-Lorton, 1976).

There is no single answer about the teacher's role in curriculum. Many beginning teachers welcome official courses of study, guidelines, and textbooks with their presentations of topics, concepts, suggested approaches, and instructional activities. Most new teachers haven't the time to develop their own vision of what might occur with unfamiliar students during a week, month, or year or do the planning and marshalling of resources required. Experienced teachers also see value in new curriculum programs and materials from external authorities. They expect that a new curriculum with its rationale, ideas, and suggested activities for students will add to their own knowledge of subject matter and teaching methods, enabling them to find better ways for promoting learning and motivation.

The particular context in which one is teaching has much to do with the teacher's role in curriculum development. By way of example, a school in a multicultural neighborhood may want to dialogue with students and others about the kind of alternative curriculum that will better serve their diverse community.

Also, magnet and charter schools need new curricula to extend their chosen themes—science, technology, the arts, or other—in ways that not only permit deeper study of an area of emphasis but allow students to reach out to other disciplines and ways of knowing, broadening their experiences while pursuing their specialty in depth. Teachers of those with special needs and talents—physical, emotional, intellectual—develop curriculum for their particular population of learners.

Some of the best curricular innovations, such as units, projects, and investigations, are developed by teachers from their own passion or expertise, be it photography, animal study, genealogy, mystery writing, investing, quilting—the possibilities are endless. Also, teachers and students may generate units of study and activities that address the concerns of learners on issues in the local community. However, success and sustainability of teacher- and student-generated curriculum depends on representing the unit of study as belonging to what the school, parents, and citizens are supposed to teach. For example, if there is a unit dealing with butterflies (how they are structured, how they migrate such long distances, why they are endangered, etc.), it is important that everyone know how this unit of study belongs and contributes to what people expect the school to teach—math, science, literacy, and so on—teachers should ask two questions: "Is the topic for this unit important in its own right?" and "Will the study of X present opportunities for students to learn more effectively the basic educational skills and academic subjects that have legitimacy in the school?" A failure to label the study so that its connection to the school's mission is unclear may threaten the legitimacy of the school and preclude survival of the innovation.

CURRICULUM IS TIED TO SCHOOLING

The teachers' role and the concept of curriculum have changed. In medieval times, there was teaching and learning but no curriculum. Students at universities such as Paris and Bologna learned what they pleased as various teachers came and went. Students attended as they chose to do and had no idea of "following a curriculum" (Reid, 1999).

Also, before the United States became a nation, individuals gained their education from whatever source was available—home, work, church, mentors. Instead of a fixed notion of what to study, at what age, or in what order, one acquired the knowledge that was offered from any source. In the 19th century, as U.S. society changed in the direction of nationalism and industry and commerce grew, schools as institutions were created with the power to determine what would count as an academic program, who could acquire the knowledge offered by the school, and the sequence for learning particular subjects. This power was backed by political and legal authorities, although the school and teachers quickly found out that the subjects taught and how they were taught could not depart very far from what the local communities and the general public expected. For a contemporary example, consider what would happen today if a teacher selects for serious study a topic such as graffiti, drawing on social psychological resources, knowledge of culture, and issues about artistic expression. If the media treat the topic as both frivolous and unworthy and a public reaction ensues, the school authorities will take action to preserve the institution's standing at all costs.

To contrast what could be learned, how, and when, as opposed to the older view of education shaped to individual circumstances in which, for example, one could have firsthand access to original authors for individual study and pursuit of knowledge, schools introduced new organizational features, many of which were made possible by the invention of the textbook. The textbook promoted the learner's dependency on a teacher for uniform course content, standardized courses of study, and learning sequences, as well as prerequisite subjects and the arrangement of knowledge on a continuum with scope and sequence by grade level. Textbooks contributed to the introduction of age-graded classrooms, tests, examinations, and report cards.

Before long, other organizational features of schools were introduced, including promotion policies and attendance records. The idea was that upon completing the continuum of the courses of study that made up a school's program (the curriculum), students could be awarded a diploma or degree. An embedded curriculum is central to what makes a school and what counts as education. Until recently, we never thought of curriculum as what is taught and modeled in the educational forms—media (especially TV, the Internet, and films), youth clubs, libraries, churches, homes—although these sources shape our identities.

Justifications for institutionalizing curriculum were the same as those for establishing the school:

- The knowledge taught will enable learners to contribute to the quality of life in the community. Public interests will be served before the interests of the individual.

- What is taught is unlikely to be acquired elsewhere. The curriculum will allow students to get beyond the limitations of local influences.

- The curriculum will simplify and manipulate events in a way to reveal patterns that are not otherwise obvious.

- The curriculum can present ideals for conduct and culture.

- The classroom will be a safe environment for examining ideas without real-world responsibility for the consequences of enactments.

- The planned sequence of instruction will have a cumulative effect on learning.

- The disciplines that are taught are organized for effective learning, connecting facts, concepts, values, and methods for understanding a subject.

- A common body of knowledge can be taught that will serve the nation's need for allegiance to principles of democracy and its institutions as well as appreciation for the national heritage.

CURRICULUM AS EXPERIENCES

In the 1920s and 1930s, the idea of curriculum as subject matter set out to be learned was challenged by the view that curriculum was a series of experiences or activities that are vital to the learner and lead to the development of understanding and attitudes helpful in meeting and controlling life situations. Accordingly, the teacher's role in curriculum was to provide learning opportunities for students in and out of school. The primary task of the teacher was to manipulate the classroom environment so that students would have educational experiences, directing and guiding learning by engaging students in meaningful problem-solving situations.

In practice, many teachers planned for such experiences by drawing on local resources (e.g., transportation, employment, food and water supply, conservation of resources). These activities were coordinated with a scope and sequence outline of the content by grade level. Regions often differed in their listing of what was to be taught, specifying a particular topic, such as in history (the California missions) or mathematics (Iowa's bushels, pecks, and rods). Teachers either followed the fixed curriculum or put the document on the shelf. The textbook became the curriculum for most teachers, although "progressive" teachers created units of instruction that took into account concerns and interests of their learners and engaged them in a range of activities that might change their comprehension and outlooks.

Today's teachers have given up much of their freedom to teach whatever they want in return for the advantages of the school's institutional support—a paycheck, instructional resources, facilities, access to students, and status derived from the school's prestige.

Although powerful forces are trying to maintain a common standardized curriculum for all, "the genie is out of the bottle." Evidence of curricular fragmentation is everywhere. In some ways, society is going back to the earlier period when people could learn what they wanted to learn from any source at any time. Activity 1–1, "Imagineering the Curriculum," illustrates the breakup of the fixed curriculum and offers you a chance to reflect on the consequences of alternative schooling and curriculum.

SOCIAL UNREST AND CURRICULUM FRAGMENTATION

In the 1960s and 1970s, schools and curriculum were in disarray because of the social unrest of the period associated with the civil rights movement and responses to the Vietnam War. Teachers and students challenged authority. Many alternative schools were created—"storefront" schools that might teach what racial and ethnic groups had been denied (e.g., black history); "schools on wheels" that carried students to theaters, laboratories, factories, and the like for the purpose of broadening experiences (exploration) and giving students a better sense of what they might want to do with their lives.

New organizational elements were introduced: block and flexible schedules, team teaching, pass-fail grading, classrooms "without walls," increased electives,

◼ ── ◼

ACTIVITY 1–1   IMAGINEERING THE CURRICULUM

Glimes (2001) creates educational futures through "imagineering"—imagining, inventing, and implementing futures without schools and without the traditional courses characterized by "scope and sequences." Here is a laundry list of changes occurring now that challenge the ideas of a common school and a fixed curriculum to be pursued in a given order and time within the confines of a school.

1. Look at the list and add additional changes of your own.
2. Imagine the consequences, including the idea of curriculum, if these changes gain acceptance.

Alternative Schooling for Everyone

Home schooling

Charter schools

Magnet schools

Tutoring

Self-selected centers and sites

Private for-profit schools

Nonprofit schools

Training by corporations

Out-of-School Experiences

Internships

Fieldwork

Independent study

Overseas experience

Technology

Chat rooms and investigations with people in other places

Learning directly from experts

Getting information when needed from any source (i.e., just-in-time delivery)

Variety of courses and programs through distance education

ACTIVITY 1–1   *continued*

Validation

Performance instead of seat work

Portfolios, not letter grades

Life experiences count

Organizational Change

Daily attendance optional

No fixed schedule

Students create own study paths

No required courses

Outsiders enter the classroom as resource people

No grouping by age or gender

Peer coaching replaces whole-class instruction

---

modules rather than semester-long courses. Teachers developed curriculum plans that introduced nontraditional topics and called for new content and ways of learning. Reading and writing, math, science, and history were taught in the contexts of addressing social issues—the environment, racism, feminism, and much more. Content was drawn from popular culture such as films, music, and cartoons, and students asked, "Whose interests are being served by this entertainment?" "What texts are hidden in the media?" Authentic and primary source materials replaced or supplemented the textbook. Teachers encouraged more class discussion, used the Socratic method, held "teach-ins," and invited outsiders to tell their stories and to bring their cultures to the classroom.

A reaction from the dominant culture was not slow in coming. The secondary curriculum was likened to a smorgasbord, belittling schools that tried to be "relevant." With support from the U.S. Office of Education, the National Commission on Excellence in Education (NCEE) issued *A Nation at Risk: The Imperatives for Educational Reform* in 1983. This report warned that what was going on in schools and curriculum constituted "a rising tide of mediocrity." Indeed, it blamed schools for the United States' failure to compete economically with Japan and to score as well on achievement tests as other industrialized nations. The report launched a reform labeled "The Excellence Movement," which is described in the next chapter.

The cultural wars were part of the reactions to curricular fragmentation and the replacement of many literary texts with multicultural sources (Cheney, 1987). The goals and content for teaching history were especially controversial with conservatives who attacked historical revisions that had introduced the lives and stories of everyday people in historical periods and offered more critical interpretations of historical events (Ravitch, 1978).

CURRICULUM FROM DIFFERENT VANTAGE POINTS

The meaning of curriculum depends on one's position and role. For policymakers, the curriculum goals are the body of educational offerings that should be available to different populations of students and schools. Today's policymakers think of curriculum as the standards to be achieved by students and the assessments to indicate attainment of the students. Publishers and specialists in the academic field view curriculum as packages of instructional material, including texts and software with learning activities and items for teaching and learning.

In the schools themselves, administrators regard curriculum as the school's educational program—areas of study, courses, and the planned activities offered by the school (athletics, drama, clubs, etc.). For teachers, curriculum is what they hope students will acquire or their expectations about the kind of persons students might become, together with the short- and long-range plans involving activities and resources that may be used in realizing these hopes. If asked, students might say that curriculum is what they have to do (assignments, activities). Perhaps a few would say that curriculum is whatever meanings they are constructing from their classroom experiences.

Curriculum scholars see curriculum as a field that studies the philosophical, political, and technical processes for determining what and how to teach. For example, they are interested in the issue of whether the school and its offerings should and do foster cultural reproduction or should and do promote social transformation.

LEVELS OF CURRICULUM PLANNING

Hierarchical models relegate certain curriculum planning decisions to levels. Table 1–1 shows one scheme adapted from a model by Romberg and Price (1999).

As presented in the table, at the design level curriculum is seen as the goals and outline of the content. A rationale for decisions is included. Although the main topics are mentioned, instructional approaches are usually not addressed.

At the blueprint level, planners take the broad outline of content and make a detailed listing of what is to be "covered" or taught, what order is to be followed, and what resources can be used to achieve the intended learning. The curriculum becomes a set of specifications, but the interactions that are to take place are not stipulated. A textbook or a textbook series is an example of curriculum at this level.

At the level of concrete interpretations, the planners go beyond specifications of materials and uses to detail what is to be done and the way it is to be done (teaching methods and other instructional considerations). At this level, the plan organizes the subject matter both sequentially and in relation to other subject matters. In many schools teachers and parents may collaborate in revising and proposing the plans so that the cultures of home and school are bridged and there is greater support for classroom undertakings.

TABLE 1–1
Educational planners

Level	Planners	Nature of Plan
Design	National/state committees	Goals; specified needs and priorities
Blueprint	Publishers and curriculum groups	Packages of curriculum materials; software
Concrete interpretations	Local curriculum committees	Guidelines for teachers Sequencing of topics Grouping of students
Utilization	Teacher or instructional team; students	Lessons; units; projects Short- and long-range plans

The utilization level involves the actual interactions of students and teachers. The curriculum becomes the planning, enactment, and learning that take place. It involves the setting of purposes, goals, and the posing of questions, determining what students already know, what knowledge is needed, and deciding how the needed knowledge can best be obtained. This is the level where students participate in the planning and revising of a plan, and as they engage in carrying out that plan, they learn and construct personal meanings from the experience.

Everyone knows more about curriculum than they realize. Individuals frequently consider how learning and opportunities to learn have affected their lives; when two or three share their concerns about what should be taught and for what purposes, they are engaging in curriculum as discourse, which is fundamental to all curricular decisions. Activity 1–2, "Generating Questions about Curriculum," is an opportunity for you to share your curriculum views and to gain new insights from your peers.

CONFLICTING INTERESTS IN CURRICULUM

There are conflicts among the planners at different levels. Reid (1999) attributes curriculum conflict to a variety of interests and notions about what purposes the curriculum should serve. He categorizes four major interests that need reconciliation: personal, professional, organizational, and critical.

Personal interests   The personal interest is what an individual administrator, teacher, parent, student, and others want from the curriculum. Often conflicts arise between personal preferences and the professional and organizational interests. In her classic study of contributions of control, McNeil (1986) documents how the personal interests of administrators are affected by the pressures placed by external forces on the school. She also describes how administrators, in acting on their own individual interests or maintaining a particular image for the school, try to control teachers. In so doing, they inhibit learning.

■ ━━━ ■

ACTIVITY 1–2   GENERATING QUESTIONS
ABOUT CURRICULUM

Break into groups of three to five students, and come up with at least three questions about curriculum. The questions may be related to concerns about what makes one curriculum better than another or the kind of a curriculum needed to meet present or future needs (international, diversity, technology, social justice, etc.). You may have questions about whether school curricula are necessary when competency can be gained without credentials and students have access to knowledge and information from worldwide sources. Perhaps you are concerned with curriculum for those with special needs or those in unique situations.

Share your group's questions with others in the class. Record the questions and keep them in mind as you read this text. These questions can guide your reading of the text, making it more relevant for your purposes.

■ ━━━ ■

Professional interests   The professional interests of teachers rest on the teacher's professional ethics and ideals for practice as well as the ability to put knowledge of how learning takes place into practice. The professional knowledge of teachers often conflicts with the school's organizational interests as expressed in aims, regulations, schedules, and so forth. The organizational interests may prevent teachers from carrying out their moral responsibilities to students and exercising their professional judgments.

Organizational interests   Organizational interests promote and preserve what official boards of education want to maintain and their desire for continuity and predictability of the school as an institution. On the other hand, organizational interests may provide the resources for new initiatives from teachers to be translated into action.

Critical interests   Critical interests are present when a group or individual challenges the legitimacy or effectiveness of the curriculum. This interest may be voiced both from within the school by students and teachers and by outsiders (parents, citizens, politicians). A critical interest helps identify deficiencies in the curriculum and initiate changes. One can see that tensions exist between those acting on a critical interest and those with an organizational interest who want to preserve the curriculum with little or no interference.

LIVE AND DEAD CURRICULA

Curriculum as policy, standards, and guidelines and as instructional materials and tests can influence both teachers and students. However, unless enacted, such curriculum is inert—a dead curriculum. Indeed, the scope and sequence listing of content allocated to grade levels has been likened to a skeleton, and

Spanish speakers sometimes contrast it to such experiences in the classroom by saying, "Muchos huesos y poca carne" (A lot of bones and little meat). Conversely, the live curriculum is when teachers and students engage in classroom activities that they find meaningful.

The curriculum message students get from the teacher and the meanings they construct from their school experiences often have more to do with how teachers go about their work than what it is that they are teaching. Teachers can create new values even when hindered in the will to innovate. For example, a teacher noticed that his students lacked motivation for real learning. They were more interested in getting a good grade on tests than learning something that mattered to them personally. They would guess what would be on the test or what the teacher wanted. Students had been indoctrinated to believe that the only evidence of learning that counted is the judgment of an external authority, such as the teacher. Hence, the teacher decided to "change the rules" to promote real learning by giving students responsibility for their learning. New rules included the following:

1. Let students set their own learning objectives and help them see whether they are achieving the objectives by writing essays about their progress and by bringing in material such as a journal entry describing their achievements and mistakes.
2. Give out the final exam questions in advance so students are clear about the objectives and what is wanted on the exam. (This practice makes cheating a thing of the past.)

WHOSE INTERESTS ARE SERVED?

The first time a person sees a dead curriculum or framework, he or she is likely to be surprised by the number of parts that are assumed to constitute a whole or contribute to an educational purpose. Most curriculum frameworks are composed of an extensive listing of content and skills by grade level and are related to a particular school subject or area of study. One can easily get mental indigestion by viewing the number of decontextualized items that are to be related to some concept, value, principle, object, or theory and be daunted by how best to connect these items to each other and to the existing schemata of individual learners.

There are differences among frameworks: Some are more detailed than others. Some reflect a compromise among scholars, while other frameworks promote a partisan view of the discipline. There are frameworks oriented to a single subject and frameworks that promote an integration of subject matters.

Frameworks are political documents implying a view of what should count as knowledge, expectations for the intended student population, and assumptions about how people learn.

Frameworks can be analyzed to show whether they are promoting a conservative position, such as transmitting traditional values and heritage or contributing to a critical view of knowledge and society by fostering inquiry and the need for social transformation.

Frameworks differ in whether they support local, national, or world interests and in their focus on general or specialized education. Frameworks for basic education seldom offer academically rigorous study and serve the interest of government rather than the individual or the academic community. Frameworks may be adapted to the socioeconomic backgrounds of the intended students.

Chapter 2 differentiates "big" standards that advocate the teaching and understanding of powerful ideas to all learners, as opposed to the "little" standards that reflect political consensus and the coverage of inert information.

SUMMARY

Curriculum has many meanings depending on social changes and the vantage points of those making curricular decisions. Although there has always been teaching without schools and learning without teaching, it is difficult to imagine a school without a curriculum.

The idea of curriculum as fixed subject matter set out to be learned came with the establishment of the school as an institution, challenging older forms of education in which the individual learned from any available source. Nationalism and the growth of industry and commerce are associated with the evolution of public schools and curriculum. Numerous arguments were made for their establishment, mostly stating how the public would benefit and how learning could be made more effective by the systematic organization of subject matter.

Companion
Website

An example of a dead curriculum can be found at *www.prenhall.com/mcneil*. Select Enter, then Topic 1: Curriculum, click on Web Links, then select Outlines and Guides. Look at the Virginia Department of Education Standards of Learning and Resources for Their Implementation. The document is a review of the K–12 curriculum of Virginia. Look at one of the standards of learning sample scope and sequence guides in a field like English, math, or science (e.g., earth science). Consider the following questions: What value or benefit do you see in this curriculum? Whose interests are served? Would the curriculum help in planning a program? What views of learning, teaching, and the purpose of schooling are implied?

A live curriculum is depicted in "The Old Man and the Sea," a lesson plan with activities that can be accessed at *www.prenhall.com/mcneil*. Select Enter, then Topic 7: Instructional Strategies, then select Lesson Plans, then Middle School, then "The Old Man and the Sea." What interests are served by this curriculum (personal, professional, organizational, critical)? Why might some students or parents reject such a curriculum? Where does authority lie in a live curriculum? What preparation is necessary before students can participate effectively in a live curriculum? How could a live curriculum make good use of both cooperation and competition?

The invention of the textbook permitted schools to introduce many organizational features by which the school and its curriculum could control what to learn, where, and for what purpose—standardization of content, sequencing of topics, grouping of students by age, and certification of learning by examination. Accordingly, in the late 1800s and early 1900s, textbooks became the curriculum for many, although the establishment of national commissions, state and local boards of education, and the superintendency led to official outlines of what should be taught, influencing what teachers taught and students learned.

An alternative view of the curriculum was voiced in the 1920s and 1930s. The notion that curriculum consisted of the activities planned by teachers and enacted by students gained support. Teachers saw that by initiating activities that engaged their students, the subject matter could be made more appealing and local concerns addressed. In practice, the hierarchical nature of curriculum making expanded with curriculum decision making at many levels—policy (national, state, district), school, and classroom—with those at each level having a different view of curriculum and their role in it.

During the 1960s and 1970s, in the context of national social unrest, many teachers ignored the official curriculum and defied external authorities by engaging students in activities and subject matter that they considered more personally and socially relevant, promoting critical evaluation of local institutions and introducing popular and diverse cultural contributions into the curriculum.

The dominant culture was quick to respond to the perceived disarray in the schools and the fragmentation of the curriculum. "Cultural wars" ensued over the content to be taught, and a campaign to undermine public confidence in the public schools was launched. Political and economic interests set the stage for school reform, tightening the fixed curriculum by aligning goals, standards, tests, textbooks, and programs for the preparation of teachers. Paradoxically, in the face of efforts to control the curriculum in the name of accountability, alternative forms of education multiplied. Information technology, particularly the Internet, and an increase in school choices are once more serving the purposes of individuals and giving opportunities to learn and teach in a range of places and ways, similar to what occurred in precurriculum historical periods.

Ideally, teachers and those engaged in curriculum decision making will reconcile four interests:

Personal   Consider the preferences of the teacher, students, and others about what to teach and learn.

Professional   The teacher has a moral obligation to students, to society, and to a valid representation of knowledge and committment to act on what is known about how people learn.

Organizational   Be aware of the need to support the school—its legitimacy in the eyes of the public—and to maintain a culture that will enable the school to fulfill its mission.

Critical   These interests entail the importance of identifying and initiating needed changes in the community, school, and classroom that will fulfill the ideals of the larger society.

QUESTIONS FOR DISCUSSION

1. There can be teaching without learning and learning without teaching, but can there be schooling without curriculum? Why not?
2. Must curriculum making at all levels—policy, school, and classroom—imply an intention to change learners in some way?
3. How much of a curriculum plan should be centered on "passing on the best of what is known," and how much should be given to questioning what is known and using what is known in new ways and unique circumstances?
4. Why do once widely taught subjects (e.g., Greek, home economics) vanish from school offerings? What level of decision making has the greatest influence on the subjects and areas of study that most schools offer?
5. The United States is undergoing its greatest effort ever at trying to control what all students must know and attain for education. Conversely, technology and alternatives to schools are making it possible for individuals to gain education for their own purpose anywhere, similar to the conditions before the establishment of schools and curriculum as institutions. How do you think this struggle will play out?
6. Consider a curriculum issue, such as the mandate that algebra should be taught to everyone. How could this issue be resolved to protect (a) the professional interests of teachers who believe that not all can learn algebra (at least as knowledge as it will be tested), (b) the personal interests of students who want to learn something else than algebra, (c) the organizational interest of the school system that wants algebra taught to show the academic rigor of the school, and (d) the critical interests of those who question whether the teaching of algebra should be for status or for a key to admission to higher education or an intellectual tool that is essential in daily living?

REFERENCES

Baratta-Lorton, M. (1976). *Mathematics their way.* Menlo Park, CA: Addison-Wesley.

Cheney, L. (1987). *American memory: A report on the humanities in the nation's public schools.* Washington, DC: National Endowment for the Humanities.

Glimes, D. (2001). Creating educational futures through "imagineering." *Wingspan, 3*(2), 9–15.

McNeil, L. M. (1986). *Contradictions of control: School structure and school knowledge.* New York: Routledge & Kegan Paul.

National Commission on Excellence in Education. (1983). *A nation at risk: The imperatives for educational reform.* Washington, DC: Author.

Ravitch, D. (1978) *The revisionist revised: A critique of the radical attack on the school.* New York: Basic Books.

Reid, W. A. (1999). *Curriculum as institution and practice: Essays in the deliberative tradition.* Mahwah, NJ: Erlbaum.

Romberg, T. A., & Price, G. G. (1999). Curriculum implementation and staff development as cultural change. In J. Rehage (Ed.), *Issues in curriculum* (pp. 201–231). Chicago: University of Chicago Press.

Shoemaker, F. (2001). Curriculum making, models, practices and issues: A knowledge fetish? In L. Corno (Ed.), *Education across a century: The centennial volume* (pp. 1–34). Chicago: University of Chicago Press.

CHAPTER **2**

CURRICULUM IN THE CONTEXT OF SCHOOL REFORM

Merl: What is school reform all about? Are teachers responsible for the competitiveness of the nation's economy? Are we supposed to make sure that all get into college so they can later get prestigious jobs with high pay?

Sara: It does seem as if much of school reform comes down to pressure for high test scores by all, but I doubt many teachers think they can make a country prosperous and ensure that everyone's among the affluent. For me, I'll keep trying to make a difference in the lives of my students by offering them something that will help them shape their lives according to their values and talents.

Sooner or later, most teachers, like Sara and Merl, will begin to question the ever-changing reforms in education. Are reforms in the interest of closing the gap between the rich and poor or to prepare a workforce that will keep the United States competitive? How can teachers best prepare students for both the uncertainty of future employment and opportunities? What should happen when the accountability demands for high test scores conflict with what is known about how students best learn? How are the on-line for-profits changing schooling and the curriculum?

THREE STAGES IN SCHOOL REFORM

The Excellence Movement

In the early 1980s, policymakers raised standards for students and teachers. High school graduation requirements called for more math and science; elementary and middle schools imposed low-level numeracy and literacy competency tests on all students. This top-down approach to reform produced no discernable increase in student learning and, in many instances, increased the dropout rate.

Restructuring Schools

Reaction to the failure of the excellence movement resulted in more freedom for schools to make decisions regarding how to achieve the higher academic goals. There was realization that if higher standards were to be achieved, the content of courses and ways of teaching would have to change and that teachers, parents, and the local community might work together in making change happen. "We've set the goals; you find out how to reach them" became the mantra. Teachers, parents, administrators, and others collaborated in decisions regarding schedules, staffing, budgeting, and curriculum planning. The ecological model for school reform was introduced in poverty areas where schools drew from parents and community resources, and, conversely, the school became the center for community life by offering school-linked social services.

Again, no noticeable overall improvement in academic achievement was noticed, and questions arose about the costs in time and money for school-based management. Also, there was tension between the teachers' unions' desire to protect the status of teachers and their exclusive role as "keepers of the knowledge that counts" and community activists who wanted the schools to serve their interests.

In their efforts to reform schools by restructuring, different curriculum programs became available. The programs represented different theories of learning and views of what schools are for. Activity 2–1 describes the theories and will help you choose the one best suited for your school.

Systemic Reform

Systemic reform is the latest stage in efforts to transform the school and curriculum. This reform has several orientations. There is the big standard movement whereby scholars and educators have created curriculum with the intent that students understand sophisticated content (concepts) in such fields as mathematics and science in which teachers use involving inquiry and projects so that students see the connections of science and math to other disciples, to the real world, and to their own lives. (National Board of the Teachers of Mathematics and the National Science Teachers Association). Big standards attempted to replace the traditional curriculum and its emphasis on mastery of procedures and reproduction of factual information.

In the little standards movement, states and districts develop their own lists of content and objectives in subject fields. These form the basis for school, teacher, and student accountability, similar to the old scope and sequence chart of the "dead" curriculum. Currently, the lists of things to know are getting longer.

All 50 states are now establishing their common set of academic standards for all students, assessing student progress and trying to align teacher preparation, evaluation, and instructional material. In many cases, rewards and punishments are given for teachers and schools that do not get the desired results.

■ ── ■

ACTIVITY 2–1   CHOOSING A CURRICULUM PROGRAM

Presented here are brief descriptions of four of these programs: Accelerated School (ACP), School Development (SDP), CORE Knowledge (CKP), and Success for All (SFA).

1. Read each description.
2. Select the program that you might want in a school.
3. If possible, share your choice with others, giving your reasons for the selection.

The following chart is an overview of the differences in emphasis:

ACP	SDP	CKP	SFA
Concern			
Rich experiences for all	Adults support each child	Common informational background	Prevent student failures
Means of Change			
Build on strengths	Bring school and community together	Order core facts on a grade continuum	New school structures: curriculum materials, methods, and training
Agreement on purposes	Combine resources in interest of students		
Provide inquiry			
Participants			
Staff; parents; students	Community members; agencies; school staff; administration	Teachers; parents	Teachers; parents
Resources			
Resource guides to school inquiry	Training instruments	Core curriculum	Teacher manuals
		Presents broad factual knowledge by grade level and exemplary practices	Training materials
Descriptions of procedures	Facilitators		Curriculum materials
Guiding principles			

(continued)

ACTIVITY 2–1   *continued*

The Accelerated School Program (ACP) is associated with Henry M. Levin, who brought the curriculum of rich schools to poor areas (Levin, 1998a, 1998b). The ACP program originates in the school, not in the district office. The school community develops its vision of the ideal school, and then it prepares a plan that will begin to make the vision a reality. Problem areas are identified, and small groups address them. Solutions are piloted, evaluated, and revised. After including more powerful learning, richer content and experiences, teachers change their views about what all students can achieve. There are opportunities for student impact. Teachers are free to try something different and to collaborate with each other.

The School Development Program (SDP) originated in the work of James Comer (Comer, 1994). The focus of the program is on bringing school and community together in supporting relationships with students. A steering committee representing the community, the school district, the school, and parents initially establishes consensus on a goal and builds community support. Curriculum is aligned with standardized tests, and standards of the program aim at having underperforming schools prepare students with the basic strengths needed for employment. Although the structure for the program is the same in all Comer schools, each school determines its own social and academic goals. In the school there are planning and management teams, and a social support team (counselor, nurse, social worker, psychologist, etc.) who minister to individual students. Also, a parent team mobilizes parents to support the school by participating in school governance and helping in classrooms, libraries, and on field trips.

The CORE Knowledge Program (CKP) originated with E. D. Hirsch, Jr., who believes that broad factual knowledge is necessary for deriving meaning from texts and further learning (Hirsch, 1987). The CKP outlines "what everyone must know to be culturally literate" and aims at familiarizing students with specific information related to a number of school subjects, but it does not present the knowledge or intellectual skills that are most valued as a discipline. The program emphasizes general knowledge and vocabulary arranged in a cumulative manner so that what is learned in one grade is extended in subsequent grades. Teachers and parents are expected to follow the outlined curriculum but are encouraged to go beyond it by offering concrete experiences with real-world activities that make a connection between the curriculum's array of topics and the everyday world. The assumption is that once learners have been introduced to a topic, they will be able and want to learn more about that topic.

The Success for All Program (SFA) is a whole school model that focuses on intervening for success in reading throughout the elementary grades. The program specifies how its materials (reading booklets, workbooks, activity sheets, and assessments) are to be implemented. Teachers are expected to follow SFA lesson plans that involve pacing of activities during 90-minute reading periods. Each activity has a time allotment as do the lessons which last 2 to 3 days. Components include the 90-minute reading period, regrouping students into homogeneous groups for instruction, cooperative learning, and one-to-one tutoring.

State Responses to Curriculum Standards

Responses to national curriculum standards and to calls for performance-based accountability have not been uniform. Although the policies at the state level have common elements—standards (their own), assessments, performance reporting and usually consequences of performance (carrots and sticks)—the states have found different ways to define what it means for schools to succeed (what indicators will be included in defining success) and what the consequences will be. Tests have become the connectors of state and district accountability systems, resulting in much controversy because the tests seldom reflect the curriculum standards, are inadequate samples of what students have learned, and do not take into account inequities that exist in opportunities to learn. It is not by accident that scores on the standardized tests can best be predicted by ZIP codes.

Policy to Classrooms

Curricular policy doesn't flow in an undirectional fashion from the state house to the school and classroom door. Fuhrman (2001) and others have described how standards-based reform has played out in the states. These authors found that large districts are better able to support the reforms and give more help to teachers in implementing the standards. Also, lower-performing schools are frequently unable to respond except superficially. Some opportunities for implementing big standards came when teachers of marginalized students wanted to protect low-performing students from traditional dumbed-down materials. The success of big standards with underserved populations brought upper- and middle-class opposition to the new curriculum because parents wanted to keep their relative achievement as measured by traditional instruments and wanted their children taught what they had been taught and in the same way.

The most serious problem is that the national standards that represent an academic professional consensus about more challenging content have been undermined by standardized testing. Also, even when school districts adopt programs that focus on achievement in the basic skills, teachers respond very differently to the interventions. For example, Datnow and Castellano (2000) found that after teachers had special training in the Success for All program, they differed in their support, rejection, and the degree of fidelity that followed in implementing the program. Almost all teachers made adaptations in spite of the developers' demand to follow the model closely. Those teachers who thought the program was beneficial for students were likely to continue implementing it. Other teachers who thought that the program constrained their autonomy and creativity adhered loosely to it (Datnow & Castellano, 2000).

Learning Community

There are teachers who implement big standards and help students acquire subject matter emphasizing problem solving, reasoning, and computing. Typically, these teachers are in schools that offer (a) curriculum-based professional development for deeper understanding of math and literacy while trying out new instructional approaches with challenging academic content and (b) a classroom and school-wide ethos that promotes caring and that nurtures individuals so that they gain more control of their own lives. In brief, a major concern about the systemic reform is that it has degenerated into a narrow focus on test results. There is a contradiction between a reform aimed at getting all students to achieve well on tests of basic skills and a reform aiming at high standards in which students identify and solve real-world problems with powerful subject matter. Accountability causes teachers to center instruction on the proximal aspects of a system (tests) rather than on the distant goals of education.

The Politics of School Reform

Educational "reforms" advance the interests of some and disadvantage others. For example, the federal legislation of 2002 mandated standardized testing that will "spread" student achievement along a normal curve. This mandate is favorable to those who have a conservative view of what counts as knowledge and who want to ensure that the federal government will not encourage multiple ways for students to show how well they can perform. The politics of this and other reforms is complex, however. For instance, the testing mandate appears to strengthen federal influence that conservatives have in the past opposed.

Interests and Agenda   The call for school reform has come from different interests: social reformers who want underserved students to have equal opportunities for mastering "world-class" standards; politicians, governors, and corporate executives seeking control of schools and the curriculum to be sure they serve an information-based economy; neoliberal reformers who believe that public education should function like the private market, replacing government control with school "choices" and charter schools; academicians and teacher educators from many professional associations endorse reform because of its promise to put students in touch with deeper subject content, newer views of knowledge, and a pedagogy that supports active learning.

Corporate leaders have been instrumental in overthrowing the political strength that educational leaders in schools once had in school bureaucracies. In large cities, CEOs from industry or government have replaced educators from positions as superintendents and other top administrative posts, and mayors have increased their influence on local school boards. Foundations that shelter personal fortunes and are required to dispense 5% of their money yearly have played a major role in school reform. The foundations have their own agenda, such as merit pay for teachers, differentiated staffing, business management practices, and wider use of technology. Schools and teachers may apply to foundations for funds, but generally their proposals must support the foundation's agenda.

Teacher unions also have supported school reforms when the reform promises to keep curriculum in the hands of professionals and for additional resources to use in attaining the new standards (Chase, 1999).

Systemic reform has shaken the foundations of public education. The idea of replacing the traditional school system by new arrangements—for-profit, nonprofit, on-line, and home schooling—is being acted upon. The federal government has become the heart of a network for transforming schools. Indeed, the 2000 presidential election put educational reform at the center of debate.

Power has shifted from the local level when the president, Congress, U.S. Department of Education, governors, and corporate leaders not only establish educational goals but endorse specific curriculum and mandated assessment. The National Assessment Board, which is appointed by Congress and the president, was established to define basic, proficient, or advanced scores on a federal test. Federal and state officers sometimes differ on such matters as teacher qualifications and the overall levels of educational quality, but the greatest dispute centers on mandated testing—what consequences should face schools that fail to improve student performance on tests. State governors want to keep the freedom of states to meet federal testing requirements by imposing their own exams.

Prior to the 2000 election, neoliberals allied with religious groups and conservatives in supporting candidates who favored such reforms as vouchers and the funding of educational choices in a variety of institutions. The alliance weakened, however, over the issue requiring students in all schools to be held accountable for their performance on national tests. Apple (2000) has described the alliance as the "Conservative Restoration," made up of those desiring a society based on individualism and a free market as well as those groups concerned about traditional knowledge and values.

Ten years ago, a national survey for a test of literacy with the passing score of 80% correct found that nearly 50% of Americans were at the lowest level of literacy. In 2002, the same surveyors, using the same instrument but with a more defensible cutoff score of 65% correct, found that fewer than 13% (5% if one excluded those who don't speak English) perform at the lowest levels (National Center for Educational Statistics, 2002).

Companion
Website

> If you are interested in the problem of seeing passing scores on tests and discrepancies among states in what counts as achievement, go to *www.prenhall.com/mcneil*. and click on Rothstein. This article describes anomalies in testing, such as in Massachusetts, where only 28% of eighth graders were proficient on the state's science exam but the international test showed their performance to be as good or better than students in every nation except Singapore.

The complaint given by the media that more than two-thirds of fourth graders "can't read," meaning that they are below what a panel of the national governing board (composed of parents, educators, business leaders, politicians, and other citizens) says is proficiency, is refuted by an international survey showing that American fourth graders score higher in reading than pupils everywhere except Finland.

State and district standards are better at standardization than on giving students opportunities to engage in the quality curriculum of the national standards proposed by academicians and teachers in the professional associations. State and district reforms standardize the curriculum, listing content by grade level, specifying performance indicators and degrees of proficiency, as well as adopting specific commercial curriculum packages that match the state and district standards. These materials provide the teacher with the instructional plans for delivering the curriculum, including activities, lessons, presentations, time allocations, grouping of students, and the like. Teachers are introduced to the materials at workshops and other orientation sessions and are monitored by peers, principals, facilitators, or coaches as they implement the curriculum.

An underlying assumption of many reformers is that if teachers, administrators, and students only work harder, achievement and test performance will improve. In contrast, other reformers have brought about changes in organization and support for teachers—class size reduction, mentors for new teachers, and teacher development through workshops and institutes where theory and content knowledge are extended as teachers try out new approaches through activities directly related to classroom instruction. Another innovation for teacher development and support is the professional development school where universities and school communities partner in research on curriculum. Obviously, there is need for more resources for teachers and students in poor schools, resources that will allow richer experiences and more opportunities for students to learn in and out of school.

An example of a reform that would greatly help poverty schools is related to changing the norm for prestigious teaching. Currently, the most inexperienced teacher is likely to be assigned to a poverty school and to a most difficult class. What difference would it make in "narrowing the gap" between poverty and affluent students if teachers adopted the norm of the elite medical institutions, in which the leading medical researchers favor the most difficult cases and are accordingly rewarded by financial and status recognition?

School and teachers respond to systemic reform in varied ways. Some try to ignore it, carrying on as usual. Some turn into grim "test factories," abdicating control over curriculum to the test contractors and "teach to the test" (Skrla, 2001). Others pursue the high-quality standards of the professional associations, engaging students in meaningful activities related to the disciplines and, if they must, reviewing the expectations of the test makers at cram sessions where they find that in the course of real investigations and projects students incidentally acquired most of what is expected by the standardized curriculum and its tests.

Companion Website

For more information on educational reform, go to *www.prenhall.com/ mcneil*. Select Enter, then Topic 1: Curriculum. Click on Web Links, then select Reform and Improvement Movements and Issues.

GOING BEYOND THE STANDARDS

Carol Jago, a teacher of high school English, prefers to see that the standards are only the first step in the big picture of what we want for students. In *Beyond Standards*, Jago (2001) describes how she inspires excellence. For instance, in her Goldilocks assignment, she asks students to present three poems, one too easy, one too hard, and one just right. Knowing that students will feel overwhelmed at first, she brings in boxes of poetry and sample copies of anthologies, checking out as many books by different authors as the library permits—everything from collections of cowboy poems to the complete works of Langston Hughes, from Shel Silverstein to William Blake. Students pick up books almost at random, drawn by a cover or quirky title, and then graze through the selection for poems that they want to read. Jago is not against standardized tests and standards but believes children can do much more than any standards document describes, and she thinks there is too much overlapping and loss of time for learning in the classroom.

Modifying National Standards

Each state has responded differently to systemic reform and the quality standards developed by the National Council for Teachers of Mathematics (Porter, 2000) and the National Research Council (1996), which departed from the traditional textbook-centered and recitation-style teaching by featuring replacement units that engaged students in active learning and put an emphasis on understanding of content. An idea of the activities and the thinking demanded of students by these curricula can be seen in Table 2–1. The table is adapted from the work of Porter and Smithson (2001), who developed indicators of cognition involved in big standards for math and science.

TABLE 2–1 Categories of activities related to standards of math and science

Understand Concepts	Collect Data
Explain concept	Make observations
Observe demonstrations	Take measurements
Explain procedures	
Develop schemas of understanding	

Perform Procedures	Analyze/Interpret Information
Use numbers in science/math	Classify/order/compare data
Do computations	Analyze data—seek patterns
Replicate/verify experiments	Infer from data—predict
Generate questions/hypotheses	Explain findings/results
Brainstorm	Organize and display data
Design experiments	(tables, graphs, charts)
Solve novel/nonroutine problems	

The California story illustrates how political forces redirected the curriculum of big standards. In the early 1990s, about half of California's teachers (40,000) were given new curriculum frameworks based on the national standards as well as replacement units, authentic assessments, and other materials for teaching in a new way (e.g., collaborative learning, inquiry lessons). These teachers also attended staff development workshops and institutes for learning about the curriculum and hands-on practices in implementing it. Subsequent evaluations after the program had been introduced found that students in the reformed schools did better in math concepts, skills, and problem solving. Little difference was found between traditional and reform classroom performance in science, although students in schools who had implemented the program for 3 years did better than those students in schools using the program for only 2 years. Noteworthy was how the academic achievement gap narrowed between underperforming students in poor areas and students in affluent areas when all were given opportunity to engage with the curriculum of the big standards.

In the late 1990s, political and policy support for national standards disintegrated in California. Reasons given for the opposition include public misunderstandings (parents wanting students taught what and how they had been taught), challenges to the reliability of the new assessments, costs of professional development of teachers, and the greater competitiveness of previously marginalized students. California moved to accountability reform characterized by the mandating of standardized tests that spread student scores along a "normal" curve of achievement predictable by socioeconomic background. These tests did not match the content and cognitive level of the quality standards.

The state rewrote the curriculum framework and adopted textbooks that reflected traditional approaches to teaching and learning. Districts and schools directed most of their improvement efforts to the teaching of basic skills for literacy and numeracy. Under the direction of principals, teachers reviewed the test scores of student performance in their schools and, after analyzing the achievement data, discussed ways to improve test scores, setting improvement goals and developing improvement plans, such as starting detention centers for students with missing homework assignments and mentoring high-risk students.

DISSONANCE BETWEEN CONSTRUCTIVIST VIEWS OF KNOWLEDGE IN TEACHER EDUCATION AND CURRICULUM DRIVEN BY TESTING REQUIREMENTS

Testing is now used to control curriculum and teaching. Under accountability, teachers and students focus on what is likely to be on the test, and most current tests do not assess broadly in content or in depth. Under the national standards in math and science, however, it was shown that high-quality examinations and performance assessments can be more valid, if less reliable, measures for assessing higher-order thinking and understanding powerful ideas. Furthermore, assessment can serve other purposes than grading students, teacher, and school; sorting students; and maintaining social hierarchies. When states and districts prescribe standardized testing and standardized procedures for teaching a subject area or module or the use of a particular curriculum package, they tend to undermine the principles and standards common in teacher education. Teacher education has been influenced by developments in cognition and learning regarding how people learn and how knowledge is constructed. Teacher educators promote pedagogical constructivism, believing that at times students should be given information directly but that it is more effective in changing students' beliefs and behavior, helping them internalize and act on new knowledge, when opportunities abound for students to understand what the information means, how it is won and validated, and how it will impact one's existing values and beliefs.

In her view of what teachers should be able to do, Darling-Hammond (1999) describes practices associated with constructivist pedagogy such as these:

- Organize subject matter so that students see how core ideas relate and how inquiry in a field is conducted.

- Interpret curriculum through their students' eyes and shape lessons that connect with what students already know and how they learn well.

- Develop curriculum with students by stimulating interactions among them so that more powerful learning occurs.

Similar views of learning and teaching are promoted through memberships in professional associations for the teaching of math, science, literacy, and other disciplines. Here are three examples of standards for teachers that call for constructivism in the curriculum of the classroom:

1. *Engaging and Supporting All Students*
   Draw from what students already know to make it easier for them to comprehend a new idea.
   Be aware of one's own cultural identity and how this predisposes treatment of students in a multicultural context.
2. *Creating and Maintaining an Effective Environment for Learning*
   Respect all students and award status to everyone.
   Foster social interactions and collaborative discussions.
3. *Organizing Subject Matter*
   Relate content to purpose.
   Connect facts, concepts, methods, values, and systems.
   Show connections among subject matters.
   Connect subject matter to the learners' concerns and interests.
   Connect subject matter to daily living and the needs of a given situation.
   Look at subject matter from its past, present, and likely future.

Activity 2–2 further considers how to assess teaching and learning opportunities.

Although the public and politicians' views of learning and teaching differ from those of teacher educators, many industrialists favor the newer views of learning that emphasize cooperative learning, real-world problem solving, making decisions, and

---

ACTIVITY 2–2   ASSESSING OPPORTUNITIES TO LEARN

Ask a student or yourself how often they have had opportunities consistent with standards for teaching and learning.

Engaging in Learning

1. I have the chance to study what I want and need.	1	2	3	4	5
2. We form teams, and everyone helps the team.	1	2	3	4	5
3. My friends and I help each other with homework.	1	2	3	4	5
4. Most problems during our projects are solved by the students themselves.	1	2	3	4	5
5. We learn how to give help and receive it.	1	2	3	4	5

Environment for Learning

1. My class makes me question my beliefs.	1	2	3	4	5
2. I have many ways to show what I have learned.	1	2	3	4	5
3. Others believe I can do the work.	1	2	3	4	5
4. In small groups, everyone expresses opinions and gives reasons.	1	2	3	4	5

Organizing Subject Matter

1. We start with a big problem, and everyone tries to figure out how to solve it.	1	2	3	4	5
2. We look for different ways to solve the problem.	1	2	3	4	5
3. Teachers let us know what they are thinking when they do the tasks expected of us.	1	2	3	4	5
4. I apply what I'm learning to situations outside school.	1	2	3	4	5

---

taking initiative. For years, classroom instruction paralleled the workplace. Teachers stressed the importance of doing your own work ("Keep your eyes on your own paper"), accuracy, speed, following directions ("Put your name in the upper right-hand corner"), and the mastery of procedures for solving particular problems.

In the 1990s, industry introduced the team concept in the workplace in which assembly lines could be regulated by workers, not just by supervisors. Worker specializations were less important. No longer would work be delayed waiting for an electrician to change the light bulb. Workers were now to suggest improvements in the production process, and teams solved problems and made decisions, making work more efficient. The team concept gave opportunities for participation in a wide range of decisions, from those related to job tasks and assignments to personnel matters (e.g., leaves and vacation time), rather than following hierarchical rules from management and unions, such as those that favor seniority.

Parallel changes occurred in teaching. Students planned and cooperated in classroom projects. The role of the teacher as supervisor gave way to the teacher as facilitator: "My teacher doesn't teach me anymore, she helps me learn." Decision making on the basis of data and the enhancement of communication skills became more important. The contributions of what small groups learned in advancing a common investigation were shared with the whole class. Students were encouraged to question traditional procedures and algorithms for math, writing, and reading as well as to validate and test alternative ways for solving problems.

MONEY AND REFORM

Recently, education has been "sold" as a commodity. Education is big business with billions of dollars at stake.

Business groups impact educational policies both in the interest of preparing the human capital they want and for creating the school market for their services and products. The public at large and parents in particular have been indoctrinated into the belief that completion of schooling is the only route to financial reward.

Curriculum and International Competition

Underlying the arguments for curriculum reform is the belief that education is the key to national and individual economic competitiveness. The excellence movement was launched on the claim that the United States was not competitive with Japan and other industrialized nations because of a failed school system. It was argued that high curriculum standards and student achievement would impact higher workplace productivity. Industry's failure to invest in infrastructure was not mentioned. Invalid international comparisons of academic achievement were featured with inadequate consideration for differences in the contexts, school curriculum, and student population.

In the prosperous 1990s, when the United States led the world in economic terms, no one suggested that the school and teachers had contributed to economic productivity and the quality of the workforce.

Berliner and Biddle (1995) have described the attack upon public schools as a "manufactured crisis" consistent with a desire to reduce taxation, to align curriculum with the training needs of industry, and to provide greater efficiency through the use of business methods and technology.

It is interesting to note that as the United States intensified accountability and testing, two of highest-performing nations on international tests of science and math—Japan and Singapore—announced that they intend to minimize performance on subject matter testing and instead implement curriculum reforms that will meet their nations' needs for individuals who can work cooperatively, demonstrate higher-order skills, and show creativity. Singapore, for example, is mandating both more collaborative and independent inquiries and open-book exams to encourage thinking and discovery in place of the regurgitation of inert ideas. Japan's political leaders, who once boasted that Japan was an intelligent society, now see negative effects on children and schools from educational uniformity, external pressure, and an exam-oriented curriculum with a narrow academic focus (Shimizu, 2001).

Another erroneous argument for curriculum reform in the United States was that educational outcomes must be standardized because of the demands of a global economy. Technology in schools was seen as a more efficient way to deliver instruction as a marketing ploy and a way to participate in a new world economy that was increasingly information based.

Failing Schools or (Business) Failing Schools?

Tensions between school funding and business breaks have intensified. The percentage of federal monies from corporations have dropped from 28% in 1956 to less that 10% today. Federal levies now contribute only about 7% of all public school funds. After Congress lowered the federal tax for corporations, companies turned their attention to reducing their state and local taxes. Nationwide, 45% of public school revenue comes from local money, and many states have recorded decreases in the tax load borne by business. About 48% of public school revenue comes from state money, and in that arena, the tax breaks for business continue to grow. The proportion of state income taxes paid by businesses fell to 15% in 1999, from 29 percent in 1979 (Tomsho, 2001). Governors, mayors, and city officials have given tax abatements to businesses as a way to get large corporations to build their headquarters and plants in a region or city in the interest of creating employment opportunities. As described by Lewis and Burnham (2001), companies themselves have found many ways to evade taxes through bailouts, off-shore shelters, and accounting practices. The tax gap of $195 billion, the cost of tax loss by cheating by corporations, cost the average taxpayer $1,600 (Lewis & Burnham, 2001).

Although business has always wanted to make schools more efficient, what is new is their view that the billions related to education is a target for income. Historically, a number of players have profited from schools—building contractors; maintenance, administrative, and classroom supply personnel; and real estate investors come to mind. Publishers of instructional materials typically have received 2% of a state or district's budget. Testing has become very lucrative, growing from $40 million to over $200 million per year in 2000. Most of an educational budget (80%–90%), however, goes to teachers.

In the 1990s, Christopher Whittle gained attention by providing classrooms with TV and news broadcasts in return for making the captive student audience receptive to commercials inserted in the broadcast. He received his income from the advertisers (Molnar, 2001). Subsequently, Whittle joined with others in the Edison Company for the delivery of instruction and the management of schools relying heavily on technology. Louis V. Gerstner, Jr., former IBM chairman and catalyst for the excellence movement, has taken responsibility for Edison's management of public education, carrying out contracts with school districts for controlling the district's finances, curriculum, and staffing as well as to initially install its program. Other for-profit schools have sought contracts from school districts for the teaching of basic skills to difficult-to-teach populations. Testing is used for monitoring student progress and for assessing the effectiveness of the program. There is an increase in on-line for-profit programs to offer students advance placement courses and preparation for SAT tests. Many students now get credit toward a university degree through their computers. The College Board, for example, offers on the Internet a complete listing of more than 1,400 examination centers and nearly 3,000 colleges that will give credit for examinations in many subjects (e.g., Spanish, business, administration). Each exam costs $45 (College Level Examination Program College Board, 2002).

Companion
Website

> For more information on exams and examination centers, go to *www.prenhall. com/mcneil* and click on the College Board link.

William J. Bennet (2001), former secretary of education, has shared his vision of the for-profit curriculum of the future. With an eye on the growing home school movement and with the support of a Milken Foundation grant, Bennet has a plan for a Web-based school that delivers a K–12 curriculum. The curriculum will be based on California standards, together with personal tutoring, supplementary course materials, and assessments. There will be a complex in which two persons, such as a student and an adult, will first read from a text and then gain additional knowledge of the topic by visiting an appropriate Web site. Although the cost of the computer, text materials, and other activities may go as high as $5,000 per family per year, Bennet plans to organize as a virtual charter school that will allow costs to be paid by taxpayers.

Curriculum and Economic Success

The notion that education is the key to a nation's or an individual's economic security is a belief stronger than the evidence. Henry Levin has refuted the claim that educational reform and standards for student performance increase higher workplace productivity (Levin, 1998). Although there is some relation between student performance and work productivity, there is no assurance that high scores on school tests will predict success in a variety of work situations. Indeed, an Urban League survey among Fortune 100 companies found that business heads oppose gatekeeper tests such as the SAT because these tests fail to show whether a student has qualities beyond the classroom—character, leadership, and effective communication. One only has to note how manufacturing companies have located their plants in states and countries with low test scores because they know that higher literacy and numeracy doesn't mean more productive workers but rather a stronger likelihood of higher wages and more unionization. Similarly, nations with high literacy rates, such as Cuba, are not necessarily economically advantaged. Economic growth and competitiveness depend primarily on economic investment in infrastructure, growth of the labor force, innovators, natural resources, and, perhaps, cultural matters—values that give hope for human progress (Harrison & Huntington, 2001).

Spokespersons from industry have argued for educational reform to serve their needs for highly educated persons in the information-based economy. In the short term at least, labor shortages have been met by importing workers from countries like India that have invested in education but have been unable to create sufficient jobs. The returns on investment in human capital, however, are great. Social benefits—health, safety, and the quality of life—are substantial.

The public has also been misled to think that all students will make more money if they are all better educated. It's true that for any individual entering the job market, the higher the level of education and skills, the better the job and salary. Although for experienced workers, work performance is more important than formal educational credits, it is generally true that higher incomes accrue to those with higher education.

It's one thing to see that most economic winners have taken a college preparatory curriculum that includes courses such as algebra, but it is irresponsible to say that if algebra is taught to all students, then everyone will have access to the most rewarding jobs (Wilensky, 2001).

Job opportunities are made by business investments, the policy decisions of government, and individual entrepreneurs. It is doubtful that reforms such as payment to schools and teachers for improvements in test scores, vouchers, and other accountability schemes will lead to equal economic advantages for all. The larger society would have to transform itself in many ways in order to close the gap between rich and poor. A teacher, however, can make a big difference in helping students find trajectories for their lives, and a rich curriculum involving active discovery and problem solving by a community of learners is an important factor in both school achievement and continued learning in life.

SUMMARY

The past decades have seen three reforms aimed at curriculum change. The first, the excellence movement, was initiated by corporate leaders and politicians as an effort to link education and the economy by setting goals and demanding more academics in the K–12 curriculum. Their arguments were that (a) the jobs of the future would require advanced subject matter content and new skills, and (b) U.S. schools were failing to compete, putting the economy at a disadvantage. Consequently, schools did raise requirements for more math and science and introduced competency testing of basic skills in math, science, and writing. This reform made little difference in student achievement, and a second reform was launched—restructuring. Restructuring gave latitude to schools, teachers, and neighborhoods to improve their schools and curriculum. Site-based management and the ecological model whereby community and school collaborated in the interest of students were prevalent.

Meanwhile, noted scholars from mathematics and science, together with teachers who represented professional organizations, created a new program on standards that would not only lead to a new generation of career scientists and mathematicians but also prepare a technical workforce and educated citizens who understood mathematics and science. The national standards (big standards) issued by the professional organizations include crucial components—curriculum instructional materials (replacement units that called for inquiry), authentic assessments, and an instructional pedagogy based on knowledge of how students best learn. The latter is characterized by attending to the learner's prior knowledge and offering purposeful engagement in higher cognitive thinking, multiple representations of subject matter, and opportunities for students to explain and argue. Collaborative learning is a central aspect of the standards.

The third reform is systemic reform. Systemic reform began with national standards developed by the scholars and teachers representing educational organizations. These standards were implemented in many states. However, there was insufficient understanding and support for the national standards, and states and districts began to prepare their own standards, which tended to be more quantitative—lists of content and expected outcomes—than qualitative. In addition, educators as leaders of school bureaucracies were replaced with business executives and politicians. Systemic reform shifted to an accountability movement with school and teachers judged by how well their students performed on high-stake and existing tests. Systemic reform came to mean alignment of goals, objectives, instructional materials (textbooks), teacher education, and standardized measures. The national testing centered on the basics—math, reading, and writing.

There is a contradiction between policies of accountability, with its emphasis on measurable results on narrowly focused outcomes, and teacher education, with its constructivist pedagogy that promotes deeper knowledge of subject matter so that teachers can engage students in tasks that are rich in content yet connected to the real world of the student, a pedagogy that fosters collaborative student learning, problem solving, and inquiry.

The focus on rewards and punishments for results fosters teaching to the test or the manipulation of favorable outcomes by teaching only middle achievers, ignoring high and low performers whose improved scores won't make a statistical improvement in class or school averages. Policy orientation is at odds with professional standards for classroom practice.

The politics of school reform shows the many interests in curriculum: social reformers (equity), politicians and corporate leaders (economy), neoliberals (choice), conservatives (traditional values), and professional educators (learning). The actions of these groups have shaken the foundations of curriculum and the public schools. New rearrangements are everywhere—for-profit, nonprofit, on-line, home schooling—redefining the meaning of *public* and making the idea of curriculum questionable.

Teacher responses to reform vary. Although most teachers go beyond the standards, some resent or ignore reforms; most make adaptions to any innovation, and some try to reconcile two distinct approaches to teaching: (a) the traditional didactic approach, in which the teacher initiates a question, students reply, the teacher evaluates, and solutions are the driving force; and (b) the inquiry approach, in which students raise questions that are the driving forces for information seeking and the negotiation of meaning.

Business has made a remarkable change from its long-standing desire to make schools more efficient and lower taxes. Now business has a new vision that there is money to be made for investors in meeting the clamor for choice, privatization, and testing. Business seeks to manage schools efficiently and to serve the great numbers of people who want information and competency without attending school and following a curriculum.

QUESTIONS FOR DISCUSSION

1. Are school subjects highly valued because they offer important skills and knowledge or because they award status?
2. What merit is there to the argument that curriculum should be standardized for the global economy? Should curriculum be context-free?
3. How can teachers best become involved in the neighborhoods from which their students come so they can understand the lives, interests, and needs of students?
4. What is the meaning for school reform as given by the poet who wrote, "Like pygmies on a pachyderm or lemmings on a leviathan and it's not easy to tell which controls which or what or who or whether anyone controls both"?
5. What kinds of curriculum reform succeed in attracting teachers who are drawn by excitement, challenges, and the infinite novelty of helping young minds grow?
6. What different meanings of *public* in *public schools* underlie the school reforms (a) supported by taxpayer monies, (b) accessible to everyone, and (c) placement of community (public) interests and values before individual interests?

REFERENCES

Apple, M. (2000). *Official knowledge: Democratic education in a conservative era* (2nd ed.). New York: Routledge.

Bennet, W. J. (2001, March 14). *Education Week, 11*(3), p. 38.

Berliner, D. C., & Biddle, B. J. (1995). *The manufactured crisis: Myths, fraud, and the attack on America's public schools.* Reading, MA: Addison-Wesley.

Chase, B. (1999, February 18). President of NEA address to town hall, Los Angeles.

Clune, W. H. (2001). Toward a theory of standard-based reform: The case of nine NSF statewide systemic initiatives. In S. Fuhrman (Ed.), *From the capitol to the classroom: Standards-based reform in the states* (pp. 11–19). Chicago: University of Chicago Press.

Comer, J. (1994). *A brief history and summary of the school development war.* New Haven, CT: School Development Program.

Darling-Hammond, L. (1999). Educating teachers for the next century: Rethinking practice and policy. In G. Griffin (Ed.), *The education of teachers* (pp. 221–251). Chicago: University of Chicago Press.

Datnow, A., & Castellano, M. (2000, Fall). Teachers' responses: Success for all: How beliefs, experiences, and adaptations shape implementation. *American Education Research Journal, 37*(3), 775–799.

Fuhrman, S. H. (2001). Introduction. In S. Fuhrman (Ed.), *From the capitol to the classroom: Standards-based reform in the states* (Pt. II, pp. 1–12). Chicago: University of Chicago Press.

Harrison, L. E., & Huntington, S. P. (Eds.) (2001). *Culture matters: How values shape human progress*. New York: Basic Books.

Hirsh, E. D., Jr. (1987). *Cultural literacy: What every American needs to know*. Boston: Houghton Mifflin.

Jago, C. (2001). *Beyond standards: Excellence in the high school English classroom*. New York: Basic Books.

Levin, H. M. (1998a). Educational performance standards and the economy. *Educational Researcher, 27*(4), 4–10.

Levin, H. M. (1998b). Learning from accelerated schools. In J. A. Bloom (Ed.), *Selecting and integrating schools*. New York: Scholastic.

Lewis, C., & Burnham, D. (2001). *The cheating of America*. New York: Morrow.

Molnar, A. *Center for commercialism in education*. Milwaukee: University of Wisconsin.

National Center for Educational Statistics. (2002, February 1). Will anyone accept the good news on literacy? *Chronicle*, p. 13a.

National Council for Teachers of Mathematics. (1983). *Curriculum and evaluation standards for teaching mathematics*. Reston, VA: Author.

National Research Council (1996). *National science education standards*. Washington, DC: National Academy Press.

Porter, A. C. (2000). *Principles and standards for school mathematics*. Reston, VA: National Council of Teachers of Mathematics.

Porter, A. C., & Smithson, J. L. (2001). Are content standards being implemented in the classroom. In S. Fuhrman (Ed.), *From the capitol to the classroom: Standards-based reform in the states* (pp. 160–180). Chicago: University of Chicago Press.

Shimizu, K. (2001). The pendulum of reform: Educational change in Japan from the 1990s onwards. *Journal of Educational Change, 2*(1), 193–205.

Skrla, L. (2001). Accountability, equity, and complexity. *Educational Researcher, 30*(4), 15–21.

Slavin, R. E., Madden, N. A., Donlan, L. J., & Nasikba, J. (1996). *Every child, Every school, success for all*. Thousand Oaks, CA: Corwin.

Tomsho, R. (2001, July 16). Public interest. *Wall Street Journal*, p. VA1.

Weiner, L. (2000, Fall). Research in the 90s: Implications for urban teacher preparation. *Review of Educational Research, 70*(3), 369–406.

Wilensky, R. (2000, May 9). Wrong, wrong, wrong—The myths of school reform. *Education Week*, p. 48.

Giving Voice to Students

Voice implies the right to have a say in policy. Giving voice to students involves putting students' efforts to understand and learn at the center of the curriculum.

Developing curriculum by listening and responding to the concerns, ideas, and goals that students have for themselves is one approach in giving voice. Another is found in curriculum that enables students to develop important concepts, understandings, and sense of possibilities that will enable them to fulfill their potentials. Voice can be extended by learning how to express private thinking so that it contributes to public knowledge and practice.

Chapter 3 features curriculum development from a constructivist view of learning, a view that holds that the curriculum is not a prior body of knowledge to be transmitted, but rather the knowledge and meanings students construct as they form goals, act on materials and other aspects of the classroom environment, and explore ideas with others. Chapter 3 also introduces the concept of an ideal activity curriculum, one that links the real-world activities of learners to subject matter that is functional for them in their everyday lives and sometimes even allows them to transform their cultural contexts.

Chapter 4 explores various answers to the question of how curriculum can best harmonize with the psychological needs of students. The writers of curriculum featured in chapter 4 do not assume that development from within—innate ability and natural unfolding—is adequate for learning and achievement or that engagement with academic content necessarily leads to the development of the person. The overriding purpose of chapter 4 is to show the importance of linking the developmental concerns of students to the academic goals.

CHAPTER 3

CONSTRUCTIVIST AND ACTIVITY CURRICULA

Sara: Thanks for letting me in on your constructivist curriculum. Some things I like: how you tease out students' existing ideas about a topic and try to generate their questioning before involving them in a search for answers and solutions.

I also like the small-group collaboration in problem solving followed by whole-class discussion where participants argue and defend their own ideas, gaining new understandings and points of view.

My concern is that your students are expected to "reinvent the wheel," to come up with scientific explanations—many of which are counterintuitive—and culture forms that have taken generations to evolve. Surely you don't think that your budding writers will create useful genres or that your young scientists will generate by themselves concepts like molecules, antibodies, and probabilities.

Merl: In my writers' workshop, children examine many genres and models that might be relevant to their purposes. Also, as these children question natural events and phenomena, they have opportunities to contrast scientific explanations with their own alternative views and to test the different ideas for viability.

This chapter deals with two curriculum trends: constructivist and activity curricula. It introduces the concept of the constructivist approach to curriculum development and illustrates curricula that follow from this approach. Comparisons are made between traditional and constructivist approaches.

The constructivist approach is concerned with uncovering the student's thinking. The teacher attends to both (a) the creative role of students in making knowledge (e.g., poetic expressions, personal stories and interpretations of world events that reflect their lives, local cultures, "views and ways of knowing") and (b) the construction of knowledge by engaging in group projects and discussion. The activity curriculum complements constructivism by casting the learner in an active role rather than that of a passive recipient. It is characterized by pursuit of goals and questions of interest to the learner. An ideal activity curriculum is one that links the real-world activities of learners to subject matter, putting students in touch with important concepts and offering them new ways of dealing with their world.

The historical antecedents of constructivist and activity curricula, particularly the work of Pestalozzi and Froebel, are presented along with modern parallels. The chapter contrasts school tasks that ignore the goals of students or that do not lead to significant learning with tasks that start with students' conceptions of their world and then extend students' knowledge in fruitful ways.

Examples are presented of teachers who are aiming at ideal activity curricula, in which the learning activities that students do actually relate to their cultural situations and may even transform aspects of these situations in positive ways.

CONSTRUCTIVIST CURRICULUM DEVELOPMENT

The constructivist approach to curriculum development is an alternative to systematic preplanning of curriculum by experts or by the teacher, which limits students to working with surface structures of organized knowledge. The constructivist approach has as its focus activities that encourage students to seek solutions and form knowledge (beliefs) rather than to repeat ready-made solutions to problems and verbalize particular constructs without really understanding or internalizing them.

It is not possible to reduce constructivist curriculum development to a set of rules. Unlike the development of traditional curriculum, in which the teacher begins with a formal structure or logic of the subject matter, the development of constructivist curriculum begins with whatever students understand about a particular phenomenon or life situation. Nevertheless, implicit in this student-centered curriculum are the familiar curriculum elements of purpose, content, activities, materials, strategies, and evaluation.

Purpose

Most teachers who follow the constructivist approach have the following as a purpose: students construct increasingly abstract concepts and procedures and reorganize their current beliefs in the interest of resolving problems relevant to them and of attaining personal and group goals.

Content

Although teachers help structure a learning environment that is likely to promote students' constructing meanings and understandings for particular subject matter, moral dilemmas, and social problems, there is no one predetermined understanding to be acquired by students. Subject matter topics are not simply covered by the teachers and passed on to students; rather, they are areas of experience and groups of ideas to which students relate their own associations and concepts.

Activities, Materials, and Methods

No specific activities characterize a curriculum as a constructivist one. However, some qualities are common to constructivist curricula. One commonality, particularly in math and science classrooms, is the introduction of manipulatives for students to act on and to use in constructing ideas. However, only when students have the intent of making sense of their experiences with manipulatives do those manipulatives serve constructivist purposes. For example, young children using blocks to calculate 34 take away 18 might only be routinizing a primitive method of counting; in contrast, other children who have been encouraged to devise their own methods for using manipulatives to solve problems may extend their initial primitive methods by constructing other mathematical relationships. Some children may see that 34 blocks = 3 tens + 4 blocks and that 18 blocks = 1 ten + 8 blocks. In brief, it is not the manipulatives themselves that are important but the students' reflections on their physical and mental actions with the manipulatives.

In constructivist curricula, materials and tasks are typically presented with a minimum of teacher talk, and students work on them in pairs or small groups. The pairs or groups attempt to reach consensus on their solutions, and subsequently, the entire class discusses the different methods and answers presented by the pairs or groups. The class has the obligation to try to understand explanations from all students. Assignment of problems that are open to a variety of different solutions or that can be solved in a variety of ways is sometimes given to help students explore multiple solutions. For example, Burns (1987) has children try to solve the following "horse problem," encouraging them to argue over it and act out solutions:

> A person bought a horse for $50.
> He sold it for $60.
> Then he bought the horse again for $70.
> He sold it once more for $80.
> Did he make money, lose money, or break even? How much?

Most problems used in the constructivist curriculum arise from students as they attempt to achieve their goals while interacting with others. Conflicting points of view are especially useful in helping individual students construct and verbalize their ideas and solutions.

Constructivism doesn't mean "anything goes." There are intended learnings as well as "just in time" learnings that arise from the problem at hand.

COMPARISON OF TRADITIONAL AND CONSTRUCTIVIST APPROACHES IN CURRICULUM DEVELOPMENT

Traditional approaches to curriculum are based on different views of knowledge and learning from the approaches taken in a constructivist curriculum. Traditionalists assume that knowledge results from information coming from outside the learner to the inside through the senses, with what is learned depending on the external stimulus presented by the text and the teacher. In contrast, constructivists believe that knowledge is created through the learner's interaction with a social and physical environment—an interaction in which the learner interprets the stimuli in light of his or her previous knowledge (prior experiences) and modifies current ideas that appear inconsistent or inadequate for dealing with new situations.

It follows that, unlike traditional curriculum planners, teachers using a constructivist framework must develop curriculum based on what is happening in the classroom. Inasmuch as the teacher must work with the understanding that individual students are showing at the moment, the classroom environment must be continually re-created in light of both individual student constructions and those of the class as a whole (Twoney, 1996).

A related tenet is that whereas the traditional curriculum uses a particular sequence that outlines a common path to prespecified understandings, constructivists expect different pathways to similar understandings and different kinds of understandings from the same subject matter task. Sense making does not dismiss "right" answers but may indicate why some answers are better than others. In a constructivist curriculum, emphasis is given to having students justify what they say and do, so that they will reveal their theories and logic. Also, the great variation among students' understandings enhances the richness of meaning that evolves as students reconcile their differences. Hence, the constructivist teacher seeks to develop a classroom community in which students are helped to communicate their reflections on the meanings of events and ideas, to express feelings, to construct new meanings, and to resolve conflicting points of view as they interact with others in their attempts to construct a consensual domain of knowledge representative of the classroom and a larger community.

Table 3–1 presents a summary of the curriculum differences that follow from traditional and constructivist beliefs.

ILLUSTRATIONS OF CONSTRUCTIVIST CURRICULA

Young children are thought to require teachers who are nurturing and older children to require models of competency. However, all learners may need both, and, as shown in the following illustration, the principles of constructivism apply to learners at all ages.

Constructivist Early Childhood Curriculum

DeVries and Kohlberg (1990) have described how curriculum for young children has been derived from constructivist goals. In the interest of helping children construct knowledge of objects that move but do not change versus objects that do change, one preschool teacher planned a blowing activity whereby 4- and 5-year-olds could act on objects to produce a desired effect. She reasoned that merely acting on objects and seeing how they react would not have the same appeal as an activity in which children blew on things for a clear purpose. This teacher selected a variety of objects on the basis of their potential for reacting in different ways—straws, Ping-Pong balls, cotton balls, spoons of various sizes, rubber bands, plastic tops, paper cups, scissors, soap, wadded paper towels, and so on.

TABLE 3–1
Traditional versus constructivist approaches to curriculum development

Traditional	Constructivist
Outcomes are thought to be attainable and predictable—standardized.	Unpredictable outcomes are highly valued.
Predetermined objectives are based on content prescribed by authorities.	The learners' current understandings of a topic are the starting point for curriculum development.
There is an optimum sequence of instruction, a continuum of skills or expected subject matter.	It is recognized that each student will have a different sequence or way of knowing in understanding a topic.
	Allowances are made for different levels of understanding of students in groups.
Specific activities are planned in advance.	The teacher and group can only provide an environment that will support, through interpersonal processes, the learner's activity in pursuit of his or her goals and contribute to further learning.
Curriculum is developed from information about a population of learners.	Curriculum incorporates data from the particular learner.
Materials assume that all learners are at a given conceptual level.	The same materials can be used by those at different conceptual levels.
Problems are given by text and teacher. There is more reliance on secondary rather than primary sources.	Problems (opportunities to learn) arise as students reach their own goals.
Emphasis is placed on a student doing his or her own work.	Students are encouraged to interact with others in solving problems and in negotiating meanings.
Students are expected to repeat official knowledge.	Students are expected to regard knowledge as interpretations of reality to which they can contribute.
Evaluation is based on the students' reproduction of official knowledge.	Evaluation is based on the students' growth in reconstructing personal knowledge.

The teacher planned to give a straw to each child for blowing and to suggest that the children find the object that would get across a water table the fastest. She also introduced activities such as games in which two children on opposite sides of the water table blew on a Ping-Pong ball, each trying to make it touch the other side. Such activities are flexible enough for the teacher to respond to children's original ideas and questions and for children to interact in ways that will encourage experimentation.

Children were invited "to see what you can do with these things," and "Can you_____?" Each child had his or her own materials and engaged first in parallel and later in cooperative play. Figuring out what the child was thinking was the greatest challenge for the teacher. Questions such as these were helpful in revealing children's thoughts about ways to act on objects:

- *Predicting:* "What do you think will happen if you do X?"

- *Determining cause and effect:* "How did you do X?"

- *Explaining:* "Why does X happen?"

In a constructivist approach, the teacher introduces new ideas when children's play becomes repetitive; however, a child should not have his or her train of thought interrupted. After an activity, it is desirable for children to reflect on what they did, what they found out, and how they produced a desired effect: "What happened when you blew through two straws instead of one?" "What did you have to do to make the straw go straight?" "What happened when the string of a pendulum broke?" "What do you want to try next time?"

Unlike traditional primary science activities, those that incorporate the constructivist approach are not aimed at having children learn to recognize and define some phenomenon or object; instead, the objective is for children to pursue the questions they come up with, to generate a variety of ideas, to see other viewpoints and solutions through the exchange of ideas, and to make and check out predictions.

Reflections in Elementary Math

Constructivist teachers hold that reflection plays a critically important role for elementary school students in learning mathematics and that just completing tasks is insufficient. In mathematics, reflection is characterized by distancing oneself from the actions of doing mathematics. In the process of reflecting, students think about what they are doing, become aware of their methods and options, and often modify their actions. Wheatley (1992) provides an example of an instructional setting that fosters reflection from the math curriculum at Florida State Lab School. A complex geometric figure is briefly shown to students, and they are asked to draw what they see (see Figure 3–1). Then they are asked, "What did you see and how did you draw it?" In this way, the students' ability to do

FIGURE 3–1
Quick-draw shape

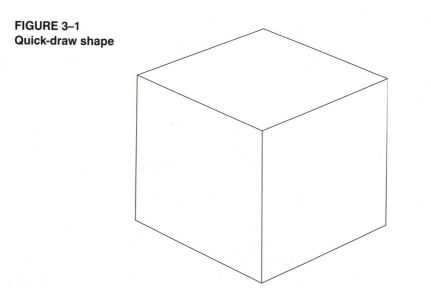

mathematical thinking is acknowledged in contrast to traditional questions that demand a single correct answer: "Did your drawing match what I showed you?" "Did you get it right?"

Students are encouraged to give meaning to their experience in ways that make sense to them. Typically students present a variety of interpretations. When some eighth-grade students were shown the shape in Figure 3–1, they reported seeing several things:

- A cube

- A hexagon with a *y* in it

- Two diamonds and two triangles

As students presented alternative interpretations, the element of surprise at another student's conclusion led to reflection, and students reported still other ways of seeing the figure. When the teacher responded nonjudgmentally, the students were free to construct their own mathematics.

In addition to selecting tasks, the constructivist teacher negotiates the social norms that encourage students to talk mathematics and learn to listen. Students assume the obligation of trying to make sense of the explanations of others. A solution presented by a student must be self-generated, and explanations can be challenged. The purpose of classroom discussion and dialogue is not to be right but to make sense. Students must be encouraged to give their reasons for their beliefs. If possible, help students see how their inferences and imaginations are impacting their perceptions. Also, let students see how their life histories are influencing their beliefs and practices. Questions raised by members of the class should be sincere and for the purpose of giving meaning to the explanation (Wheatley, 1992).

For a firsthand experience with constructivist teaching, you may want to carry out Activity 3–1.

ACTIVITY 3–1   EXPERIMENTING WITH KNOWLEDGE ABOUT SOLUTIONS AND DENSITY

Richards (1991) uses the following set of four experiments to help fourth-grade students generate knowledge about solutions and density. You may wish to try the experiments with your learners and to note how students learn by explaining their theories and listening to conflicting views.

Experiment 1

Sand and water.   Students are shown a 100-milliliter cup filled with sand and a 250-milliliter cup filled with water. "If I pour this amount of sand into this cup of water, will the water level (a) rise, (b) fall, or (c) stay the same?"

A vote is taken. Students try to persuade one another, giving reasons and using prior experiences with sand and water.

A second vote is taken. Students see the demonstration and are then asked to write about the empirical evidence, their explanations, and the names of any children who persuaded them to change their thinking or whose arguments made sense.

Experiment 2

Salt and water.   Students review the previous experiment and then are shown the materials for the new experiment. They are asked, "If I pour the same amount of salt into this cup of water, will the water level (a) rise, (b) fall, or (c) stay the same?"

A vote is taken. Students try to persuade each other, giving their reasons and prior experiences with salt and water.

A second vote is taken. Students see the demonstration and are then asked to write about the empirical evidence, their explanations, and the names and arguments of children who persuaded them to change their opinions.

The students might want to double the solute experiment by finding out what would happen if they continue to pour salt into the water. The terms *dissolve, solution,* and *saturated solution* may be introduced.

(continued)

ACTIVITY 3–1   *continued*

Experiment 3

Water, salt, and sand.   Students review the previous experiments. The teacher points out that the contents of the container with the salt look like plain water and asks the students how they can be sure the container holds saline solution. Discussion follows.

Students are shown a 250-milliliter cup filled with plain water and the cup with the saline solution from Experiment 2. They are asked, "Will the saline solution for Experiment 2 weigh (a) more than plain water, (b) less than plain water, or (c) the same as plain water?"

A vote is taken. Students try to persuade each other with their reasoning and prior experiences.

A second vote is taken. Students see the demonstration and then write about the empirical evidence, explanations, and what changed their thinking. The concept of density (mass and volume) may be discussed.

Experiment 4

Water, salt, and ball.   Students are shown the materials and asked, "Will the ball float (a) higher in the saline solution than in plain water, (b) lower in the saline solution than in plain water, or (c) the same in the saline solution as in plain water?"

A vote is taken. Students see the demonstration and write about the empirical evidence, explanations, and arguments that changed their thinking.

The concept of density (mass and volume) may be discussed.

Constructivist Curriculum with Adolescents

Increasingly, teachers of English in the middle schools are designing curricula that focus on the interaction between personal concerns of adolescents, the social concerns of the world at large, and the language arts. One seventh-grade teacher began her experience with constructivist curriculum using literature-based materials thought to address the personal and social needs of students (Smith & Johnson, 1993). The teacher surveyed her class a month before the thematic unit was to start, asking, "What is your greatest concern for the world?" and "What is your greatest fear?" Global concerns included "war," "pollution," and "the environment." Fears ranged from "failing at school," "dying of AIDS," to "going to hell," with the majority revolving around one's own death. The overlap of personal and social concerns about death suggested a tentative theme.

In her preplanning, the teacher decided she would negotiate the parameters of the study, allowing students to make choices about what to read and assume responsibility for their learning within a structure that included journal writing, whole-class discussions stemming from journal entries, and small literature study groups. At the center of the studies, however, was a desire to hear student voices. The selected literature presented the topic of death in a variety of settings and from various perspectives. Novels such as *Sheila's Dying*, *Park's Quest*, and *Z for Zachariah* were introduced.

Enactment of the plan began with students constructing the topical framework for the unit, stating what they were going to study, how they would approach it, what materials they would use, and what their responsibilities would be. Students gave their ideas of what death and environmental problems meant to them. They raised questions about the topic. They wanted to know about spirits and who believed in ghosts; they wanted to know what happened to us as we die and after we die. The conversation gradually shifted to talking about the death of the planet.

Figure 3–2 shows the semantic map created by students for their study of death and dying. The students chose the books that different groups would read and decided on group projects, individual papers, and persuasive pieces. They also accepted responsibility for studying a specific aspect of the topic—the death of a place, crime, euthanasia, disappearing rain forests, endangered animals, AIDS, and the like.

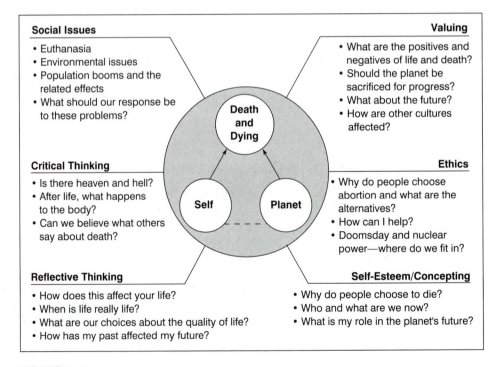

FIGURE 3–2
Semantic map of students' ideas about death and dying

Journal writing began in response to the prompt "What do you expect to learn in the next 6 weeks?" During group sessions, students made decisions about how to work together and kinds of activities to pursue; they identified problems to consider and solutions to problems. Typically class members were given tasks that would contribute to a common goal. Individual journal entries often revealed problems related to implementing the group activity, particularly ones associated with group dynamics. During the last week of the study, groups presented their projects, showing what is possible when students are given responsibility for their own learning. The presentations showed a diversity in designs—original information pamphlets about the ozone layer and the dangers of its disappearance, dramatic skits about hate crimes and their impact on the United States, persuasive posters for saving the rain forests, a seminar about AIDS and its prevention, and a panorama of types of pollution. The studies allowed students to use their own knowledge, as well as a variety of outside sources, in addressing their own questions and concerns. Although discussions were prompted by individual journal writing, they led to groups participating in clarifying and understanding why certain problems exist. The selected books served many purposes—as tools for reflection, bases for exploring ideas and feelings, and sources for stimulating intellectual curiosity.

Not all constructivists believe it wise to extend each and every student construction. In her Algebra 1 constructivist curriculum, Magidson (1992) limited the constructions addressed. She believes that because of the sheer number of students and the fact that some constructions are not fruitful, the teacher must strike a balance by creating situations that encourage student constructions yet limit those selected for full-class discussion. Discussion validates student constructions and allows different levels of understandings within shared core ideas. Her curriculum unit "Functions and Graphs," for instance, had as its centerpiece the computer program Grapher, which allows students to manipulate the parameters in equations and observe the graphical consequences of the manipulations. The curriculum unit involved two types of activities:

1. Computer labs and other activities in which students worked in small groups to explore, extend, and apply ideas
2. Whole-class discussions in which the results of the lab explorations were probed

In an effort to limit the direction of individual experiments in the interest of some common knowledge about slope, Magidson restricted the computer lab activity to the challenge of finding an equation that produces a line that is part of a starburst (a problem that invokes the ratio of directed line segments) and cautioned students to use equations that begin with the form $y =$ (which deals with slope and not the reciprocal of slopes). Students still invented alternative forms of the equation, which extended the task of generalizing about the effect of slope numbers on the resulting lines. Magidson learned that the diversity of students' mathematical knowledge generated a variety of approaches to a problem and that the sharing of small-group discoveries led to both new knowledge and new questions far beyond the realm of the traditional algebra course:

- "Why isn't a line with a slope twice as steep?" (Twice the angle of a line with a slope of 2—the student is attempting to reconcile previous knowledge of angles with new knowledge of slope.)

- "Does the origin of the Cartesian plane signify the exact middle of the whole plane?" (The student is exploring the ramifications of the standard definition.)

- "Where does the name Y-intercept come from? Why isn't it the X-intercept instead?" (The student is trying to understand a connection that doesn't appear to make sense.)

- "What is the difference between fractions and equations?" "If you have a rise and a run of 2/4 can you reduce it so it is easier to find the slope?" (Is the slope just a regular fraction, or is it different in nature?)

Some students' constructions are variations on a theme: larger numbers produce steeper lines; others address distinct aspects of a slope's behavior; some combine subjects in different ways.

The need for clarifying and relating fragmented ideas was met through whole-class discussions in which ideas were pooled, strengthened or eliminated, and related to an underlying structure. (In the starburst activity, student ideas were integrated by the concept of slope as a circular continuum from -00 to 00.) The selection of a large structure or concept to which individual constructions can be connected precludes the teacher and class attending to and refining a large number of constructions from individual students. However, although the class construction is in the direction of creating public knowledge, individual constructions for the domain remain.

ACTIVITY CURRICULUM

The notion of curriculum as activities that will affect the learning, development, attitudes, or behavior of the learner was hotly debated in the 1920s and 1930s (Schoonmaker, 2001). Dewey (1910) cautioned that activity for activity sake was not enough. He placed great importance on reflection in the activity curriculum. Teachers should help students learn and reflect on what they are doing and what actual sense they are making from the activity. Reflection requires attitudes of open-mindedness, whole-heartedness, and respect together with making suggestions, defining problems for study, forming hypotheses, reasoning, and testing the plans in action by determining the consequences.

Teacher Strategies That Foster Active Learning

Basic to many constructivist curricula in mathematics, social science, science, reading, and writing are teaching strategies that foster active learning. These strategies follow three phases: (a) a preparation for learning phase, (b) an inquiry phase, and (c) an application and integrative phase.

1. In the *preparation phase,* students think about the problem, phenomenon, or topic to be studied. Often this entails that students discuss their present knowledge of, and prior experience with, a problem situation, sensing what they do not know but would like to find out. Observation of discrepant events, provocative questions, the making of predictions and dialogue, and debate about the phenomenon are used. Often conflicting student preconceptions become the starting point for inquiry. Discussion of where to obtain the data, information, and resources for resolving the problem is part of the preparation phase.

2. In the *inquiry phase,* students attempt to answer their questions and clarify their views. Sources of new information—texts, films, interviews, computer programs—are explored; often experiments and investigations follow. Students select relevant ideas from the sources and experiments, comparing the new ideas with previously held concepts. Both students and the teacher process the information and attempt to understand its meaning.

3. The *application and integrative phase* is characterized by judging whether the goal of learning has been met and, if not, what further activity is appropriate. The new information is summarized and critiqued, a problem is solved, and old ideas are contrasted with the new. The newly generated knowledge is applied in other situations, especially to tasks in everyday contexts and to other tasks in the same subject field.

Following are some examples of how active learning can occur in the classroom.

Active learning in the science curriculum usually begins with observation, such as where to stand in order to see someone else in a mirror, what a pencil looks like in a glass of water, or which direction light is traveling when one looks out of a window. Dialogue and debate among students help them become aware of other ways than their own to think about the observed objects and events. Although students can discover many interesting things about plants, light, and other phenomena on their own, constructivist teachers introduce scientific concepts related to the problem at hand, not as facts or definitions to be learned but as alternative conceptions for the students to evaluate.

Active learning in the reading of literature means encouraging students to connect their prior experiences with those described in the text while keeping themselves open to new social, cultural, and economic perspectives. Although learning to interpret text may still call for students to learn about the rhetorical strategies for reading different genres and understanding symbolic meaning, and author's intentions and perspectives, the newer practice of giving students opportunities to write their own opinions rather than repeat correct answers about a text increases the level of interpretation. Participation with others in judging the sufficiency, relevancy, validity, and insightfulness of student interpretations helps students assess their own performance and create meaning from the text.

Activity 3–2, which follows, demonstrates how background knowledge determines comprehension and how beliefs are changed through interaction with others. Activity 3–3 is an opportunity to engage in mental rehearsal for planning an active learning lesson.

ACTIVITY 3–2   NEGOTIATING MEANING
WITH LITERARY TEXTS

Where does meaning lie? Of course, some believe that meanings of text are those intended by the author and that these meanings can be deciphered by learning the syntax and other communication symbols and structures of the text or by becoming acquainted with the backgrounds of authors and their times. Others are convinced that the text carries meanings that were unrecognized by the author and that what is *not* said is often significant. Still others believe that meanings are constructed through the interaction of readers who bring their past experiences and cognitive frameworks to the text, and others know that texts are forever new as changing circumstances give rise to fresh meanings.

Test for yourself the range of interpretations a selection generates, and explore techniques to help students or peers gain more powerful ways for constructing meanings.

1. Choose a literary text—short story, play, or film.
2. Have students read, view, or recall the selection.
3. Initiate discussion of the text with a series of sentences to complete. The sentences should draw out individual feelings about the human relations issues provoked by the selection.
4. Encourage students to share their ideas with others in the class, pointing out how considering the full range of ideas of those in the class expands the knowledge of everyone.
5. Encourage students to support their ideas with evidence from the text, to go beyond their own sense of the characters, and to see how characters fit in the context of the text.
6. Feel free to introduce any aspects about the text (important details or historical background) that you think are important for understanding the text.
7. Together, try to effect a consensus on meanings that will link individual interpretations.
8. At the conclusion of the activity, discuss whether or not the activity opened understanding of students into new possibilities about the meaning of text.

ACTIVITY 3–3   PLANNING LESSONS FROM AN ACTIVE LEARNING PERSPECTIVE

1. Select a subject matter topic of interest to you.
2. Describe activities that might take place in the three phases of active learning: (a) preparation for learning, (b) inquiry phase, and (c) the application/integrative phase.
3. You may wish to consider under the preparation phase such activities as presenting a dilemma, previewing, activating prior knowledge, raising questions, and making predictions.
4. For the inquiry phase, illustrate how you might encourage clarification, elicit preconceptions or contradictions, establish focus, and determine the information or data students need.
5. For applying/integrating phase, think (a) about the product and audience (report, dramatization, exhibit) that might follow from the inquiry and (b) about possible extensions.

Application of the active learning strategies in teaching other content areas may include the same three phases. Most important is that at the closing of lessons, students share what they have learned and how they might use their knowledge. They may say why they find something difficult as well as tell what helps them the most with their problems.

ANTECEDENTS TO CONSTRUCTIVIST AND ACTIVITY CURRICULA

Most of us are surprised at the similarities between contemporary curriculum in the United States and the practices and insights of early teachers. Some point to John Comenius (1592–1670) for his use of manipulatives and other teaching aides in developing learners' sensory experiences before verbalization; others tell how Johann Herbart (1776–1841) stressed the linking of the child's previous knowledge and interest to whatever newer content is introduced. Of course, many refer to Maria Montessori's (1870–1952) curriculum, in which children were free to learn at their own pace and to discover by themselves using self-teaching aids.

Two teaching approaches from the past, however, are closely associated with the antecedents of important current trends in learner-centered curricula: constructivism and activity curricula, in which learners pursue real-world goals of interest to them. Not only is studying the work of these two styles a way to better understand contemporary trends; doing so may encourage others to find better ways for helping students expand their lives.

Teachers who place their learners at the center of curriculum planning have ties to two early 19th-century teachers: Johann Heinrich Pestalozzi (1746–1827) and Friedrich Froebel (1782–1852). The sections that follow emphasize Pestalozzi's concern for initial concrete experiences (as opposed to verbal abstraction in learning to learn) and Froebel's efforts at connecting the learner's developmental stages, inner potential, and desire for expression to the learning of important subject matter, symbolic thought, and specific educational goals.

Learning by Doing: The Broad Curriculum of Pestalozzi

In about 1776, Pestalozzi began his teaching by bringing 37 abandoned children of different ages to his Swiss farm. There he clothed, fed, and treated them as his own children. They were always with him, sharing work in the garden and the field, domestic duties, weaving, spinning cotton, and learning music, French, arithmetic, reading, and writing. His act was in response to the prevailing misery of the day. Poor children were exploited on the grounds that they were by nature vicious and depraved. In consequence, these children were left without any spirit or energy, often giving up any attempt at a useful life. Pestalozzi attempted to regenerate children who would otherwise have been lost as vagabonds or criminals. He developed a new, broadly based curriculum involving hand, heart, and head. Under his curriculum, children learned to work with their hands to make a living; they experienced gentleness, kindness, and trustful behavior; and they acquired basic subject matter as tools for independent use.

One of the first of Pestalozzi's curriculum plans called for students to cultivate small plots of land. Students were to learn how to lay down pasture, understand the uses of manure, recognize the different sorts of grasses and the importance of mixing them, the nature and use of marl, the effects (disputed at the time) of the repeated application of lime, and the management of fruit trees and some forest trees.

Pestalozzi's view of instruction began by exposing the learner to an environment that would make a personal impression, whether physical or moral, and then supporting the development of impressions through other activities. Thus, Pestalozzi emphasized doing and talking before reading, precepts before concepts, and firsthand experience before confirming generalizations. Nature study and activities that required the manipulation of objects and materials were used to form the sense data (e.g., observation of color, structure, number) necessary for understanding objects and their uses.

Pestalozzi spent the next 50 years in different schools with different kinds of students designing programs that would help children be the agents of their own knowledge. The study of geography, for instance, was sometimes introduced with a trip to the valley where the children first gained a general view of the valley and then examined its exact nature. They took some clay that lay in beds on one side of the valley. On their return to the school, the students, using the clay, reproduced in relief the valley they had studied. Over the course of the next few days, the students made more explorations and further extension of their work. Only when the relief was finished were they shown a map; they would not see the map until they were able to understand it. Also, from the first day, students sought connections between geography and their other studies, such as natural history, agriculture, and geology.

Similarly, the children were to discover the truths of geometry for themselves. After being given problem situations and a clear picture of the end to be reached, students were left to work alone. They first distinguished among vertical, horizontal, oblique, and parallel lines; right, acute, and obtuse angles; different kinds of triangles, quadrilaterals, and so on. They then formed questions such as how many angles, triangles, or quadrilaterals could be formed from them, leading to the first problems of theoretical geometry.

Pestalozzi's concern for self-directed learning relegated the teacher's role to evoking purposes and to supplying appropriate resources for the child to pursue these purposes.

City Building: A Current Pestalozzian-Type Curriculum

Similarities are found between Pestalozzi's curriculum and Doreen Nelson's celebrated city-building curriculum (1985). Modern city-building classrooms emphasize self-directed learning as students construct a scale model of their own city or community projected into the future as part of an ongoing classroom activity. In an introductory phase of the activity, students explore what they know of their environment and draw maps of the major features of their community—landmarks, streets, significant buildings, vegetation, and so on. Individual maps are combined to form a large common map. In one implementation of the curriculum, students walk around their community observing geographical features and then learn to convert their community to scale, making a relief map out of Styrofoam depicting the natural landscape of mountains, valleys, lakes, and open land. The map becomes the basis for other, more abstract city-building activities. The students create a list of what they want and what they don't want in their own city. This list of criteria is used to guide decision making and to evaluate transformations of "the city." The "site" is divided into governmental districts, and students serve as representatives on a city council and commissions. Students develop housing, transportation, and other services and facilities to keep up with growing population and environmental concerns.

Early in the project, students explore the world of objects. Each student selects and builds a model of an object—a toothpaste tube or a film reel at actual, decreased, and increased scale, and at the scale of the student's own body. Thus, students become familiar with the concepts of structure, scale, ratio, proportion, and geometry. They begin to see that cities are merely spaces fitted with objects that have grown vertically (e.g., a skyscraper) or horizontally (e.g., tract homes).

At the same time, concepts of community, structure, and transportation are related to questions of organization and design. Constructing a three-dimensional model of a classroom interior gives students the opportunity to experiment with change before committing to it, thus acting as an empowerment tool. Students learn that there are many ways to arrange classrooms depending on the immediate needs of the classroom community.

The students research the basic forces acting on their community, theories of land division, and actual forms of government. They decide on their own governing structure and begin the planning, design, and construction of their own city. Professionals from the community—architects, city planners, environmentalists, lawyers—serve as consultants and resource people for the students, contributing information the students use as they design and construct a model of their community projected into the future.

A large flow chart serves as a visual and organizing aid for the activities over the course of the entire year, and events are documented on a "history wall." (Once city building is launched, students may work on the city at random hours or one day a week, using the activity to integrate formal lessons.)

Building a "city," like the work Pestalozzi recommended for his students, helps students recognize that they live in a world of objects that affect them and that, if they desire to influence that world, they must know the nature and essence of these objects. For example, a student may learn to find the radius and circumference of a circle in order to construct models of a film reel. Ultimately, any subject can be explored through city building—movement, mathematics, science, ecology, verbal skills, and visual skills.

Froebel and the Inner World of the Child

Friedrich Froebel worked with Pestalozzi, acting as a teacher of drawing in his school and then as his assistant. Early in his career, Froebel taught students of various ages in his elementary school at Keilham, Germany, and in schools in Switzerland. Later, he became preoccupied with early childhood education and opened the first kindergarten. Excerpts from a state evaluation of the school at Keilham reveal Froebel's emphasis on the personal construction of knowledge:

> What the pupils know is not a shapeless mass, but has form and life, and is, if at all possible, immediately applied in life. . . . There is not a trace of thoughtless repetition of the words of others, not of captive knowledge among any of the pupils. What they express they have inwardly seen. Even the objections of the teachers cannot change their opinions until they have clearly seen their error. Whatever they take up, they must be able to use, and what they cannot think, they do not take up. Even dull grammar begins to live with them, inasmuch as they are taught to study each language with reference to the history, habits, and character of the respective people. (Hailman, 1887, pp. 86–87)

Froebel capitalized on the inner, active forces of learners and gave them encouragement and direction. He regarded them somewhat as plants that need cultivation and protection in order to realize their potentials, yet he believed that, unlike plants, children can direct the process of their own growth through conscious perception and reason.

In his kindergarten, Froebel sought to understand the child's inner life, not merely attend to external behavior:

> For the child that seems good outwardly is not necessarily good inwardly, i.e., does not desire the good spontaneously or from love, respect, and affection. Similarly, the outwardly rough, stubborn, self-willed child that seems outwardly not good, frequently is filled with the liveliest, most eager, strongest drive for spontaneous goodness in his actions; and the apparently inattentive boy frequently follows a fixed line of thought that withholds his attention from all external things. (Hailman, 1887, pp. 86–87)

Froebel's kindergarten curriculum was an activity curriculum that gave children an opportunity for self-expression that would draw them out and reveal their potentialities. He regarded written language as a fundamental way for students to express themselves and to reveal inner needs. Hence, he encouraged young children to engage spontaneously in pictorial writing, to invent their own alphabets, and to seek assistance with squibble writing in their attempts at expression (Hailman, 1887, pp. 86–87).

Similarly, children's love of story, story drawing, and rhythms was seen as a manifestation of their inner development. Activities that incorporated them, as well as nature study, handwork, and physical activity, were part of Froebel's curriculum. Such activities were also intended to help children free themselves, to differentiate self from external things, and to differentiate external things from one another.

Play was central to Froebel's curriculum. The play activities were organized systematically to correspond with developmental needs of children of a given age and to point to larger symbolic meanings. His curriculum included many types of cooperative play and group games, physical activities that aimed at developing children's strength and dexterity, games that initiated joy and imagination, and intellectual games that demanded reflection and judgment. Some activities, called "gifts," entailed children's manipulation of balls, blocks, and other materials in a sequential order and were introduced to help children discover universal or conceptual ideas that were thought to correspond to an external world—colors, shapes, number (divisibility), proportion, and the like. (Of course, today many regard the idea of universal concepts as an illusion, just as the notion of an external world where students can "discover" through observation is challenged by the view that any "real" world is in one's mind and that any common view of reality must be constructed in given social situations.) Other activities, called "occupations," promoted invention as students worked with furnished materials to make a product. In doing "occupational" activities, such as those involving clay, wood carving, and painting, children applied the concepts discovered through the gifts to create something new.

The importance of relating the "inner" world of the child with powerful principles or concepts for dealing with the universe is illustrated in Froebel's view of the ball as an educational device. He recommended giving one to a child at the age of 3 months, believing that the play it stimulates trained the child's senses, muscles, and power of attention, while at the same time building the child's confidence in his or her abilities. The ball, now held, now lost, teaches the meaning of such key concepts as space and time (past, present, and future). A caretaker singing a description of the motion of the ball helps a child learn the meaning of such significant readiness concepts as *up, down, out, around, middle,* and *first.*

Froebel introduced nature study and manual construction for older children. Accordingly, children took trips through neighborhood fields and along lake shores, making observations, drawing, connecting their work in science with their studies in language and art. Mathematics was frequently introduced in connection with laboratory work as well as with the "occupations" found in the manual training room where students made the equipment for their studies of nature and other activities (Cremin, 1961, p. 133).

THE ACTIVITY CURRICULUM: AN AMERICAN RESPONSE TO FROEBEL

By 1900, Froebel's ideas had become a basis for elementary school practice in the United States. School gardens formed an integral part of the school environment and of schoolwork. The care and observation of living things—plants and animals—occupied a place in the curriculum. Storytelling, as well as recognition of the importance of promoting children's love of stories, was also integrated into the curriculum. Activities involving music, art, and physical education reflected a change from viewing subject matter as something set out to be learned to emphasizing activity and an appeal to the developmental needs of children.

In his study of the American kindergarten at the turn of the century, Brosterman (1997) found evidence of Froebel's influence. Indeed, Brosterman believes that much of what the giants of modern art and architecture knew about abstraction was due to the gifts and other educational toys of Froebel. R. Buckminster Fuller, the inventor of the geodesic dome, traced his discovery of the superior strengths of triangles, the building blocks of his domes, to Froebel's curriculum, in which children were challenged to build the strongest structure using toothpicks and moistened peas. Similarly, Frank Lloyd Wright's Robie House of 1906 resembled a textbook house made by Froebel's geometric blocks. At 88, Wright recalled sitting at a kindergarten table and playing with the maple blocks "as in my fingers to this day" (Brosterman, 1997).

J. L. Meriam's Activity Curriculum

In 1904, Junius Meriam developed an activity curriculum based on four categories: observation, play, stories, and handwork (Meriam, 1920). This curriculum is noteworthy for its consistency with Froebel's belief that concrete objects could be used to connect the inner world of the child to powerful ideas related to the external world.

The following list of play activities taken from Meriam's curriculum illustrates the potential of play for developing concepts of science:

■ *Water.* Playing with water, pouring, wading, splashing, watching objects in water, throwing objects into water, building dams and waterwheels, watching the actions of water on land, "erosion models," and so on—all of which present problems in fluids

■ *Air.* Playing with air, sailboats, kites, windmills, airplanes—which present problems in air pressure, air currents, wind, temperature, humidity, rainfall, and so on

■ *Fire.* Watching fire, making fires, observing friction and heat, playing with toy steam engines and thermometers—which present problems in heat, combustion, expansion, contraction, and the effects of heat

■ *Mechanical devices.* Playing with hoops, tops, pulleys, wheels, toy machines, gyroscopes, pendulums, levers; watching thrown objects; balancing objects; and so on—which present problems in motor dynamics

■ *Sound.* Vocalization; beating and drumming; blowing on toy instruments; "listening to shells"; speaking through tubes and telephones; experimenting with conduction through air, water, timbers; and experimenting with vibrating bodies, echoes, and so on—which present problems in vibration, noises, tones, and music

■ *Light.* Playing with reflectors, mirrors, prisms, lenses, water refraction, glasses, and telescopes—which present problems in light, color, optics, and time

■ *Electricity.* Experimenting and playing with magnets, induction coils, telephones, telegraph instruments, dynamos, electric motors, electric lights, and so on—which present problems in electrodynamics

In playing with such phenomena, students shared their experiences with others, used their imaginations and constructed useful objects, investigated and experimented, and acquired knowledge of materials and processes. Incentives to learn reading, writing, and arithmetical processes arose from the activities involved with the materials. The teacher's role was to help students plan what they wanted to do, how they would do it, and how they would evaluate their undertakings. The teacher's role was also to help students pursue purposes that would offer the greatest possibility for further learning.

The entire class seldom worked on the same materials at any one time. While some were constructing objects, others used books and reference materials dealing with the problems growing out of the activity, and still others were preparing reports or displays.

Difficulties and Promise of the Activity Curriculum

Two kinds of difficulties confront the activity curriculum. One centers on the selection of content: the failure of students to develop powerful concepts or content that can enhance their efforts as they pursue their goals. In part, this problem can be solved by the teacher stimulating or knowing the goals of students and helping them extend their existing perspectives, procedures, and solutions in creating more fruitful methods and tools. A second difficulty is one of context: the failure of the teacher or school to consider the cultural context in which learners live so that the content of the curriculum can become functional in the lives of the learners and perhaps even help them transform these contexts.

The promise of an activity curriculum rests on two points:

1. Constructivism and its contributions in suggesting ways to arrange classroom conditions for extending the knowledge of students
2. Situated learning, in which subject matter is related to the everyday activities of learners so they can be more inventive and effective in their everyday life

In the past, many teachers found it difficult to place control of learning in the hands of students. Often nature study became object study with formal and analytical questions posed by the teacher to shape children's thinking. Cubberley (1934) tells how if common salt was the "object" of the lesson, the class would be expected to learn its chemical structure, its uses, how and where it is found in nature, how it is mined and refined, that its crystalline form is cubical, that it varies in color from white to bluish and reddish, that it can be made translucent, that it is soluble in water and saline in taste, and that it imparts a yellow color to flame (p. 353).

The principle of self-activity was often corrupted to "busywork." Inasmuch as the child's active nature called for a busy life, teachers found many devices to keep students employed—activities such as designing words with beans and clipping and folding paper. Instead of constructing their own knowledge, children were expected to meet organizational demands by obeying authority, behaving uniformly, and acquiring information in common.

Meriam himself cataloged 15,000 activity units from different school systems in the United States and found that more than 50% of the activities were assigned by school officials, 31% by teachers, and only 18% by students. Many of the activities were inappropriate—for example, serious and advanced topics in the lower grades and trivial topics in the upper grades. Meriam faulted the imposing of activity topics that appealed to children's interests but were unrelated to daily living and the continuity of the learning experience. One teacher chose the topic of a music band on the grounds that noise appeals to children; another chose the topic "candles" because messy handwork attracts children. In general, activities were formed more from what teachers wanted students to be interested in than from information about the interests of students. Also, teachers had concern about the transitory nature of student interests—"fads"—and how these interests could promote progress toward significant educational goals.

A recent analysis of elementary curriculum materials found that many of the problems identified by Meriam persist in many of today's learning tasks and school activities (Brophy & Alleman, 1991). These problems include the following:

- Activities that do not contribute to significant learning because they are built around peripheral content rather than key ideas (e.g., identify clothes that would be worn to a birthday party) or are busywork (e.g., word searches, memorizing names of state capitals and state symbols, cutting and pasting, coloring, connecting dots)

- Activities that induce misconceptions instead of accurate understanding (e.g., forced categorizations, such as exercises in distinguishing foods eaten today from foods eaten long ago and classifying foods as breakfast, lunch, or dinner foods)

- Activities that do not justify the trouble it takes to implement them (e.g., pageants, culminating activities, complicated simulations, collage and scrapbook activities that call for a lot of cutting and pasting of pictures but not thinking or writing about ideas linked to major goals)

- Activities that are not matched to students' competency or readiness levels (e.g., students already know what the activities are intended to teach or activities whose procedural complexities make them too difficult for students to understand)

Some parents overplan the activities for their children, depriving them of challenges and opportunities to exercise autonomy and collaboration with others. Activity 3–4, conducted at a workshop for teachers, illustrates the importance of giving responsibility to students for the design and conduct of learning activities.

Toward an Ideal Activity Curriculum

It's easy for a teacher to present educational tasks, but ideal learning activities require that the teacher know the students' lives outside school. Stories of student alienation and resistance to school tasks are legion. "Do we have to do what we want to do today?" "Would you like to get out your green math books?" Peter springs upright in his seat. "Do we have to? You said, 'Do we want to?'" The teacher grins with a wry twinkle. "Well, I guess I just meant to ask you nicely to get out your books." The teacher pauses; then, nodding to Peter but addressing the class, says, "*Please* get out your green books and get ready."

ACTIVITY 3–4   RATING THE TEACHER

This activity is based on an actual activity carried out in a Foxfire workshop for teachers.

1. On a scale of 1 to 10, with 10 closest to a good developer of an activity curriculum, rate the teacher described here.

   When the teacher noticed that her students were having problems with map skills, she applied for a minigrant from a local corporation to plan a large square map of her county to scale and properly oriented due north on a cement slab in the schoolyard. She located the town and major highways and took her students outside for their lessons on the slab. Later she presented the results of activity at a banquet hosted by the donors.

2. Imagine that you are talking with others about all the other things the teacher described above might have done, from leading her students through the process of choosing a project, to helping them plan the events—presenting the plan to the principal, drafting the minigrant proposal, giving the rationale and drawing up the budget, having the students design the prototype map to scale (as did Pestalozzi), receive the money, purchase the supplies, paint the map, document the process, plan how other classes might use the map, invite them to do so, produce an article about the project for the local paper, present the results themselves (complete with slides) at the banquet. What more could the teacher have done to make the activity educational for the students?

3. Now rate the teacher again.

Teachers often assign tasks or arrange situations in hopes of initiating educative activity—exploratory activities or problem solving on the part of students. Ideally, school tasks link subject matter (content or thinking skills) with the students' own motivations for various kinds of knowledge. The ideal activity curriculum requires that tasks both relate to the students' world and offer them the possibility of transforming that world.

Prior discussion in this chapter about constructivism highlighted the importance of uncovering the motives, goals, questions, and perspectives of students as they act on materials and other aspects of the classroom environment. It also recommended that students create knowledge in a social environment in which collective learning takes place through group and classroom discussion and projects. However, the ideal activity curriculum requires the teacher to gain broader insights into the real-world activities of learners, as well as insights into the thinking and behavior of students as they undertake classroom tasks. The additional challenge for teachers is to understand the life situations of students so that school tasks involve subject matter that is functional.

Approaches to this challenge are found in Part 5, which presents extensive accounts of teachers and students creating ideal activity curricula, particularly with respect to long-term units of instruction. For this chapter, however, the concept of designing educational activities that are in harmony with students' social contexts is illustrated by the two accounts that follow.

Deriving School Tasks from Life in the Community

Four 6-year-olds were brought to the roadside and for 5 minutes were asked to do three things: (a) count the number of cars driving toward the town, (b) count those coming from the town, and (c) write down the results. The children were organized into pairs, with one to do the counting and reporting to the other who was to write the information down. Children typically solved the problem of how to write by using a symbol for each car, such as 1111 or xxxx, and the like. On returning to the classroom, pairs presented the results, which were written on the chalkboard for interpretation, counting, and discussion.

Subsequently, groups did the activity at different times and the variations in the results were discussed: When did the most cars pass? In the morning? Afternoon? What about when there was a ceremony near the church? Later, questions were asked and answered about how many people a car can seat. (Unexpectedly, the children's mode number was 7, which probably reflected their experience rather than the experience of the teacher, who wanted 5.) Then the children were grouped in fives, and each group took a place near the wall to do some driving—two children in front, three in the rear. The 24 members of the class were transformed into four full cars and one with an empty seat.

The children repeated the activity at the roadside, this time counting cars and the number of people in them, recording the number of occupants from one to five. They transformed the results into graphs. Their graphs were impressive, showing from 1 to 30 cars with one occupant to 6 cars with five occupants. The children also counted and reported the number of buses seen and estimated how many people the buses could seat. These children used their own symbols for the recording, which they then compared and discussed.

Spoken mathematics was encouraged in the classroom. Questions such as the following were discussed:

- "How many are absent today? How many were absent yesterday? The day before? Is a flu epidemic around? Is it mostly children from one specific area who are absent?"

- "How many pages are left?"

- "You will have to go 4 by 4 to the nurse."

- "We have 8 minutes per group. Will we finish before lunch? How many minutes will groups have by then? Could you show us your method? So you drew the clock and counted like that? Very clever. Does anyone else have a method you would like to show?"

As indicated, this activity curriculum was connected to the lives of beginners and involved powerful math content—counting, graphing, classifying and grouping, variation in data as a function of time, and the function of mathematical symbols—all in the context of using mathematics as a tool to solve problems.

Companion
Website

> If you are interested in Lev Vygotsky's contributions to activity theory, in which, the teacher "scaffolds" the thinking of children so that what they do today with the help of the teacher, tomorrow they can do by themselves, you can read a collection of papers about the works of Vygotsky at *www.prenhall.com/mcneil*. Select Enter, then Topic 2: Child/Adolescent Development. Click on Web Links, then Developmental Theories.

Relating Popular Knowledge to School Knowledge

Steig Mellin-Olsen, a Norwegian teacher of mathematics, aims at an ideal activity curriculum that includes cultural aspects—the way people outside school use mathematics (Mellin-Olsen, 1987). He starts with folk mathematics, such as sawing a piece of wood along a given angle or the designing of a skirt pattern. Such everyday activities can lead to theoretical learning and formalizations, such as $\angle a = 90$ degrees for angles, or to the use of proportion for designing. Mellin-Olsen wants students to engage in those activities that are required for effective functioning in their own community and also to extend their knowledge of subject matters.

By way of example, knowing that knitting and carpentry have deep roots in Norwegian culture, he connected the folk mathematics of these activities to the learning of formal mathematics. Knitting involves wool left over—blue and red yarn in two balls. The decisions about what to make—socks, mittens, scarf, or something else—depend on the quantity and quality of the wool, time of year, and the like. If students decide to make red-and-blue socks and know that 100 grams of wool are necessary for a pair, then they have to design a pattern and figure out the ratio of the colors in the pattern compared with amount of wool available in the two colors. In Mellin-Olsen's example, students consider several ways of dividing the wool based on the design, including one in which there is almost twice as much red as blue. This problem lays the basis for instruction in proportion and symmetry.

Carpentry activity centers on the use of off-cuts of wood for building a hut, in which Euclidean geometry is presented as a way to solve questions that arise during the building process. For example, in traditional Euclidean geometry, two triangles are congruent if their corresponding sides are equal in length. In carpentry geometry, when a rectangular frame is built, a diagonal base is needed to prevent the frame from collapsing, and whenever a triangle is built, the builder has to make sure that the whole doesn't fall down. Also in traditional Euclidean geometry, a quadrilateral is a parallelogram if, and only if, both opposite sides are equal, but in carpentry, diagonals must be measured using the theorem that a parallelogram in which the diagonals are equal is a rectangle.

Back in the classroom, Mellin-Olsen puts his carpenters on the road to Euclid with problems like this:

> You have materials of these dimensions for a frame of the floor of a hut:
> 7.5 centimeters
> 9 centimeters
> 10 centimeters
> 6 centimeters
> Don't think about what else you will need for the hut. How would you make the frame and how would you check that it is OK?
> Draw what you would like it to look like, and write the measures for it.

Most teachers don't live in areas where knitting and carpentry are so popular with young people, but the point is that all teachers can observe students carrying out the tasks of their culture, can listen to what students say while thinking about how best to perform the tasks, and then can use this information in planning classroom activities.

Using School Knowledge in Activities for Transforming Aspects of Daily Life

In the traditional elementary school curriculum, students are assigned artificial tasks so that they can have experience with data and some analysis of the distribution; for example, they may be asked to quantify their day and night activities. In contrast, the ideal activity curriculum features projects in which students address actual problems and use math investigations as part of a plan for approaching the adult world—for example, with the idea of improving the neighborhood. In one instance, a new housing project failed to provide recreational areas for children, so teachers of three elementary classrooms involved their students in a project related to the problem. For the project, students generated suggestions for recreation and then interviewed other students about their preferences. Data collection, statistics and data analysis, and other mathematical tools were important in documenting the issue and possible solutions. Subsequently, students prepared and carried out a plan of action whereby they presented their conclusions, supported by their data, to various boards and councils that could act on their demands for change. An ideal curriculum activity emerged as analysis and discussion developed into action for transforming an aspect of the students' daily life.

Companion
Website

> John Singer and others have created four middle school units on water quality, an eighth-grade unit on force and motion, and an eighth-grade unit on communicable diseases and the immune system. The units are interesting in their own right, but, more important, they show in curriculum terms the principles of social construction, inquiry, and ties to big standards reform in science. They also show how technology can be used to support students in intellectually challenging tasks. To see how they developed these curricula, go to *www.prenhall.com/mcneil* and click on Singer.

SUMMARY

The trends toward constructivist and activity curricula are giving students more responsibility for their own learning. Preparing students for uncertainty and change is a dominant impetus behind these trends. Although differences in student outlooks are recognized and appreciated in the new curricula, teachers make a conscious effort to help students extend their outlooks in the direction of more encompassing, mature, and public views. The classroom is a community where meanings are negotiated.

A meaning-based approach to curriculum development is an alternative to the traditional model of planning that has dominated schools. Instead of using the organized subject matter of the adult and the prespecification of instructional objectives as the starting points for curriculum design, constructivist teachers begin with the multiple goals and backgrounds of their students. Tentative plans of teachers give way to an enacted curriculum whereby teacher and students determine the validity of goals and content as they reflect on their experiences in instructional activity.

This chapter has shown that the student-centered curriculum does not imply that scientific and other knowledge or subject area systems are excluded. On the contrary, essential content is introduced when it is likely to serve student purposes and address their issues and problems.

Although a constructivist approach is effective, it is not the only way to facilitate student learning of subject matter, and constructivism is not only valued because of its effectiveness in academic achievement. Constructivism has gained prominence because it contributes to other values—cooperation, demystification of where knowledge comes from, critical awareness of the tentativeness of knowledge, and the fostering of multiple perceptions (Burbules, 2000).

The contributions of Pestalozzi and Froebel to constructivist and activity curricula, and their viable alternatives to a formalized curriculum, have been described. The work of those early teachers demonstrates that teachers can initiate mighty winds of curriculum change. The accounts of modern teachers who follow these educational innovators may inspire others.

This chapter has acknowledged the difficulties involved with placing control of learning in the hands of students and has drawn contrasts between sterile school tasks and those learning activities that relate to the actual concerns and lives of students. It has featured examples of teachers who are relating students' real-world activities to the classroom and setting up environments in which students construct knowledge by reorganizing their thinking and beliefs and, in some instances, transforming the quality of life in places where the students live.

QUESTIONS FOR DISCUSSION

1. How does the teacher's view of human nature affect classroom practice? What are the consequences of believing that children must be controlled and shaped versus believing that students have predispositions to goodness and should be given freedom to pursue their own inclinations and goals?
2. What are some curriculum implications for believing that students bring their own resources to the learning context and construct their own meanings from it?
3. Indicate how curriculum materials might best reconcile two sometimes conflicting concerns:
   a. Encouraging individual thinking
   b. Learning rules and procedures established by the wider society
4. What are some reasons that teachers might have for not implementing a constructivist curriculum? How might such constraints best be overcome or circumvented?
5. In what way does a constructivist curriculum address problems associated with increasingly diverse student populations and the conflicts and contradictions between popular culture and academic knowledge?
6. Ask two or three people to talk about and explain what they "know" about something—the concept of an atom, electricity, poetry, prime numbers, multiplication of fractions, the Bill of Rights, the Federal Reserve system, use of geometry in solving real-world problems, origin of the self, time, respiratory system, or any other topic. Have them avoid textbook generalizations but instead give their own understanding of the topic. What are the gaps and uncertainties in their explanations? Are there conflicting views on the topic? Relate the inquiry to the constructivist curriculum.
7. Is it the unpredictable rather than the predictable outcomes from student actions that make education worthwhile? If so, what are the implications for curriculum development?

REFERENCES

Brophy, J., & Alleman, J. (1991). Activities as instructional tools: A framework for analysis and education. *Educational Researcher. 20*(4), 24–30.

Brosterman, N. (1997). *Inventing kindergarten: Nineteenth century children and twentieth century art.* New York: Abrams.

Burbules, N. (2000). Moving beyond the impass. In D. C. Phillips (Ed.), *Constructivism in education: Opinions and second opinions on controversial issues* (pp. 330–331). Chicago: University of Chicago.

Burns, M. (1987). *Math lessons.* Sausalito, CA: Math Solutions.

Cremin, L. A. (1961). *The transformation of the school.* New York: Knopf.

Cubberley, E. D. (1934). *Public education in the United States.* Boston: Houghton Mifflin.

DeVries, R., & Kohlberg, L. (1990). *Constructivist early education: Overview and comparison with other programs.* Washington, DC: National Association for Education of Young Children.

Hailman, W. H. (1887). Superintendent Zechs' report of his visit to the Educational Institute at Keilham, 1826. In *The education of man.* New York: Appleton.

Magidson, S. (1992). From the laboratory to the classroom: A technology intensive curriculum for functions and graphs. *Journal of Mathematical Behavior, 11*(4), 361–377.

Mellin-Olsen, S. (1987). *The politics of mathematics education.* Norwell, MA: Kluwer Academic.

Meriam, J. (1920). *Child life and the curriculum.* Yonkers, NY: World Book.

Nelson, D. (1985). *City building education.* Los Angeles: Center for City Building Education Programs.

Richards, J. J. (1991). The implementation of a Japanese science education method in the United States. Paper presented at the American Educational Research Association Annual Meeting, Chicago.

Schoonmaker, F. (2001). Curriculum making, models, practices and issues: A knowledge fetish? In L. Corno (Ed.), *Education across a century: The centennial volume* (Pt. 1, pp. 1–33). Chicago: University of Chicago Press.

Smith, J. L., & Johnson, H. A. (1993). Content in the classroom: Listening to adolescent voices. *Language Arts, 70,* 18–30.

Twoney, C. F. (Ed.). (1996). *Constructivism: Theory, perspectives, and practice.* New York: Teachers College Press.

Wheatley, G. H. (1992). The role of reflection in mathematics learning. *Educational Studies in Mathematics, 25*(5), 29–54.

CHAPTER 4

PERSONAL DEVELOPMENT
IN THE ACADEMIC CONTEXT

Merl: Any ideas on how a curriculum can relate to the interests and needs of children of different ages?

Sara: Hey, I'm not a recreation director or a psychiatrist. I'm responsible for closing academic gaps and there are plenty. The range in backgrounds of my students is overwhelming. Age doesn't tell me what they know.

Merl: I agree that it is difficult to target curriculum on some assumed developmental stage based on age. The cultural experiences of the students are as influential as age. In fact, I have three students that are better in handling math than many adults. It makes me wonder whether there is something to the charge that "age-appropriate" is a phony idea to control children or overprotect them from ideas some adults abhor.

This chapter looks at personal development—that is, the development of identity—as a curriculum aim. It describes efforts to relate curriculum to the psychological and biological needs of learners and illustrates how social interactions play an important part in determining who one is.

Teachers are sometimes asked to think about putting the learner's needs first and then selecting subject matter to relate to those needs, versus putting the subject matter first and then trying to relate the subject matter to a learner's personal concerns. Curriculum exemplars in this chapter illustrate ways to capitalize on students' strengths and to extend them through social arrangements.

Furthermore, the chapter challenges the constraints imposed by stage theorists— those who believe that individuals move through similar stages of development and that curriculum content should match one's stage of development—cognitive, moral, physical, and the like. The curriculum exemplars relate to the forming of personal identities, taking advantage of the individual's endowed strengths and extending them.

CURRICULUM FOR PERSONAL DEVELOPMENT

Personal development is generally viewed in terms of autonomy, self-knowledge, or the formation of personal values. Abraham Maslow proposed a hierarchy of universal needs that must be met for optimum personal development: physiological needs, safety needs, belongingness and esteem needs, the need to develop one's potential talent and capabilities (self-actualization), and the need to understand and appreciate aesthetically. Although personal development and the meeting of human needs can serve as a broad aim, no one-to-one correspondence exists between such aims and the answer to the teacher's question "What should I teach?" Specific situations determine how human needs can best be met. The eloquent reply in 1744 of leaders of the Six Nations to an invitation from commissioners of Virginia to send Native American boys to the College of William and Mary illustrates how responses to universal needs are shaped by culture:

> We know that you highly esteem the kind of learning taught in those colleges, and that the Maintenance of our young Men, while with you would be very expensive to you. We are convinced, that you mean to do us Good by your Proposal; and we thank you heartily. But you, who are wise, must know that different Nations have different Conceptions of things and you will therefore not take it amiss, if our ideas of this kind of Education happen not to be the same as yours. We have had some experience of it. Several of our young People were formerly brought up at the Colleges of the Northern Provinces: they were instructed in all your Sciences; but, when they came back to us, they were bad Runners, ignorant of every means of living in the woods . . . neither fit for Hunters, Warriors, nor Counsellors, they were totally good for nothing.
>
> We are, however, not the less oblig'd by your kind Offer, tho' we decline accepting it; and, to show our grateful Sense of it, if the Gentlemen of Virginia will send us a Dozen of their Sons, we will take Care of their Education, instruct them in all we know, and make Men of them. (McLuhan, 1971, p. 57)

Universal Needs

The idea of universal needs is useful to curriculum makers in several ways. First, the concept suggests content fundamental to human nature. Decci, Valerane, Pellitier, and Ryan (1991) postulate that three needs are innate and inherent in human life:

1. *Competence*—understanding how to attain various outcomes and be able to perform the requisite actions
2. *Relatedness*—developing secure and satisfying connections with others in one's social milieu
3. *Autonomy*—self-initiating and self-regulating one's own actions

Second, the teacher's theory of universal human needs serves to help the teacher make sense of a multitude of student behaviors. Observations and facts regarding a student's participation in activities, academic performance, attitudes toward school, plans for the future, peer and parent relations, and the like can be connected through an interpretation based on a human needs perspective. Working from this interpretation, the teacher conceives and implements a plan of action regarding the learner.

Third, the concept of need allows one to specify the contextual conditions that will facilitate a student's academic performance and development. This point has special relevance for those who want to see students achieve in particular subject areas. Accomplishment in a field requires conceptual understanding and the flexible use of knowledge. Curriculum contexts that support student competency, social relations, and learner autonomy are linked to these two requirements. A central theme of this chapter is that unless a curriculum contributes to the basic psychological needs of learners, that curriculum will diminish students' motivation, impair their developmental process, and lead to poorer academic performance.

How Teachers and Peers Meet Developmental Needs in the Academic Context

Newman (2000) has marshaled evidence showing how teachers and peers contribute to the development of the relatedness, autonomy, and competence necessary for successful academic learning.

Roles of the Teacher

Relatedness

- Establishes personal relationships with students

- Involves him- or herself in multiple ways depending on student age and other factors: (a) showing affection (liking, appreciation, enjoyment); giving resources (aid, time, energy); attunement (aware of the student's problems and abilities)

- Takes the student's perspective and understands his or her thinking

- Brings to class his or her own academic strengths and interests and describes his or her own thinking when confronting tasks and problems in learning

Autonomy

- Sets challenging academic goals that focus on mastering critical tasks

- Helps students link personal goals to the academic goals

- Makes students responsible for pursuing goals

- Encourages students to seek assistance only when necessary

- Avoids external rewards that increase student dependency on the teacher and puts grades ahead of learning

- Lets students figure out problems for themselves

- Shows how students' efforts—what they are doing—is related to achievement, avoiding the negative effect of belief in ability as determining success

- Gives feedback tailored to the individual that is specific, not a global assessment—that is, offers guidance, not answers, notes strengths as well as weaknesses, and includes encouraging comments

- Records the student's progress, not normative grades

Competency

- Helps student learn how to ask questions

- Sees that questions flow from student to teacher and from student to student; less teacher-to-students flow

- Employs different activity structures: individual, whole class, small groups—each with norms for expectation, management, and communication

- Makes sure students know how to collaborate, downplaying competitiveness

Roles of Peers   Peer collaboration is essential for development of positive identities and the social construction of knowledge. Influential peers have learned to perform the following roles:

Relatedness

- Share experiences, exchange information, and learn from each other

- Build friendships by supporting each other and offering self-disclosures and intimacies

Autonomy

- May make social comparisons if they are constructive and nonjudgmental

- Avoid comparisons that are a threat to self-worth and inhibit help seeking

- Focus on learning and completing tasks, not on comparing individuals

- Exchange perspectives and ideas

- Model ways of thinking and doing

- Elaborate on explanations

- Listen to what others have to say

- Don't give answers to problems, but show how to solve them

- Receive suggestions and then try them out

Competency

- Seek help only when necessary

- Know when help is necessary and how to get it

■ ——— ■

ACTIVITY 4-1   DETERMINING DEVELOPMENTAL GOALS FROM INFORMATION ABOUT LEARNER(S)

Any instructional program should be responsive, at least in part, to the individual learner's nature and needs. This activity offers you the opportunity to explore different ways of gathering pertinent information about a learner population, to reveal your own interpretation of what this information means—what you consider to be positive or negative—and, finally, to state what educational responses would be appropriate to your findings and interpretation (individual goals, content, or activities).

1. For the purpose of this exercise, select the learner(s) for whom you might actually develop a curriculum (e.g., a peer, a partner, or a family member).
2. State the area or areas in which you will seek information about the learner(s)—health, interests, activities, peer relations, attitude toward school, learning expectations, and so on.
3. Conduct an interview, survey, or observe your learner(s) in specific situations, or examine any readily available school records about the learner.
4. Record a summary of the information collected, the generalizations or interpretations you draw from the information, and state what implications you see for either *what* should be taught the learners or *how* something should be taught the learners in light of your study.

Figure 4-1 presents a suggested form for your report.

■ ——— ■

■ Monitor own performance

■ Attend to goals, tasks, and learning, not grades

Activity 4-1 requires making educational responses to student needs. Educational responses may be different from responses provided by other professionals and nonschool institutions.

ACADEMIC APPROACHES TO PERSONAL NEEDS

It is assumed that among those who completed Activity 4-1, some drew opportunities for learners to advance their own interests and to pursue their own concerns. Others would help learners increase their motivation, find new interests, and enhance their self-concept. Some would focus on learners' recognizing sources of help or recognizing their own talents and becoming aware of how they are inhibiting or facilitating their personal decision making. Some would help

Summary of Findings	Generalizations and Interpretations of the Findings	Curriculum Implications (a logical answer to what you have uncovered—the action, content, or goal you would introduce to help the learner)
Health		
Interests		
Peer relations		
Attitude toward learning		
Other		

FIGURE 4–1
Curriculum implications from studies of the learner

learners set more realistic standards, to engage in multiple ways to express themselves, or to consider alternatives to their intuitive beliefs. The possibilities are numerous.

Immediately, however, some teachers will question the extent to which such goals should be pursued in the classroom, where they believe that academic subject matter should be the focus. Other teachers believe that students' personal development is the function of other people and agencies—parents, medical specialists, psychologists, and social workers, for example. Most teachers, however, understand that they have a unique contribution to make to the personal development of their students through expansion of knowledge, social interventions, and learning activities. These teachers know that overemphasis on achievement tends to increase a sense of detachment, loneliness, emptiness, and discontent. Hence, they emphasize community learning and social connections. Teachers sometimes divide in their approaches, with some giving priority to developmental issues and introducing a wide variety of resources for addressing them, while others capitalize on student psychological and social concerns, using them as a means to activate the learning of academic subjects. The following sections illustrate curriculum from the two perspectives.

A Curriculum That Prioritizes Personal Concern

Goodman (1991) has described how Ursina, a teacher in an Indiana middle school, has responded to the growing sexual maturity of early adolescents by designing a curriculum that breaks out of the subject matter mold in addressing an important student concern. Although biological information regarding adolescent development and reproduction was introduced in her science class, Ursina ensured that the social and psychological context within which adolescents become sexual beings also received attention. Among the themes of Ursina's human sexuality curriculum were these:

1. Communication—the ability to openly discuss sexual feelings and behavior in mixed-gender groups of peers and with adults. Communication was necessary to avoid the mistrust and fear associated with gender separatism. Students were expected to respect the information that others gave, others' right to privacy, and student-generated questions. A communicative climate was established as students discussed topics that were formerly taboo—anal sex, transvestites, incest, birth control methods, and the like. All materials for the course (films, guest speakers, books) were available for both girls and boys. Boys role-played fathers, explaining physiological and emotional aspects of development to the girls as if the girls were their 10-year-old daughters. In turn, girls explained the same information to their "sons."

2. Appreciating one's own body—examining attitudes toward students' own bodies. Students performed activities such as viewing themselves in front of a mirror. They critically analyzed the images of "beauty" conveyed in advertising, films, and television. They viewed photographs of external and internal sexual organs, and they discussed the "beauty" of human sexuality and the wonder of conception. Students discussed the implications of taking full responsibility for the health of their bodies.

3. Dynamics of sexual development—considering cultural consequences of living in a society that follows a patriarchal rationality. For example, students discussed how the "negative" characteristics of being a girl in American society could be a positive given a different cultural worldview. In response to the statement that "anything that two consenting people do (sexually) is OK," content emerged regarding government's role in an individual's sex life, sexual exploitation, subtle forms of coercion, and the concept of informed judgments. The issues of date rape and the evaluation of intimate relationships were treated. In pursuing their concern about homosexuality, students interviewed male and female members of the Gay Alliance. Throughout their study, students gained understanding of the responsibilities and caring necessary for a healthy love relationship.

4. Teenage pregnancy—demystifying teen pregnancy. Students interpreted facts about social, economic, and health costs of teenage pregnancy. They discussed reasons so many teenagers in the United States become pregnant. They sought answers to the questions of who are responsible for this situation and how the social issue could be addressed. Issues of adoption, abortion, and birth control—and their ethical dimensions—were considered by students and guest speakers.

A Curriculum of Concern That Puts Biology First

Heller's (1993) Human Biology curriculum (Hum Bio) is a response to the negative aspects of adolescent lifestyle—drugs, violence, and unplanned pregnancy. However, Heller is as much troubled by student disaffection and alienation from science. He focuses on human and adolescent concerns in the belief that in doing so, more science will be taught than in a standard curriculum.

In each unit of the Hum Bio curriculum, Heller emphasizes information from the behavioral sciences, biological sciences, and safety and health. When teaching about the heart and circulation, he provides information about the effects of fatty foods, cholesterol, and stress. The "Your Changing Body" unit describes what happens during puberty, the role of hormones, and the menstrual cycle. Discussion of feelings about body changes, gender, attractiveness, dieting, anorexia, and steroid abuse occurs. Active learning is promoted through such activities as students calculating how much blood their hearts pump per hour, finding the blind spots in their field of vision, and creating scenarios for an adolescent whose wish for independence conflicts with parental standards.

Hum Bio is primarily a life science curriculum. The conventional topics such as the nervous system and how it works together with scientific concepts are viewed as essential. However, each topic is related to a personal concern of students. Study of the topic of the brain, for example, includes discussion about the effect of drugs on the brain.

The underlying assumption of this curriculum is that if the teacher can capture student interest with topics that adolescents find relevant, students will learn and retain more. Instead of starting with Mendel's pea plant, Hum Bio starts with human genetics, sex determinates, and genetic disease, capitalizing on adolescent concerns as the springboard to appreciation of science. In turn, a relevant information base should help students make wiser decisions in their lives.

CURRICULUM USING THE THEORIES OF ERIKSON AND PIAGET

Two major theoretical sources that explain human development and influence the way teachers respond to learners are the writings of Erik Erikson (1968) and Jean Piaget (1991). Both of these theorists follow Froebel in adhering to the *epigenetic principle,* which holds that just as certain organs of the body appear at specified times and allow the individual to perform life-sustaining functions, so, too, do the personality and intellect of an individual form through a series of interrelated stages.

Linking Curriculum to Erikson's Developmental Concerns

The idea of linking academic content to psychological needs is powerful. Unless curriculum is tied to basic needs, it is unlikely to lead to high academic performance. Erikson's (1968) stages provide a vehicle for effecting such linkages. To the extent that a teacher of mathematics, art, reading, or any other subject succeeds in addressing a developmental task through the subject matter, that content will be valued. A teacher of history, for example, became aware of how her adolescent students' concern for identity (an Erikson concept) was reflected in the conflict between parental expectations and peer expectations for certain social behaviors. Responding to this, she encouraged a project in which students conducted a historical study related to the social practice in question (e.g., diet, dress, recreational habits). The students used primary and secondary sources in their investigation into the origins of the practice. Subsequently, the students evaluated the current social context that was responsible for changed beliefs regarding the practice. The research resulted in great gains in student interest in history, historical information, methodology, and interpretation. It also led to better student–parent understanding.

A further example of how academic goals in conventional subject matter—reading, writing, and arithmetic—can be related to psychological needs is found in Terry Borton's "Curriculum of Concern." Borton selected the concern of self-identity and encouraged students to explore the disparity between what they thought about in school, what they were concerned about in their lives outside school, and the ways they acted. The curriculum outline consisted of a series of questions designed to lead the students to a personal sense of identity and finally to an examination of actions that would express that sense of self. Some of the questions were these: "What is 'human' about humans?" "Who am I?" "How can we find activities to express our thoughts and feelings?" Additionally, students engaged in many activities, such as a trip to the zoo to contrast humans with animals, improvised drama to imitate the movement of animals, and discussions of animal metaphors in the characterizations of humans. All activities reflected the teacher's commitment to the three Rs. In addition, students made generalizations about identity, such as "If a consciousness of self is one of the major differences between animal and human, then one of the most effective ways to make people more human or more humane would be to help them explore the significance of their own diversity."

Erikson's Developmental Stages

Erikson (1968) has proposed eight stages of development, each of which poses a critical task and consists of positive and negative qualities. Individuals adapt to the world best when they successfully possess more of the positive quality of a given stage than the negative quality. The following outlines the tasks, qualities, typical age ranges, and characteristics of the stages.

Trust versus Mistrust (Birth to 1 Year)   The basic task to be learned by infants is that they can trust their world. Trust is acquired by consistency, continuity, and sameness of experience in satisfying the infant's basic needs by the caretaker. If the care infants receive is inadequate, inconsistent, or negative, they will approach the world with fear and suspicion.

Autonomy versus Shame and Doubt (2 to 3 Years)   A sense of autonomy develops when toddlers are permitted and encouraged to do what they are capable of doing at their own pace and in their own way. If caretakers are impatient and do too many things for young children, then the children may doubt their ability. Also, adults should not shame young children for unacceptable behavior for this will contribute to feelings of self-doubt.

Initiative versus Guilt (4 to 5 Years)   When children are 4 and 5 years old, they want to be active. If given freedom to explore and experiment (and if caregivers take time to answer their questions), the inner drive of these children toward initiative will be encouraged. If children are restricted and made to feel that their activities and questions are bothersome, they will feel guilt about doing things on their own. Froebel's words are appropriate here:

> Show no impatience about their ever-recurring questions. Every repelling word crushes a bud on a shoot of their tree of life. Do not, however, tell them in words much more than they can find themselves without your words. . . . [I]t is, of course, easier to hear the answer from another, perhaps to only half hear and understand it, then to seek and discover for oneself. Do not, therefore, always answer your children's questions at once and directly, but as *soon* as they have gathered sufficient strength and experience furnish them with the means to find the answers in the sphere of their own knowledge. (Hailman, 1887, p. xiv)

Industry versus Inferiority (6 to 11 Years)   On entering school, children are dominated by curiosity and desire for performance. They are ready to learn by producing things, developing a sense of industry. The danger at this stage is that they may feel inadequate or inferior. If the child is encouraged to make and do things well, to persevere, and to finish tasks and if the child is praised for trying, industry results. If the child is unsuccessful, derided, or treated as bothersome, a feeling of inferiority results. Children who feel inferior may never enjoy intellectual work and take pride in doing things well. Worse, they may feel that they will never excel in anything.

Identity versus Role Confusion (12 to 18 Years)   At this stage, adolescents are concerned about the kind of person they are becoming. The goal at this stage is "the accrued confidence of sameness and continuity." The danger at this stage is role confusion, such as doubt about sexual and occupational identity. If teenagers succeed, as reflected by the reaction of significant others (parents, teachers, peers), in integrating roles in different situations so they experience continuity in their perception of self, identity develops. If they are unable to establish a sense of stability in aspects of their lives, role confusion results.

Integrity versus Isolation (Young Adulthood)   The goal at this stage is to establish an intimate relationship with another person. A willingness to be truthful about oneself and the other contributes to this goal. Failure to achieve the goal will lead to a sense of isolation.

Generativity versus Stagnation (Middle Age)   Generativity refers to productive and creative efforts that will have a positive effect on younger generations. Teaching, research, curriculum development, and political and social action that benefit children and youth are cases in point. The negative qualities of this state are stagnation and self-absorption.

Integrity versus Despair (Old Age)   Integrity is the acceptance of one's life as something that had to be and that by necessity permitted no substitutions. Despair is the feeling that time is too short to take alternative roads to integrity.

Implications for Curriculum Planning   In planning curriculum, teachers sometimes identify the development stage of the learners to be served and attempt to shape learning opportunities so that they contribute to the positive qualities of each stage. Examples of curriculum that assist students with their needs for *industry*—the feeling of competence—are found in many Montessori schools. The "practical life" area of many Montessori programs includes a large set of activities that prepare young children for success in tasks of daily life, such as personal hygiene, cleaning, care of the environment, courtesy, repair of machines, and nutrition and food preparation (see Activity 4–2). Prerequisite skills for these real-life tasks, including pouring, spooning, and using tools, are taught to enhance success and a sense of competence.

In the academic area, also, many children in Montessori schools have success because they are presented with materials that interest them, offer clear tasks that can be independently undertaken, and have a built-in feature whereby the child can tell whether his or her actions have been appropriate (e.g., when a child is constructing a tower, a cube placed out of order will result in an unstable structure).

An illustration of a curriculum that advances understanding of the subject matter of history by meeting developmental needs is "Teaching the Holocaust," which follows.

Teaching the Holocaust

Carmon (1980) has developed a moral curriculum in history called "Teaching the Holocaust." It places the adolescent and the problem of identity at the focal point in the presentation of history. This curriculum is based on Erikson's belief that people are confirmed by their identities and that society is regenerated by their lifestyles. To enter history, students must be able to relate their childhoods to the childhood experiences of former generations. They must be able to identify with the ideals conveyed in the history of their culture. According to Erikson, in youth, childhood dependence gives way; no longer is it the old teaching the young the meaning of life, it is the young who by their actions tell the old whether life as represented to them has some vital promise.

The major purpose of the Holocaust curriculum developed by Arye Carmon is to heighten the student's awareness of the critical question of adult responsibil-

---

ACTIVITY 4–2 GENERATING ACADEMIC ACTIVITIES THAT ARE ALSO RESPONSIVE TO DEVELOPMENTAL CONCERNS

1. Identify a developmental concern—trust, initiative, industry, identity, or other—for a learner or learners with whom you are familiar.
2. Sketch an idea for a learning activity whereby the above concern can be related to the learner's progress in a subject matter of importance to you.

ity. This purpose is achieved by fostering young students' awareness of the human tendency toward stereotyping, prejudice, ethnocentrism, and obeying authority as an escape of responsibilities. The subject matter is organized into units: the socialization of a German adolescent in Nazi Germany, the socialization of a Gestapo member, the moral dilemmas of individuals and groups during the Holocaust, and the meaning of life in the post-Holocaust era. In each unit, students are given documents from the historical period. These documents provide historical background and serve as a basis for discussion of the moral dilemmas.

There are opportunities for both individual inquiry and group exchanges. Each person deals with a specific document; students then form small groups to exchange feelings and opinions regarding the topics and their individual studies. Finally, the entire class completes the discussion of the topic at hand. The content is not alien to the students, and they cannot remain apathetic to it. Students face questions that are relevant to their own lives:

- Why favor the sanctification of life rather than martyrdom?

- What are the dilemmas that confronted individuals at the time of the Holocaust and the dilemmas that confronted Jews as members of a community?

- Which of these dilemmas touches you personally? Why?

- What is the common denominator of the dilemmas?

Discussion of the issues results in a dialogue between the student and his or her conscience and among the student and peers.

During the first phase of this curriculum, resistance toward the subject matter arises; students tend to resist giving up their stereotypical attitudes and other protective mechanisms. Gradually, this resistance fades, only to be replaced by a feeling of helplessness. At this point, the study has opened students to the possibility of critical thinking and moral judgment. Students then begin to formulate the universal questions for confronting moral dilemmas:

- How would I have behaved if I had been in this situation?

- How should I have behaved?

Thus, the curriculum helps each student formulate a set of personal moral rules (Carmon, 1980).

Applying Piaget's Theories

From his investigations, Piaget concluded that cognitive development occurred in stages: the infant (birth to 2 years) acquires understanding of the world primarily through sensory impressions and motor activities; the young child (2 to 7 years) learns to think with symbols such as words; the preadolescent (7 to 11 years) generalizes from concrete experiences and arrives at an understanding of logic-based tasks such as conservation (matter is not created or destroyed when it changes shape or form) and classification of items by constructing hierarchical relations among items and arranging them in particular orders; and older students (11 years and older) acquire mental structure and ways of learning that allow them to deal with abstractions, form hypotheses, and conceive of possibilities and ideals that conflict with existing reality.

Piaget viewed mental structure as a product of both biological systems and learning from interaction with the world. Central to his theory is that learners must construct their own knowledge and assimilate new experiences in ways that make sense to them. Children create new knowledge by reflecting on their physical and mental actions. Telling students what they are to know does not work (Piaget, 1991).

Companion Website

> To read a biography of and essays by Piaget, go to *www.prenhall.com/mcneil,* select Enter, then Topic 2: Child/Adolescent Development. Click on Web Links, then Developmental Theories.

Initially, teachers used Piaget's theory as a *screen,* a basis for deciding what could be taught effectively to students of specified age. For instance, activities involving cause–effect relations or inductive and deductive reasoning were postponed until the intermediate grades. Unfortunately, the use of Piaget's theory as a screen conflicted with the Piagetian values of freedom, expansion, and optimal development. The screen led to a restricted view of what students are ready for and limited the methods and content that might be introduced to them. Furthermore, the practical problems that arise from trying to match learning opportunities with assumed mental ages are immense. Students are likely to have a high level of ability in an area where they have much experience and are likely to conduct themselves at lower levels in unfamiliar areas.

Today teachers are giving more attention to Piaget's interest in how outside stimulation affects an individual's initiative in pursuing the relations among ideas. Curriculum developers are giving more attention to Piaget's views that children are like scientists who are attempting to make sense of their reality and that learning best takes place when one is confronted with cognitive dissonance; that is, one's present ideas and practices are not compatible with the logic of others, or one's ideas and practices don't work in new situations. Cognitive dissonance occurs when fundamental beliefs and the logical basis for these are challenged. Students then create new beliefs and new ways of acting in the world in response to the conflicts.

In her work with children's science curriculum, Metz (1997) has challenged the Piagetian assumption about children's scientific reasoning abilities—that they can comprehend only ideas that are linked to concrete objects because they are "concrete thinkers" and that not until adolescence can children grasp the logic of experimental control and inference. She does not accept the assumption that the core of intellectual strength of children centers on playing and classifying, so that only making observations, ordering, and categorizing are "developmentally appropriate" science activities for children. Indeed, in her own curriculum enacted with young children, Metz has engaged second-graders in generating their own questions about insects, setting up controlled experiments for gathering data that might help answer their questions, observing (after recognizing the need to differentiate an inference from an observation), collecting and organizing their data, and determining what conclusions can be drawn on the basis of their findings.

Divergent Ideas about the Development of Identity

There is general agreement that social relations are important for identity. Language and social roles tend to place us in relation to someone or something, to define what we can and cannot do. However, despite the overriding importance of social structure, individuals can still give their own meaning to the structure. The curriculum can encourage students to consider new possibilities in the situation in which they find themselves, recognizing that they don't have to be dependent on existing structures.

Learning today means learning about oneself—a perspective of who one is in given circumstances. Although there may be a sense of an inner self that transcends the way we are at different times and place (similar to Erikson's unified view of identity), individuals find themselves in situations where they may be guided by different perspectives, some of which may be incompatible. Hence, teachers need to be aware of student needs for handling the various changing circumstances and contradictions so they can manage their own development. Openness, pluralistic attitudes, and ways to deal with contradictions are responding to today's diversity in culture in contrast with a time when roles were limited and fixed.

Implicit throughout this chapter is the question of how the curricula relates to the innate capacity of the learner (private world) and to the social contexts (the public worlds) that together determine the possibilities for an individual's identity (see Activity 4–3 for more on this point).

Curricula derived from Eleanor Duckworth's concept of "the having of wonderful ideas" and Howard Gardner's theory of multiple intelligences are singled out as models for enhancing the active construction of knowledge, including the use of a cognitive dissonance for knowing the world in new ways and helping students identify their strengths and pursue areas of personal interests where they can expect to make contributions.

Duckworth's "The Having of Wonderful Ideas"

Duckworth's curriculum first puts students in touch with concrete examples or experiences related to the area to be studied (math, science, art). Students are encouraged to notice what is interesting in the phenomena and challenged to think and wonder about what they have observed. Next, students are asked to share what sense they are making, and the teacher and peers try to understand the meanings students are creating from the situation. Students are helped to examine

ACTIVITY 4–3   HOW DOES CURRICULUM SHAPE IDENTITY?

1. Pick any student text, workbook, or test, or observe any interaction between student(s) and teacher.
2. Analyze the selection in terms of language and implied roles by answering as many of the following questions as you can:
   a. *Frame*. What is the intended purpose (stated or unstated)? What possible future for the learner does it point toward? Whose interests are served?
   b. *Tenor*. What social relations are implied? What is the distance between teacher and student? Who is marginalized? How is "student" defined? Where does authority lie?
   c. *Mode*. What is the role of language? What is being achieved by language? What practices are encouraged? What ideas about math, reading, writing, or other subjects would students form from this text or interaction?

conflicting notions and to recognize inadequate explanations, modifying their views as they resolve conflicts. Duckworth's curriculum offers situations in which learners at various cognitive levels come to know parts of the world in new ways, using multiple routes to knowledge—perception, action, and theory.

In a curriculum for teachers, Duckworth incorporates a unit on "Moon Watching," an aspect of astronomy. This unit is a vehicle for helping teachers better understand teaching and learning. The study of the moon by teachers who have had little scientific background is analogous to the school curriculum where students have as yet little interest and few ideas of their own. "Moon Watching" begins with a discussion of when the teacher-students last saw the moon, what it looked like then, when they think they'll see it next, and what it will look like then. This preliminary discussion gives rise to conflicting ideas and some involvement on the topic, although some of the students think a study of the moon is a waste of time.

The teacher-students are asked to keep and bring to class a notebook in which they make an entry every time they see the moon—when and where and what it looks like. After the first week's reporting, some students have something specific they want to look for, and little by little, the tasks change from ones that are arbitrary and trivial to ones that are absorbing and serious.

Excerpts of accounts from students illustrate the responses:

I keep my notebook on my bedside table, and every night it's there to remind me to look out the window. It takes only two to three minutes to write down my observations and draw my pictures, but later when I sit down and read several weeks' notes all together, I can spend fifteen to twenty minutes just generating questions and checking answers. I get excited when the moon moves across the sky just the way I thought it would, and I'm so disbelieving when it does something unexpected that I check my notes again and again.

My questions caused my observations to change. I'm now concentrating on the path of the moon each night, not on its color or shape, although I'm still shaky enough to always note those, too. . . . [E]verything is expanding—my questions and observations are getting broader.

My biggest problem in this class is forgetting about being a teacher and relearning how to be a learner. The notebook is a big help. I can make hypotheses and they can be wrong and that's OK. I can share observations and theories and be proud when someone says, "Ah, that's good." I can move at my own pace and ask my own questions. I like it.

I felt I knew a great deal about the moon. (I'd taught about the moon as part of a unit on astronomy with sixth-graders.) I knew things about orbits and distance and reflected light. The first class discussion clued me in to the fact that my knowledge of the moon falls short of an understanding. My knowledge was only from a perspective of out in space looking in. It was always easy to think about those three objects in space and their interaction (sun, moon, earth). With this new perspective, I had many questions without answers; not knowing can be much more fun than knowing. It has opened my eyes to look for understanding.

After observing and engaging with real phenomena and fellow learners, as well as the teacher, teacher-students are encouraged to reveal the meanings they are generating and to make their thoughts clear for others:

Class discussions have helped a lot. Often people have seen the moon at different times than I did, and they tentatively fill in some of my gaps in knowledge. (The gaps won't really be filled in until I see things for myself.) I also like to hear other people's hypotheses because they give me other avenues and ideas to check out. I especially like it when I can't believe what someone else has seen. It makes me slow down and reevaluate my own notes and theories.

Duckworth's students come to recognize knowledge as a human construction. As the teacher of the course, she centers her efforts on helping students to see that their own ideas are reasonable and the best starting points. She does, however, offer ideas for consideration when she has a point of view that no one else has mentioned, not as the "right" idea but simply as an alternative to consider (Duckworth, 1987).

Gardner's Multiple Intelligences

Gardner envisions a developmental trajectory for children with special reference to the issues of intelligence, giftedness, and creativity. He believes young children develop abilities related to language, numbers, music, two-dimensional depictive art, and other like important abilities, or "intelligences," by their own spontaneous interaction with the world in which they live.

Gardner sees the child of elementary school age as wanting to know the rules of domains of knowledge and the conventions of culture: children are apprentices en route to expertise in some specific domain. Adolescents, on the other hand, can achieve a high level within a domain and may solve problems in novel but appropriate ways. Mature practitioners fall into two categories: those who continue to function as contented experts and those who consider ideas and practices that have not been attempted before, challenging the domain.

More important is the implication that curriculum should respond to those with different combinations of intelligences. In Gardner's view, individuals differ in their intellectual potentials and proclivities related to his eight intelligences: (a) linguistic, (b) musical, (c) logical-mathematical, (d) spatial, (e) bodily-kinesthetic, (f) interpersonal understanding, (g) intrapersonal understanding, and (h) naturalistic intelligence.

Validation of these categories of intelligence is found in the following: (a) psychological studies in which students master a specific skill but fail to transfer that ability to another area, (b) newer studies of the brain that associate specific parts of the brain with particular mental activities, and (c) the fact each intelligence has its own unique or notational systems.

In fact, according to Gardner, every person possesses all eight intelligences (and probably more), and these intelligences interact with one another. Yet most individuals are more highly developed in some intelligences, modestly developed in others, and underdeveloped in others.

Gardner argues for a curriculum that is responsive to these differences. Instead of uniform schooling, Gardner would (a) let students immerse themselves in a domain that draws heavily on a particular intelligence and (b) offer opportunities for students to learn subjects using their particular strengths.

Eight teachers from the Indianapolis public schools inspired by Gardner's ideas in his book *Multiple Intelligence* opened their own inner-city school, which proved a remarkable success. One of its founding principles was that each child should have his or her multiple intelligences (MIs) stimulated each day. In the first part of the day, all children in the class have experiences related to all the intelligences; later in the day, each child is given enriched activities with his/her area of intellectual strength.

Every student participates in the activities of computing, music, and "bodily kinesthetics" in addition to a theme-centered curriculum that includes standard literature and subject matter. Daily each student goes to a "pod" to work with children of different ages and knowledge levels in a craft or discipline related to given intelligences. In the pod, the student gets to see an expert engaging in productive work. There are a dozen pods, ranging from architecture to gardening, cooking to "making money"—all of which relate to the real world.

Also, once a week an outside specialist demonstrates an occupation or craft to all the students. Typically this specialist complements the topic of a current theme. If the theme is protection of the environment, the visitor might talk about garbage disposal, the political process of lobbying, or the selling of environmental rights.

Students also extend their interests in a given intelligence by spending several months as apprentices at the Center for Exploration at the local children's museum, engaging in such activities as animation, shipbuilding, journalism, or monitoring the weather.

During the school year, the curriculum features three different 10-week themes. Activities related to the themes give rise both to the need for skills and concepts

---

ACTIVITY 4–4   SETTING THE STAGE
FOR DEVELOPMENTAL GROWTH

Ask others (class members, peers, family) about their exposure to music: what type of music they prefer, how music affects their moods and behavior, and how they interpret its messages. If possible, conduct a "conversation" with your respondents to further their—and your—intellectual and emotional development.

---

in mathematics, language, science, and other subjects and to opportunities for students to apply the academic knowledge that has been previously learned.

Each student carries out a project related to the theme, and the projects are placed on display at the conclusion of the unit. Students present their projects, describing the origin of the project, problems, and future implications. All presentations are videotaped and become part of the student's portfolio, documenting the student's evolving development over the course of his or her life in the school.

Projects reveal a student's particular intellectual propensities (multiple intelligences)—for example, musical (see Activity 4–4 for an example), linguistic, logical, mathematical, spatial, interpersonal, or bodily-kinesthetic. Projects also indicate the student's disposition toward taking risks and persevering. Each project is an instance of a particular genre—a comic play, a science experiment, a historical narrative—perhaps reflecting Gardner's concern that students gain familiarity with the criteria of a genre and increase their ability to think in a given domain or subject matter (Gardner, 1993).

Companion
Website

To read reports on the Project on Schools Using Multiple Intelligence Theory, go to *www.prenhall.com/mcneil*. Select Enter, then Topic 2: Child/Adolescent Development. Click on Web Links, then Multiple Intelligence Theories.

SUMMARY

This chapter began with traditional approaches to developing curriculum on the basis of students' psychological needs and interests. An argument was made for curriculum aiming at students' personal growth and at the same time educating them for competency in academically valued fields. The methods of teachers who departed from strict domains of knowledge in addressing student concerns, predispositions, strengths, and talents were discussed, as well as those of teachers who used the concerns of learners as a way to enlighten them about a particular academic subject and its relevance. Attention was given to modern theorists and teachers who follow the tradition of Froebel in giving voice to students by involving them wholly—mind, body, spirit—as they explore aspects of nature and culture. Exemplars of curriculum derived from the theories of Erikson and Piaget were presented to show how students can be helped to connect their own experiences and inner world to the interests and ideas of others. Powerful ways to help students construct knowledge were illustrated in Duckworth's curriculum, and ways to respond to individual strengths were found as teachers apply Gardner's theories of multiple intelligences in the classroom.

QUESTIONS FOR DISCUSSION

1. How might the following assumption be used in setting priorities in curriculum planning? If intrigued by the opportunities of a domain of knowledge, most students will make sure to develop the skills they need to operate within it.
2. In the planning of curriculum, should children of all ages have the right to be heard and have their views taken into account?
3. Regardless of student ability, performance is best in classes that are enjoyable. Why don't we, then, stop worrying about coverage of content and concentrate on how to make learning enjoyable?
4. What is the best "test" to show that a particular program, learning opportunity, text, or content is developmentally appropriate for a student of a given age?
5. How can a teacher best resolve the dilemma of balancing a student's need for choices and self-control with curriculum mandates and requirements set by those outside the classroom?
6. Piaget suggested that development can be encouraged by inducing cognitive dissonance—confronting children with evidence that contradicts their beliefs or having to deal with students from cultures that have opposing views of the world. In which classroom is intellectual growth most likely to be fostered—one where students are homogeneous in their beliefs or a classroom where students are heterogeneous in their beliefs? Give reasons for your answer. How might you use this suggestion in dealing with the issue of mixed-age groups and variability among learners versus homogeneous groupings?
7. The lives of geniuses and profound scholars are associated with three factors:
   a. Capacity to concentrate on central questions of personal concern
   b. Assistance of a model or mentor (including distant teachers of a previous generation)
   c. Openness to collaborating, together with the ability to go it alone
   What are the curricular implications of this finding?
8. What gender differences should be taken into account in developing a curriculum? Which of these differences are wittingly and unwittingly fostered by culture? Which ones are innate?
9. Is there a danger that if students are encouraged to be attentive to their own well-being, they will turn out to be egoists? Or does an enlarged conception of well-being include care for others?

REFERENCES

Carmon, A. (1980, July). Problems in coping with the Holocaust: Experiences with students in a multinational program. *American Academy of Political and Social Services Annals,* p. 450.

Decci, E., Valerane, R., Pellitier, L., &Ryan, R. M. (1991). Motivation and education: The self determinist perspective. *Educational Psychologist, 26*(3 and 6), 25–347.

Duckworth, E. (1987). *The having of wonderful ideas.* New York: Teachers College Press.

Erikson, E. (1968). *Identity, youth, and crisis.* New York: Basic Books.

Gardner, H. (1993). *Multiple intelligences: The theory in practice.* New York: Basic Books.

Goodman, J. (1991). Redirecting sexuality: Education for young adolescents. *Curriculum and Teaching, 6*(1), 12–22.

Hailman, W. H. (1887). Superintendent Zechs' report of his visit to the Educational Institute at Keilham, 1826. In *The education of man.* New York: Appleton.

Heller, H. C. (1993). The need for a core interdisciplinary life science curriculum in the middle grades. *Teachers College Record, 94*(3), 644–652.

McLuhan, T. C. (1971). *Touch the earth: A self-portrait of Indian existence.* New York: Simon & Schuster.

Metz, K. (1997, Spring). On the complex relation between cognitive developmental research and children's science curriculum. *Review of Educational Research, 67*(1), 151–163.

Newman, R. (2000). Social influence on the development of children's adaptive help seeking: The role of parents, teachers and peers. *Developmental Review, 20,* 350–404.

Piaget, J. (1991). Adaptation and intelligence. In *Organic selection and phenocopy.* Chicago: University of Chicago Press.

3

Labyrinth of Curriculum Relevance

Few problems in the curriculum field are more difficult than those related to deciding on relevant purpose and content. To what should the curriculum be relevant—to the individual, the world, the nation, or the local community? To a past, present, or future way of life?

Part 3 provides an opportunity for you to evaluate your own views about whether curriculum should adjust to present and likely future social conditions, transcend negative features of society, or encourage social change by fostering skepticism about social practices and institutions, making critical inquiries, and taking political action. The curricula, including those of past generations, presented in these chapters show the range of options available in answering the question "In postindustrial society, what knowledge is of most worth?"

CHAPTER **5**

RESPONDING TO SOCIAL CHANGE

Sara: Must all teachers link their subject matter to what's going on in the world at large—environment, globalization, health, racism—or at least how these events are playing out locally?

Merl: I don't want my subject matter to just sit there and not function in the lives of my students. I want it to help them understand and deal with changes in the world.

Teachers and students find their spaces for curriculum development as they select the events, issues, and problems of the real world to which they will connect to whatever standards, subject matter, or official curriculum is imposed on the school. It is the real world that gives rise to the need for academic interpretation and high-level thinking, increasing student interest in content.

CURRIULUM ALTERNATIVES IN RESPONDING TO SOCIAL CHANGE

Teachers have responded to postindustrial society by centering on the local manifestations of world conditions. They try to answer the question of how their curriculum can best prepare students for dealing with local problems in the environment and society—jobs, health, recreation, safety, immigration, and the like. Their answers fall into three categories:

1. *Social adaption* attempts to help students fit into the society as it is.
2. *Social revisionism* aims to help students transcend excessive individualism, consumerism, and materialism by encouraging local self-sufficiency and mutual aid and by focusing on relationships, rather than on the pursuit of material wealth.
3. *Social criticism* develops knowledge about society and critical perspectives on it, its practices, and its institutions, raising the consciousness of the uses and abuses of power in our lives and projecting a vision of a better society.

By way of example, in responding to the issue of multiculturalism—differences arising from race, gender, class, ethnic origin, and economic status—teachers take different approaches. Some teachers are indifferent to the inequalities among students, seeing these inequalities as natural or something to be expected because of home background or inherited ability. Others regard multiculturalism as an opportunity to improve human relations by encouraging students to help one another both academically and in personal relations, learning to appreciate the different cultures from which they come. Still others focus on giving special assistance to those who depart from the dominant culture—teaching English as a second language and providing opportunities for all students to succeed. Some teachers choose social criticism for their approach. These teachers regard multiculturalism as a moral issue coupled with critique of institutions and the culture at large in explaining racism and discrimination. A few teachers even encourage students to work with others in acting politically and trying to influence institutions to change in the interest of equity.

Those who carry out Activity 5–1 will find their knowledge of the "students' world" enhanced and their teaching more culturally relevant.

Social Adaption

Adaption occurs through the introduction of new content, new ways to present content, and varying the nature of relations with students. The most obvious example of curriculum adaptation during the past decade is associated with the computer and its uses. Teachers at all levels and fields have adapted their curriculum to the computer. Cases in point are, in language arts, writing using word processors, and, in mathematics, increased attention to estimation, discrete mathematics, graphing, and simulations. Other adaptations reflect the needs of a changing workforce. Curricula that impart both vocational and academic skills,

---

ACTIVITY 5–1   VISITING A PARENT

The gap between teachers—linguistic, ethnic, economic—and the community where they are working creates classroom problems. Students have difficulty learning the culture of the teacher until the teacher learns enough about the students' cultures to understand what the words and actions of the students mean. Also, too often, the gap keeps diverse students and their families in subordinate positions.

This activity encourages teachers to listen to the perspectives of parents and to elicit ways parents can contribute to the curriculum, helping the teacher see the strengths of diversity in constructing curriculum.

1. Arrange at least three visits to the home of at least one student.
2. Consider in your visits the parents' views of school, how learning takes place, and the expectations they have for their child.
3. Share your ideas with parents for a possible classroom activity—your learning goal—then have the parents suggest how the activity might be enhanced to result in benefits you haven't considered.

---

such as mathematics for nurses, attempt to meet the demand for better-educated workers. Similarly, classrooms change to match the changed workplace of the postindustrial society.

Adapting to the World of Work

The *New Youth Entrepreneur* (2000) is an example of curriculum that addresses the new economy and its need for entrepreneurs. In this curriculum, students create their own jobs while exploring entrepreneurship. After discussing the characteristics and qualities of entrepreneurs, students search for business opportunities in their neighborhood (i.e., identify needed services and products). They consider business ideas for meeting community needs and prepare an extensive business plan that includes such matters as how to get funding; determine the best location, when to get help, and how to anticipate a market; and determine break-even points, how to market their products and services, and how to keep records.

In creating their businesses, students draw on numerous subject matters—mathematics (rates, graphing); writing (persuasive informative); government and law (regulations, contracts); finance (credit, banking); sociology (culture, population and income).

Federal policy, such as the School-to-Work Act of 1994, has had great influence on vocational offerings in schools. This act signaled a departure from programs that taught particular skills to programs that (a) introduced students to all aspects of an industry and (b) integrated academics with work experience, educating through occupations rather than for occupations. Students were to learn what school can and cannot do for them in terms of employment. When one considers that nearly half of the 18- to 24-year-old population is working in low-paying service jobs and that of those high school graduates who continue to the community college, only 38% will get any kind of a degree 5 years later, the heavy emphasis in public schools on preparation for college to the exclusion of personal and social pursuits seems misguided.

Currently, the principal curriculum adaptations for the world of work are as follows:

- School-to-work programs in which large companies, such as Toyota, offer high-level training, mentoring, and apprenticeships

- Collaborative school-based programs in which teachers, students, and local businesspersons design a curriculum related to one or more industries

- A joint high school–community college vocational program

- Career magnet schools, such as a high technology school in which technology is the theme running through the curriculum and pointing to careers in such fields as communications and health science

One such magnet school, Foothill Technology High School in Ventura, California, is of interest, not only because of its success in developing project-based learning in which all academics are integrated into real-world projects that call for research, delivery of Power Point presentations, designing Web pages, and the like, but also because of what it reveals about social class and the schools. This magnet school was established to track middle achievers, but, to the surprise and dismay of teachers, counselors, and educators in the district's other high schools, affluent and high-achieving students are going to the "vocational school" thereby threatening enrollments in advanced placement and honors classes in the neighboring academic high schools.

■ Placement of individual students in small businesses in which the employer and trainee agree on the experiences to be provided. Placement may permit job shadowing or paid internship.

■ A training credit plan in which students are awarded funds—usually about $3,000 for training purposes—and must find whatever employer is available and willing to offer training. Unfortunately, few highly qualified opportunities are available and unsophisticated youth are viewed by marginal employers as a cheap source of labor (Finkelstein & Grubb, 2000).

Companion Website

Service learning is a popular way for teachers and students to engage in social revisionism, performing services through projects that benefit communities. Usually the service experience is connected to the subject matter of a course. If you wish to learn how service learning affects community or student achievement or a course outcome measure—academic, values, leadership, and the like—go to *www.prenhall.com/mcneil* and click on the UCLA or Servenet links.

Social Revisionism

Concern about AIDS, parenting, alienation, discrimination, and other social problems have prompted teachers to develop units of instruction and full courses on those topics. Sometimes the topics are included within a traditional academic subject as an added topic or as an application. Other times the topics are regarded as important in their own right, and a range of subject matters is brought to bear on the study. Social revisionism can occur in the context of both disciplinary and community approaches to problem solving.

Illustrating social revisionism in the disciplines, a teacher of literature was concerned about the psychic consequences of life today, especially the loss of a sense of self and the primacy of one's perceptions and emotions in a postmodern world. She selected novels whose authors offered strategies for coping with the current condition. Her curriculum included works of Saul Bellow, who helps readers contemplate their own special resources; Joan Didion, who depicts the tragedies of postmodern life; Don DeLillo, who offers possibilities of self in a repressive world; and Thomas Pynchon, whose options range from the avoidance of commitment to acceptance of the multiple contradictions of life today.

Other social revisionists follow the tradition of the old community school, with its primary aim of sustaining a community that nurtures interdependency, the well-being of the group, and a sense of moral responsibility both to the natural environment and to one another.

Foxfire: A Modern Curriculum That Connects to the Community

For more than 25 years, Eliot Wigginton's (1985) students have published Foxfire books and magazines, reporting their studies of the traditions and history of their community. This is one example of a major initiative beginning from the work of one teacher. The Foxfire experience evolved with this curriculum philosophy:

1. *Student choice and responsibility.* The tasks flow from student needs and wants. Students choose, design, revise, carry out, and evaluate the worth of the activity. Most problems that arise during the project must be solved by the students themselves.
2. *Local connection.* Connections of the work to the surrounding community are clear. Whenever students study real-world problems, such as changing climate patterns, acid rain, racism, or AIDS, they must "bring them home" by identifying local attitudes about them, as well as illustrating and stating the implications of these problems in their own environment. Also, members of the community serve as the resources from which the students draw.
3. *Challenge.* Rather than the students doing what they already know how to do, all are continually led into new work and unfamiliar territory.
4. *Cooperation.* There is emphasis on peer teaching, small-group work, and teamwork. At the end of the project, each student can identify his or her specific contribution to the project.
5. *Teacher role.* The teacher is not the repository of all knowledge but acts as collaborator and guide.
6. *Audience.* There is an audience beyond the teacher for student work, an audience the students want to serve. The audience may be another individual, a small group, or the community at large. The audience in turn must affirm that the work is important, needed, and worth doing.
7. *Subject matter.* The academic integrity of the work is clear. Although texts are regarded as reference works, not as content to be covered, content such as grammar and mechanics are blended into purposeful writing activities, not isolated drill.
8. *Evaluation.* Evaluation follows the teacher's challenging question, "In what ways will you prove to me at the end of this program that you have mastered the objectives it has been designed to serve?" Students are taught to monitor their own progress, to devise their own remediation, and to understand that the progress of each student is the concern of every student in the room.
9. *Continuity.* New activities grow from the old. A finished product is not the conclusion of a series of activities but the starting point for a new series.

Questions that characterize the moment of completion include these:

- "So what?"
- "What do we know now and know how to do that we didn't know how to do when we started together?"
- "How can we use the skills and knowledge in new and more complex and interesting ways?"
- "What is next?" (Wigginton, 1989, p. 28)

Typical of Foxfire stories is one about two ninth-graders who researched and completed an article for publication about Dan Crane, who demonstrated for them the almost lost art of hewing railroad cross ties by hand. In the introduction to the piece, the boys wrote:

> The second reason John and I wanted to interview Dan is because he is our grandfather. He has about every issue of Foxfire magazine, and he knows many of the people who have been interviewed, but he has never been interviewed himself so John and I decided to get him into one of the magazines. We thought this might make his life a little brighter, so this is our gift to him.

A network of teachers is now applying the Foxfire approach. Among their accounts is one about Elain Briscoe's sixth-graders, who had a concern about the fact that a local child had been abducted and killed. At the students' request, community resource people were interviewed, and existing safety booklets were critiqued and found wanting. The students decided to produce their own booklet, and one student created the booklet's main character—a dog named Fido—and illustrated the pages and cover. All students were involved in conducting the research, writing the text, creating word games, and designing the pages. Toward the end of the school year, the completed 24-page booklet was given to every elementary school student in the school.

As another example of the Foxfire approach, one can point to the Media Academy, a supportive school community within the Fremont High School in a ghetto area of Oakland, California. Four teachers initiated a program for the school's predominately African American, Latino, and Asian students. The program links the curriculum to possible future vocational opportunities and to communities beyond their own (Wehlage, 1987). The students issue a Spanish-language community paper as well as other publications, and they air their words on radio and television. Field trips to telecommunication and other media centers, as well as internships, offer students experience in the media profession. Advisers from the media assist with curriculum support. For example, a reporter may help students follow leads and develop a story. Students are responsible for developing topics for articles and are encouraged to write about issues of immediate concern to themselves and the broader community—for example, date rape, reverse discrimination, abortion. An unresolved question for the academy is whether the cooperative skills and talents students develop under the curriculum should be viewed as a means for the students to escape from their ghetto neighborhood into lucrative employment opportunities or to regenerate their own neighborhood and deal with the larger political and economic practices that have contributed to their poverty.

The garden ethic is popular among revisionists as a way to help students and community become creative caretakers of the land, working with nature rather than against it. Judy Karasky's National Service program, in which young men and women create a garden curriculum for an early childhood development center, is a case in point. The curriculum begins with team members talking with the children about the soil and about how life comes from the earth. The children look at pictures of fruits and vegetables, decide what to plant, and then draw the many shapes and colors of leaves and flowers. The garden is used to teach nutrition, as well as ecology, botany, art, writing, and thinking. The goal is for children to feel that the garden is theirs and that when the plants come up, they made it happen. All are mindful of the danger of building something that could be abandoned, a garden gone to seed, and of the need for children to accept responsibility for the watering and weeding. An excellent description of social revision through environmental projects is provided by Nagel (1996).

Another illustration of a revisionist curriculum in environmental studies is found in a text written by the people of Rock Point Community School on a Navajo reservation. *Between Sacred Mountain: Navajo Stories and Lessons from the Land* (Rock Point Community School, 1984) functions as a curriculum in history, science, and social studies. The text describes the relationships of the Navajo to their land. An overriding theme of the text is that the survival of all people depends on our abilities to keep peace with the land that sustains us. The book grew out of the need to teach about Navajo life and the concern of the community that teaching conform to the Navajos' view of themselves. Parents wanted their children to understand the ecology of the land and to comprehend their relationship to both the land and the animals that support their way of life.

Social Criticism

An excellent example of social criticism is found in the protest against the Massachusetts Comprehensive Assessment System Test by Will Greene, a sophomore student at Monument Mountain Regional High School in Great Barrington, Massachusetts, and others of the activist group Student Coalition for Alternative to MCAS (Flynn, 2000). Greene is not opposed to showing what he does and does not know, but he claims that the state test is too narrow in its focus, discourages critical thinking skills, and is unfair to minorities and the poor.

"Three years from now, this is not going to be a graduate requirement", the 15-year-old Greene told hundreds of student protestors, educators, and parents gathered on the Boston Common. "We need to start talking to the people in power" (Flynn, 2000, p. 1).

Greene and nearly 40 of his peers declined to take the standardized exam that was to have become a "high-stakes" exam to be passed if one expected to receive a high school diploma. Subsequently, students across the state boycotted the test, opting instead to pursue special projects that they felt more adequately measured their skills. After school, the teens turned out in droves on the Common where they rallied for more than 3 hours, blasting the test in speech, song, and signs and delivering a petition to the statehouse asking the legislature to remove the high-stakes component of the test. Other students expressed their determination to see the process through in the legislature where the proponents argue the test will ensure accountability among teachers and schools. Students made it clear that they were "totally for raising standards and improving schools, but don't think this is the way to do it."

In addition, Jim Bougas, a middle school teacher, said he would rather lose his job than administer the test to his students. As he began a 2-week unpaid suspension from the school, Bougas said he would not back down from the fight even though his recalcitrance puts his teaching career in jeopardy, saying, "There is a monster in my classroom every day that is known as the MCAS. We have to get rid of it" (Flynn, 2000, p. 2).

This chapter describes curricula arising from social criticism—the fomenting of social change. One example of a critical curriculum that effected a change in an institution or social structure was developed by staff and students at Queenscliff High School in Australia. The curriculum arose as part of a larger network of schools, linked by computers, engaged in water quality studies. Students at Queenscliff broadened their focus from a study of freshwater quality to a critical study of sewage pollution at local beaches. They found bacteria counts far in excess of acceptable guidelines for safety.

After being rebuffed in their efforts to discuss their findings with the local water board and to obtain the board's own record of bacteria count, students invoked a Freedom of Information Act to gain access to the water board's data. Students then published an account of their findings in the local press. This triggered a powerful community response, including the local health center's recording of complaints about infections that were possibly associated with the bacteria in the seawater and the state government's requiring the water board to justify its action and ultimately to improve, at great expense, their sewage treatment facility.

Not all went smoothly in the project. Although the media initially accelerated the controversy initiated by the students, they later reinforced the water board's position and brought forth the financial implications of the proposed remedy. Nevertheless, by taking social action, the students engaged in an environmental curriculum that did more than impart environmental content. Students developed working knowledge about the power relationships among agencies and about their own capacity to influence the issues through the media. Rather than helping students adapt to society as it exists, the Queenscliff curriculum encouraged students to question institutions and to work to change them. (See Activity 5–2 for another example of a curriculum arising from social needs.)

WORLD-VIEW OF POSTINDUSTRIAL SOCIETY

Although there is no single world-view of postindustrial society, many recognize that such a society is characterized by challenging ideas from the Enlightenment such as the scientific method (the "objectivity" of science), faith in universal

■ ── ■

ACTIVITY 5–2   DEVELOPING CURRICULUM PURPOSES IN RESPONSE TO LOCAL SOCIAL NEEDS

Consider a local community with which you are familiar.

1. List some of the most important trends or social facts about this community, considering health, recreation, environment, employment, social relations, and family life.
2. Form one or more generalizations stating the most pressing community needs as indicated by the trends and facts listed in step 1.
3. State what students might learn or do so that they will understand the community needs or help them adapt or engage in effecting a change in the existing situation (e.g., your curricular purposes). Your response may be within your field of expertise (math, language, science, or some other area) in which the subject matter is adapted to community needs, or the response may call for students tapping resources that are not now in the curriculum.

■ ── ■

reason, and the belief that the natural and social world can be controlled so that human life can have higher levels of material comfort.

Technological and economic developments created new industries and social realities during the 20th century and into the 21st century. New technologies such as information systems, mass media, and computers that produce images and information rather than products have brought many social consequences. Too often, television determines what is real and brings loss of a sense of one's perceptions and emotions. A consumer ethic dominates society: things have no value unless they can be sold.

Globalization is blurring the meaning of the nation-state. We are seeing the rise of extraterritorial companies, the free flow of capital, regional organizations (created as, e.g., the European Community, North American Free Trade Agreement, Association of Southeast Asian Nations), and the need for international cooperation in dealing with problems of peace and the environment. Conversely, the fading of the superpowers is associated with growing popularist nationalism, which on the positive side offers more local determinism and political democracy and seems to satisfy people's needs for connectedness, honor, and loyalty; and on the negative side gives rise to suspicion of others within the same nation who do not seem to agree with the dominant ideology and harms the lives of those termed "minority" through discriminating practices.

Workers in the United States have been affected by these world events—the rise of consumerism and service industries, and relocation of jobs and workers, and the widening of the gap between the haves and the have-nots. Within the manufacturing plant, assembly lines with their emphasis on routine, accuracy, speed, and close supervision have given way to the team concept and its value of flexibility, cooperation, problem solving, and decision making by workers.

Postindustrial society is associated with a litany of gloom and doom—overpopulation; pressure on the land; pollution of the air; depletion of water, forests, and natural resources; problems in social relations; loss of community; personal isolation; detachment from the suffering of others; and a sense of one's own mortality. Activity 5–3 explores how to use data on society to determine a curriculum.

The thoughts and practices of distant teachers are influencing teachers today. Their accounts contribute to our reconciling tensions between those who focus

ACTIVITY 5–3 DETERMINING CURRICULAR IMPLICATIONS FROM DATA

About Postindustrial Society

Here is a sample of acts and generalizations about the postindustrial society. Check those that you accept as valid, and then indicate what students should learn in relation to each:

1. There is a prevailing attitude that society can collapse around us and our lives will not be affected (i.e., the gated community).
2. The security of the privileged will be jeopardized by global warming, ozone depletion, contamination, and terrorism.
3. The knowledge now propagated by schools will not be appropriate for the experiences children will face in the 21st century, when economic contraction rather than expansion may be the norm.
4. What counts as knowledge is not found in reason but determined by the judgment and values of particular academic communities.
5. How to learn is more important than specific knowledge and skills.
6. The loss of species and energy resources indicates that we are eroding the life system that supports us.
7. The exportation of firms to locations where labor is less costly reduces individual opportunities.
8. Among all social classes, there is an increase in life expectancy but also an increase in suicide, drug abuse, family breakdown, and child abuse.
9. Population pressures produce different outcomes in different settings.
10. The Soviet lesson is that to rely on defense for securing goals is not effective in the postindustrial world.
11. Mass migration across national boundaries is associated with social-racial tensions.
12. The global village is becoming more fragmented even as it becomes more unified by systems of communication.
13. Add your own.

on a universal, intellectual, and ornamental curriculum and those who want a practice curriculum in context.

In a broad sense, adaptations in the past as well as the present reflect the tension between those who believe that the curriculum should focus on the universal, the intellectual, or the ornamental and those who want a curriculum that is practical and contextual. At policy levels, curriculum decisions have swung between several curriculum orientations:

1. *Academic*—the view that the development of the mind through the study of great works and abstract subject matter is most important
2. *Social meliorist*—the position that curriculum should make a direct contribution to improving the society, principally by creating classroom conditions that mirror the ideals of a democracy
3. *Social efficiency*—a concern for the practical affairs of life—business, vocations, and the duties of daily living—as well as for the preparation of students for work and social functions
4. *Student centered*—the placing of students and their interests at the center, with a curriculum that offers students rich experiences, encouraging their imaginations and self-expression

At the classroom level, a different orientation has predominated at different times and places. Current thought would interpret such shifts in practice to the ascendancy of different political interests. A particular orientation is matched to a social class—the academic or student-centered curricula with the affluent, the meliorist and social efficiency curriculum with the middle and working classes.

Although power relationships are central in deciding how curriculum is adapted to changing circumstances, one should not discount the nature of the circumstance and the initiative taken by individual teachers.

Companion
Website

The PBS program *School: The Story of American Public Education* is a documentary of the nation's attempt to offer universal education. For information on this KCET/Hollywood Presentation and other information on the series, go to *www.prenhall.com/mcneil* and click on the PBS link.

CURRICULA FOR PRACTICAL VERSUS INTELLECTUAL PURPOSES

The meeting of Old and New World cultures at the start of the colonial period is an instance when those of intellectual tradition—those concerned about beauty, wisdom, truth, and justice through study of prestigious and abstract subject matter— found it necessary to accept an authentic curriculum or face the possibility of not surviving.

A Native American Curriculum for Survival

The Native Americans offered the most important curriculum to the early American colonists. For example, consider the account of one Native American, Squanto, who had been kidnapped and taken to England. Back in America, he became the pilot, interpreter, and teacher of the Pilgrims who founded Plymouth Colony in 1620 in what is now Massachusetts. He helped the early settlers until he died in 1622. Squanto's students recalled how he taught them, among other things, "how to set their corn, where to take fish, and how to procure other commodities" (Axtell, 1974, p. 248).

Squanto was only the first of many Native Americans who shared agricultural and other knowledge with the early settlers from Europe. As the English acknowledged, "Our first instructors for the planting were the Indians who taught us to cull out the finest seeds, to observe the fittest season, to keep distance for holes, and fit measure for hills, to worme it and weede it, to prune it, and dress it as occasion shall require" (Axtell, 1974, p. 248). The Native Americans' generosity in teaching what they knew about the natural life of their woods and fields gave the English a chance at survival and kept them from starving in the new environment.

Reading and Latin Grammar

The survival curriculum contrasts with the one that was soon established in the early American colonial schools. The new settlers brought with them educational traditions and concerns in which it was essential that students learn to read and interpret the Scripture. Pilgrims and later colonists in New England established schools for children to receive religious instruction from catechisms, to learn songs of worship, and to read the Bible. Instruction in reading began by using the letters of the alphabet with the names of biblical characters ("*A* is for Adam"). Reading material consisted of Bible stories and moral lessons based on passages of Scripture.

Although most formal schooling in colonial America ended with children learning to read by spelling out words, those who were to be church leaders received additional training in some of the languages in which early versions of the Bible had been written or translated, especially Latin and Greek, as well as instruction in theology. Preparation for college training in theology was provided at the Latin Grammar School in Boston, which offered instruction in Latin and Greek. This school was established in 1636 and remained the important institution of secondary education in the colonies for more than 100 years. The curriculum of this school emphasized memorization of the rules and paradigms of Latin grammar, first through the study of Cheever's accidence (Eziekel Cheever was a schoolteacher in this early period who had written his own summary of Latin grammar) and then the study of Lily's grammar (with its 25 kinds of nouns, seven genders, 15 pages of rules for genders, and 22 pages of declensions of nouns). After students mastered grammar, they read the Latin classics including the major works of Cicero, as well as the Bible in Latin. The rudiments of Greek—

declensions of nouns and conjugation of Greek verbs—were also included as a requirement for college entrance.

On completing the Latin Grammar School, the future leader was eligible for college and the continued study of Greek grammar, as well as study of the New Testament, Hebrew, and perhaps Sanskrit. Language study was supplemented by further literary and theological instruction. Such a curriculum was intended to prepare selected young men for leadership roles, guiding the daily lives of their fellow colonists according to the Scriptures.

In colonial America, experience was the great teacher. Daily living on the farm taught the settlers how to make and repair wagons and harnesses, to build and repair buildings, to take care of animals, to sow and reap, to interpret the signs of weather, and to provide the food, clothing, and other necessities for existence. The apprenticeship system, in which students received technical instruction from a master in a craft or trade in return for labor (and in some cases a premium of money), was common.

In the 1770s, the demands for a more practical curriculum than that offered by the Latin Grammar School was met by "venture" schools and academies. For a fee, teachers in these schools taught the subject matter of most use to those interested in trade—modern languages, geography, bookkeeping, navigation, and surveying.

Ben Franklin's Curriculum

Benjamin Franklin had proposed the academy in 1749 as an agency to prepare students for the duties of life. Franklin's proposal offered both classical languages for those who wanted college preparation and utilitarian subjects that could be chosen in light of one's desired future occupation. Husbandry and science were offered through formal studies, together with practice in planting and grafting, as well as measures for preserving health, such as inoculating. The curriculum called for teaching the history of commerce, including study of the invention of the arts and manufacturing, and instruction in the mechanics, commodities, and materials that would increase industrial and agricultural productivity.

Franklin wanted the academy to have a well-equipped library, a garden, orchard, meadow, and a field or two. Students were to be "frequently exercised in running, leaping, wrestling, and swimming" (Franklin, 1749/1907, p. 389). He anticipated the modern literature-based curriculum and focus on the writing process in his recommendations for teaching English through the study of the best writers and the practice of students writing to one another, making abstracts of what they read in their own words, and expressing themselves by writing their own stories.

SCIENCE VERSUS CLASSICS IN 19TH-CENTURY CURRICULUM

By the 19th century, teachers in the primary school had broadened their curriculum from the teaching of the alphabet and the memorization of biblical sources to a study of the three Rs. Although most primary teachers focused on reading as oral expression, a few wanted students to also focus on what they read. Arithmetic was taught with an emphasis on numeration, counting by groups, addition, multiplication, and division of integers. Writing was undervalued and taught chiefly as related to spelling and handwriting.

Near the end of the 19th century, the primary curriculum was extended by development of an elementary curriculum. This new 8-year elementary curriculum reflected demands from the disciplines and the sciences that children need to be prepared for every area of life by learning to think through the study of mathematics and grammar. The practice of teaching arithmetic for its practical uses gave way to teaching mathematics for its value as a discipline. English grammar replaced Latin grammar, and it, too, was taught for its value as a discipline. Its teaching was patterned after the divisions of Latin grammar—orthography, inflection, syntax, and prosody.

The scientific view was that content from the natural and social sciences would be more useful than the classics in preparing students to adapt to a changing world and better prepare them for the new scientific studies that were being introduced in colleges (e.g., those of the various biological and physical sciences) and the expanded social sciences (e.g., history, geography, and political economy). The concept elementary school was derived from the idea that children should learn the elements of knowledge found in the new scientific fields. The teacher was expected to select from the sciences those facts, principles, and laws that would be most frequently found and used in daily life. Studying music, good manners, principles of morality, and physical education was also regarded as important for personal and social living.

The curriculum of the new public high school was broad, with courses for those preparing for college, those who wanted an academic program but who had no plans for college education, and those who wanted vocational preparation. The classical emphasis on Latin and Greek continued for college preparation. Both college and noncollege programs stressed algebra and geometry because those subjects were thought to be useful both in developing the mind and in helping students deal with the technical and scientific applications of the developing industrial society. Physics and chemistry gained entrance on the grounds that their disciplinary values were equal or superior to the classics. English was first introduced for those not going to college, but it eventually won acceptance as suitable for preparing students for college. History and geography were at first in the inferior position of content for the noncollege-bound student, but they gradually were offered as part of the college preparation program, even though their disciplinary claims could not be established. The vocational studies—industrial arts, home economics, commercial studies, and agriculture—remained without prestige, unsuitable for academic purposes but necessary for their vocational and practical purposes. The arts and physical education were included for their values in developing the individual.

Public support for high schools rested on the claim that these schools were beneficial to the community, but few attempts to buttress this claim were made. In 1881, David Hoyt assessed what high schools did for the city and state. He found that all classes of society attended the school but that the middle class was most fully represented. His follow-up study of graduates showed that most were in the mercantile business, manufacturing, and mechanical pursuits, employed as bookkeepers and accountants. Only 13% were in the learned professions—law, clergy, medicine. Hoyt recommended that the curriculum include manual training, mechanical drawing, and the study of mechanical operations, to help better prepare students for positions in businesses other than as sales representatives and accountants. He believed that the community's need for people able to engage in the practical operation of manufacturing was paramount and that the school had not been responsive to this need. Hoyt anticipated what today is considered a problem in American productivity—the need for people with both the intellectual attainment and the practical skills required for planning and guiding manufacturing enterprises.

CURRICULUM RESPONSES TO THE INDUSTRIAL SOCIETY

The relation of curriculum to the change from an agricultural society to an industrialized nation took many forms.

Conceptualization: John Dewey's Curriculum

In the early years of the 20th century, John Dewey implemented a curriculum for young children that addressed the negative consequences brought by large-scale industry and the corporate form of business organization—the loss of community as the interests of a working class conflicted with the interests of a business group, and specialization of functions that robbed work of the social and economic meanings it had previously possessed. Dewey's curriculum focused on occupations that served social needs (Mayhew & Edwards, 1936).

In Dewey's curriculum, 4- and 5-year-olds studied the familiar occupations of the home; 6-year-olds studied large social industries such as farming, mining, and lumbering, so they could begin to learn about the complex and varied occupations on which life depends. For instance, in one project, 6-year-old children found the connection between raw material and the manufacturing of a finished product as they removed seeds from cotton plants, baled the cotton, and went through other stages in the manufacture of cotton cloth.

In the curriculum, 7-year-olds experimented with raw materials and various metals, noting the materials' qualities and uses. Older students studied the development of industry and invention, to understand the steps of industrial progress to realize what enters into the makeup of society and how it came to be, thus gaining insight into social life.

History was taught as a pageant of techniques and cooperation rather than a chronicle of violence and oppression. The land was the center for science study because all work related to it sooner or later. Also, children at all ages were expected to engage in experimental work as a way for them to awaken their consciousness of the world, develop powers of observation, and acquire a sense of the method of inquiry. Teachers and subject matter specialists cooperated so that intellectual resources necessary for solving problems initiated by students would be available.

Linkages in the Lincoln School Curriculum

Teachers at the Lincoln School of Teachers College, Columbia University, in the 1920s continued to help students find connections between modern society and its antecedents (Triplell, 1927). These teachers also gave more emphasis to the immediate quality of life in the classroom than to preparing students for some prespecified future. Gaining a maximum meaning from the present was thought to be the best preparation for the future.

The Lincoln teachers followed a "unit of work" procedure in their curriculum development. A unit consisted of an extensive project that would make use of many subjects. The selection of a unit or project was guided by several criteria:

1. *Realness.* The unit must develop from a real-life situation. The topic for study may be an individual or group suggestion and represent a past experience or a present need. Resources for conducting the project should be available.
2. *Breadth of opportunity.* The topic or question should stimulate many kinds of activities and provide for individual contributions—constructing, dramatizing, exploring, and expressing creative energy (appealing to multiple intelligences). The activity of each child must contribute to the unit as a whole.
3. *Personal growth.* The study should allow each child to exert effort in improving higher skills, habits, and attitudes. The unit should be rich enough to lead students in the discovery of new interests and possibilities for further study.
4. *Cultural resources.* The social meanings found in art, history, geography, mathematics, science, literature, and the like, should be brought to bear in the unit and serve as a springboard for future study.

One unit for sixth-graders evolved from a student's concern about daylight saving time and the question of who had the right to determine the correct time. Early discussion centered on various types of clocks, the master clock at the Naval Observatory, and arguments for and against daylight savings. Among the questions that arose from this discussion were these:

■ What causes the midnight sun?

■ How did early people tell time?

■ How is the master clock regulated?

To answer such questions, students located the important observatories in the world; they discussed the contributions of Galileo; and they studied sphericity, rotation, revolution, and their consequences. Students made daily observations of the sky and reported results. These observations began with smoked glass, old films, and compasses. To express themselves, students formed concepts for such terms as *celestial sphere, zenith, horizon, altitude declination,* and *degrees.* The moon as a way to measure time was also a focus for study. With the help of the monthly *Evening Skymap,* the class knew what to expect to see each night. Activities with compasses led to interest in terrestrial magnetism and magnetic poles. Investigation of how to determine direction at night, the North Star, and sidereal time followed. Observations of Mars led students to collect newspaper and journal articles on the topic. Theories and facts about the planet were explored.

Some of the questions that led to instruction in science as well as work in literature and history were these:

■ What is atmosphere? Where does it end?

■ What causes wind?

■ How did the planets and stars get their names?

Students' imaginations were stirred by the natural causes discovered. Poems with titles such as "Night," "Snowflakes," "Spring," and "Mars" were written. Students were stimulated to compose original myths and adventure stories such as "My Adventure in Star-Catching," "Professor ZoDiak and Me," and "The Heavenly Twins." Students considered the notions of astronomy and time of the ancient Mesopotamia, Egypt, Greece, Rome, and the early peoples in western England. The astronomical discoveries of the Chinese and Native Americans were reviewed.

The activities students did in the unit were extensive, involving using telescopes; making a zodiac calendar; inventing time instruments; using principles of shadow sticks, sundials, clepsydras, and time candles; using a hectograph; dramatizing a play of "The First Water Clock"; making a time line of history; and visiting museums that featured relevant exhibits. Some students set poems to music; others created dances based on their ideas of the revolutions of the planets and their satellites. Geometry was used in estimating light and position of stellar objects above the horizon and below the zenith.

Curriculum of the Community School

The community school concept, which developed in the 1930s, was locally centered and directed toward the health, recreational, vocational, and other needs of the community in which students were a part. The curriculum was seen as a means to improve living conditions and, at the same time, help students think more intelligently about how national and world affairs were affecting their lives. Engaging in some useful work was a key element in the program. Community needs were analyzed by students and programs of action developed. Students not only read about problems but worked out solutions. Parents participated and aided in addressing the problem selected.

One illustration of a community school's curriculum is found in the story of Holtsville, Alabama (NEA Education Policies Commission, 1940). The Holtsville school, grades 7 to 12, took as its ideal the creation of better living conditions for all. The teachers shifted their emphasis from teaching subjects as ends in themselves to a functional view, asking how the subjects could enrich the life of the community. In their study and analysis of needs of the community, students found that many of the commercially canned fruits and vegetables bought in the community could have been raised there as a source of income. They also discovered that the community's heavy meat spoilage could have been avoided if refrigeration and canning facilities had been available. Teachers secured federal and state aid to construct and equip these facilities for community improvement. The home economics department of the school took charge of the cannery, and students were trained to maintain the refrigeration plant and cold storage room. A chick hatchery was installed under the management of students. A power spray machine was acquired so that students could spray orchards.

Students also engaged in terracing, corridor plowing, and planting and pruning fruit trees as service to the community. Home economics students engaged in home redecoration projects, remaking clothing, and designing draperies for home use. Students edited the only weekly paper for the community and ran their own print shop; they opened a cooperative store that sold many of their own products, such as toothpaste made in their chemistry department; they showed films for the community; and they maintained a library loaning out games as well as books. Students formed a home nursery for the care of babies and operated a dental clinic, a beauty parlor, a barber shop, and a bowling alley as well as a building devoted to crafts.

Another teacher who created a community school was Marie Turner Harvey of Porter, Missouri. Harvey worked with a group of interested women in galvanizing the community to make the school the focal part of Porter's social life. She formed clubs and organizations to come to grips with Porter's economic and social problems (Dewey, 1919).

Other detailed accounts of the nature and funding of community school curricula have been given by Elsie Ripley. She describes how teachers in Kentucky and West Virginia became closely involved with their communities and educated themselves about the needs and resources of these localities as bases for further education of the community (Ripley, 1939, p. 38). For instance, in response to health needs, teachers and parents raised funds for a trained pediatrician to examine children, provided midmorning meals for undernourished children, offered courses in budgeting, obtained the services of dentists who would visit the community monthly, operated a nursery school for parents to observe the right conditions for children's well-being, and organized a "sick committee" whose members volunteered to assist the doctor and help ailing neighbors. These and other activities improved personal and family hygiene in the community.

Less well known about Ripley's community school is that it was largely dependent on funding from government and business as secured by Eleanor Roosevelt and Bernard Baruch. Furthermore, the community did not represent an ideal democracy but reflected the racial discrimination of the time in excluding African Americans. Indeed, W. E. B. Du Bois, a prominent African American leader of the

ACTIVITY 5–4   GIVING REASONS FOR THE REAPPEARANCE OF CURRICULUM ADAPTATIONS FROM THE PAST

Many curriculum trends from early periods are resurfacing today. Identify the trend(s) that are part of a curriculum reform in your community. What social factor(s) are associated with the reappearance of the following:

- School—the center for community needs
- Offering Latin and other classics
- Integrating academic (theory) and vocational (practice)
- Algebra and geometry required for all
- Work-study programs (internships)
- Schooling at home
- Teaching phonics and computation
- Learning to write by expressing oneself to a real audience
- Investigating nature and the environment
- Conducting community projects (social service requirements)
- Using interdisciplinary units that draw from different subject matters

period, argued for equal funds to establish a segregated African American community.

Activity 5–4 explores why some of these curricula of years ago are becoming popular again today.

SUMMARY

There are three kinds of curricular responses to social change: *social adaption*, in which students are helped in fitting into the society as it is; *social revision*, which encourages students to look at social issues and problems, connecting courses and subject matter to world conditions as played out in local contexts; and *social criticism*, offering opportunities for students to learn the language of critique, hope, and possibility and thus raising the consciousness of uses and abuses of power and setting the stage for a radical curriculum aimed at transforming aspects of society and its institutions.

Attention was given to postindustrial society and its challenges to the nationalism that schools and curriculum were designed to serve. What happens to the traditional curriculum as students pursue learning by generating ideas, negotiating meaning, and finding resources beyond the school?

As background to the present situation, this chapter included accounts of how distant teachers adapted curriculum to changing circumstances and dealt with the tensions and interests between those advocating a practical education and those who value a classical and abstract approach to intellectual development.

QUESTIONS FOR DISCUSSION

1. Give your opinion of the growing practice of moving an array of social services (e.g., a program for babies and their teenage mothers, health care, family counseling, or substance abuse) into the schools.

2. Mandatory service programs as a way to instill citizenship values and to make students take responsibility for others have become controversial. The controversy arises particularly when the service becomes a requirement for a high school diploma. What are the assumptions about the functions of schooling, the nature of a valid learning experience, and the role of the teacher held by those in favor and those opposed to mandatory service?

3. Public support for schools has always rested on demonstrating that schools are beneficial to the local community. In what ways does the curriculum in a school familiar to you contribute to life in the community? If this curriculum were eliminated, what difference would it make to the community?

4. Joseph Pichler, chair of the National Alliance of Business, is a hard-shell believer in the liberal arts as the best training for life at work: 2 years of Latin, 2 years of Greek. On the other hand, Robert Bjork, chair of a national research committee on training, says that excellent performance in the classroom does not necessarily predict good performance on the battlefield, on the shop floor, or in the sports arena. What is the validity of these two viewpoints, and what are the curricular implications of the two views?

5. The official educational hierarchy at national, state, and district levels is said to impede efforts of teachers to address the needs of their immediate communities. What are some of the ways teachers can link the official curriculum to the local situation? Should teachers be responsive to both the hierarchy and the local community? If so, how?

REFERENCES

Axtell, J. (1974). *The school upon a hill.* New Haven, CT: Yale University Press.

Dewey, J. (1919). *New schools for old.* New York: Dutton.

Finkelstein, N., & Grubb, W. (2000, Fall). Making sense of education and training markets: Lessons from England. *American Educational Research Journal, 37*(3), 601–663.

Flynn, E. E. (2000, May 16). County students join Boston MCAS protest [On-line]. Available: *http://www.newschoice.com* and click on *The Berkshire Eagle.*

Franklin, B. (1907). Proposals relating to the education of youth in Pennsylvania. In A. H. Smyth (Ed.), *The writings of Benjamin Franklin* (pp. 388–396). New York: Macmillan. (Originally published in 1749.)

Hoyt, D. (1881, March). Relation of the high school to the community. *Education, 6*(5), 429–441.

Mayhew, K. C., & Edwards, A. C. (1936). *The Dewey School.* New York: Appleton-Century.

Nagel, N. (1996). *Learning through real-world problem solving.* Thousand Oaks, CA: Corwin.

NEA Education Policies Commission. (1940). *Learning the ways of democracy.* Washington, DC: National Education Association.

The new youth entrepreneur: Youth can make their own jobs. (2000). Kansas City, MO: Kauffman Foundation.

Ripley, E. (1939). *Community schools in action.* New York: Viking.

Rock Point Community School. (1984). *Between sacred mountain: Navajo stories and lessons from the land.* Tucson: University of Arizona Press.

Triplell, J. (1927). *Curriculum making in the elementary school.* Boston: Ginn.

Wehlage, G. (1987). *Dropout prevention and recovery: Fourteen case studies.* Madison, WI: National Center on Effective Secondary Schools.

Wigginton, E. (1985). *Sometimes a shining moment.* New York: Doubleday.

Wigginton, E. (1989). Foxfire grows up. *Harvard Educational Review, 59*(1), 24–50.

CHAPTER **6**

FOMENTING SOCIAL CHANGE

Sara: Teachers as revolutionaries? Get real! Critical pedagogues won't go beyond having their students recognize and analyze power relationships. Teachers won't change society or their institutions, and they're not about to form new identities for themselves by interacting with the dispossessed.

Merl: Some teachers will form alliances with the "oppressed" in their communities and effect social and school changes. As for me, I'm less interested in marshaling a political solidarity than in opening—for both me and my students—new and untapped perspectives, in increasing self-confidence and in awakening consciousness that will help us change our world. It has happened.

Social activism in the classroom is described by the story of Mrs. Garrison, a teacher of English and Social Studies for sixth-graders (Windschitl & Joseph, 2000).

In planning a required Central American unit of study, Mrs. Garrison read about Jennifer Harbury, a lawyer who had assisted immigrants, including refugees from the Guatemalan civil war and who later married a freedom fighter there. Her husband's disappearance led Harbury to search for information about his fate and eventually to charge that her husband had been captured and tortured by a Guatemalan army colonel on the payroll of the U.S. Central Intelligence Agency (CIA).

When Mrs. Garrison read about Harbury's hunger strike to call attention to her need for information, Garrison decided to build her unit around the people, events, and issues surrounding Guatemala and the Harbury case.

Accordingly, her students studied the lives and circumstances of the people in this civil war. The unit included visits to the classroom by a reporter covering the Guatemalan story, and Jennifer Harbury herself. Students engaged in a letter-writing campaign to the chair of the Foreign Relations Committee and made presentations to peers, family, and community members at which time they drew upon their own artwork, background writing, and artifacts.

Initially, Mrs. Garrison had doubts about centering the curriculum on a topic of political controversy involving challenges to U.S. policy and the conduct of federal officials. However, as the unit progressed, she became convinced of the rightness and importance of the Harbury project, the Guatemalan liberation movement, and the need to challenge U.S. policy and CIA operations. She saw how student activism in the interest of fairness, justice, oppression, and freedom could connect to the official curriculum, making its abstractions comprehensible and laden with meaning.

Mrs. Garrison's story prompts questions about fomenting social change through curriculum. Some teachers won't pursue a curriculum that bears upon political education; others think it cannot be avoided. As indicated in chapter 1, there are four interests to consider in constructing curriculum. How well did Mrs. Garrison reconcile these interests?

It's clear that the critical interest was met as students sought to critique and improve institutions. Mrs. Garrison's personal preferences, interests, and commitment were served by the curriculum, but we don't know about the preferences of all the students. One can argue that the professional and moral interest was met by Mrs. Garrison's careful reflections on the decision to proceed, although we might want to know whether the activity gave students a message of cynicism about U.S. institutions or if it generated hope that it is possible to improve institutions through democratic means. Was the institutional interest of the school maintained? Perhaps if the media followed the story and presented the student undertaking in a favorable light—democracy in action, student thoroughness in collecting facts, and using academic skills for a worthy cause.

BACKGROUND FOR CRITICAL CURRICULUM

For many years, some teachers have sought to develop curriculum that would bring greater equity and justice. They feared that too often the traditional curriculum contributed to structured inequality, environmental pollution, gender, and racial disharmonies. The following section describes curriculum efforts of radical teachers in the past.

Antebellum America and the Slavery Question

Most teachers in the United States before the Civil War played little part in the slavery question. Most of them—in both the North and the South—accepted slavery and drifted along with the sentiment of their community. Teachers were expected to indoctrinate children with the community attitude toward slavery whenever the community on the whole had one or to avoid the subject entirely. There were, however, notable examples of teachers who expressed their dislike of slavery.

Reuben Crandel, a teacher of botany, was arrested and thrown into prison in 1835 for an alleged curriculum of abolitionist literature. Although it was proven that the "abolitionist" newspapers found in his trunk were wrapping his botanical specimens and the "incendiary" pamphlets were articles opposing slavery, the district attorney sought his execution on a capital offense. The jury cleared him, but 8 months in damp confinement caused his death of tuberculosis (Beale, 1941).

In 1857, J. C. Richardson, a Kentucky teacher, was seized by a mob for giving a sermon against the rise of slavery. The mob beat him and threw him into a guarded cabin. Expecting the mob to return and further punish him, two of his students rescued him and managed to hold off the mob with their rifles until the teacher and his wife escaped northward. Another Kentucky teacher, John Fee, was more persistent. Although he founded an abolitionist school in the mountains away from slaveholders, he was greeted in another county by a riot, and his school was burned. In all, he was mobbed 22 times and twice left for dead. Finally, he was driven from the state. Three times Fee tried to return, succeeding the last time under protection of Union soldiers when he reestablished his school, which later became Berea College (Beale, 1941).

Socialistic Curriculum

Kenneth Teitelbaum's (1993) *A Curriculum for "Good Rebels"* gives an account of the socialist Sunday school at the beginning of the 20th century, revealing ways in which radical activity attempted to instill students with understanding and concern for more equitable social and economic relations. In their effort to encourage children (ages 5 to 14) to become "good rebels," teachers used three kinds of texts:

1. Appropriate mainstream texts
2. Adapted radical materials
3. Focused discussion on socialistic themes

Robert Louis Stevenson's "Where Go the Boats," an example of a mainstream text that could serve a socialist idea, was used to reinforce a perspective of the interrelatedness of individuals in society: what happens "up the river" has an effect on children who play "away" a hundred miles or more.

Some texts were adaptions of radical materials that were not originally written for Sunday schools. An adult economics textbook became the basis for a curriculum criticizing capitalism and the ownership of "the machines and the buildings by a few individuals," and it offered socialism as an alternative that would put "an end to the relation of master and servant" and ensure equal opportunity for able men and women as well as an equal voice in the management of the industries carried on for the use of everybody (Teitelbaum, 1993). Through such a curriculum, children were expected to gain an introductory understanding of capitalism and the everyday conditions of working-class life in a capitalistic society—poverty, unemployment, and unhealthy and unsafe working conditions. Such content pointed to the need for rebels and stimulated an awareness of how conditions could be improved under socialism.

Some texts featured discussion questions that focused on the relationship between socialistic themes and the social conditions of most workers, such as the following:

■ Name some instances of political injustice.

■ What is justice?

■ What do you know about oil wells? Any near here?

■ Is it easy or hard to get coal or oil?

■ Who does the work?

■ Who makes the money?

■ Who owns the coal mines and oil wells?

■ Who ought to own and control them? Why?

■ Would they cost less or more under socialism? Why?

The primary aim of such materials was to show that all things necessary for our support come from the land. The earth, of course, belongs to all people; therefore, no one should be deprived of any of the necessities of everyday living.

Biographic sketches of socialistic leaders and excerpts from the writings of Dickens, Tolstoy, Sinclair, and others were used. Storybooks with accompanying radical lyrics like the following were common:

> The earth was made for brother men
> To live in peace, they say;
> But men have turned it into hell
> In competition's way. (Teitelbaum, 1993)

The socialistic curriculum was a model of useful knowledge. The outcomes sought were students' pride in their working-class backgrounds; a sense of solidarity with other oppressed groups; a vision of social interdependence, insight into the relationships between current social problems, and an understanding of the nature of the dominant economic and political interests; and a recognized need for fundamental social change.

Teachers as Activists in Segregated and in Freedom Schools

Everell Dawkin, an African American teacher of mathematics, illustrates one way that teachers resisted an unfair structure in the 20th century prior to the civil rights movement. He opposed school board policy that prohibited the teaching of advanced math in segregated black schools as a way to label African Americans as academically inferior. Dawkin taught advanced math to his African American students until forced to stop, at which time he pressed the issue of who should control curriculum for educating African Americans. Other African American teachers, especially those who were well educated, were given opportunity to teach in white schools, but they refused because they felt their service was more needed in the segregated schools for African Americans (McLaughlin & Tierney, 1993).

In addition to serving as role models, African American teachers encouraged their students to achieve beyond what society expected of them, a surreptitious activism (Ladson-Billings, 1994). Also, the narratives of radical Catholic nuns, Jewish women of the left, and African American women teachers show how these teachers offered new ways of being political, not only by struggling with state and institutions but also by nurturing others in the home and school (Casey, 1993).

Florence Howe was among many who faced danger in challenging the power structure of Mississippi. In 1964 she started the Freedom Schools to assist young African Americans in their education and to foster collective community work in social and political areas. Her teaching was innovative in confronting students with the realities of exploitation. Academic competencies were important but not as much as social change. Activities included participating in student forums for community change, publishing community newspapers, writing and presenting plays promoting change, participating in picketing, and exploring other ways of demanding fairer treatment. In the process, Howe found her own identity (Chilcoat & Lignon, 1994).

CURRENT CRITICAL CURRICULUM

In the late 20th century, some teachers began following the liberation pedagogy of the late Pablo Freire. Freire (1970) developed a revolutionary curriculum model for the Third World that helped students learn to "problematize" their situations, differentiating those social conditions that are determined politically from those determined by natural necessity, and then to take actions that are possible and just. Teachers in the affluent world also have found Freire's ideas of value. The goal of these teachers is to empower students to build a just and equal society at peace with itself and other nations, as well as in accord with the environment. The teacher invites students to examine problems and structure their investigations of these problems, comaking the curriculum. Typically, students are expected to look at situations with such questions as the following in mind:

- What is happening?

- How did it get this way?

- Whose interests are served by it? Whose interests are not?

- What are the consequences of the practice? Or text?

- What are its underlying assumptions?

Consider William Bigelow's (1989) work described in "Discovering Columbus: Reading the Past." Bigelow wanted his students to be critical of their textbooks and their society and to ask, "Why is it like this? How can I make it better?" His approach was first to have students examine the word *discover* and think of possible substitutes—*rip-off, steal, invade, conquer*—to see that *discover* is a word of the conquerors and to recognize that when the word is repeated in textbooks, it becomes the propaganda of the winners. In his introduction to the study, Bigelow feigned ownership of a student's purse on the grounds that he had "discovered" it. He then prepared students to examine critically the history textbooks they had used by considering alternatives to Columbus's enterprise—that the primary motive for his trip was to secure profit and wealth for Spain and himself (Columbus had demanded a 10% cut of everything for himself and his heirs).

Bigelow then introduced letters and records written by Columbus and others of the period revealing the generosity of the Indians and Columbus's idea for subjecting and making slaves of the Indians. Moving accounts of how Columbus and his brother sent slaves to Spain and the terror those people experienced were also presented. Even more revolting accounts were presented, telling how Columbus extracted gold from the Indians and the systematic ways the Indians were hunted and killed when they fled when unable to meet quotas for tributes in gold.

After students considered the topic of what "discovery" meant to the victors, they examined textbooks with accounts of Columbus's discovery, including those used in grade schools, and wrote critiques of the texts' treatment of Columbus and the Indians. Guidelines for the critique featured factual accuracy, consideration of omissions, motives given, points of view, function of pictures in the text, reasons given for the portrayal, and groups in our society who might have an interest in presenting an inaccurate view of history.

In keeping with Bigelow's desire that students read texts skeptically, students were asked to question how the text was written, bringing writers' assumptions and values to the surface. The students were able to find instances of omission, avoidance of reality, untruths, and disregard for negative consequences, and were able to give reasons for the rosy accounts in the texts. The relevance of Columbus to present events—U.S. involvement in other countries, motives for exploration, wars for profit—was discussed. Bigelow had evidence that the curriculum was working when students spontaneously asked, "What is your 'interest' in offering this curriculum?"

In his book about liberating teaching, Shore (1987) presents the work of teachers in diverse settings who have social criticism and change as their goals. One of these teachers, Marilyn Frankenstein, has developed a critical mathematics curriculum. In her course "Statistics for the Social Science," Frankenstein (1987) provides many opportunities for students to examine how subjective choice is involved in describing and collecting data and in making inferences about the world. For instance, students prepare critiques of the official treatment of the military portions of the federal budget, while at the same time learning about percentages and circle graphs. Students find that the government makes military spending appear smaller by including funds held "in trust" (e.g., Social Security) under Social Service and by counting war-related expenditures under nonmilitary categories. Production of new nuclear materials is charged to the Department of Energy; veterans' benefits are categorized as Direct Benefit Payments. In contrast with the government's claim that 25% of the budget is for national defense, student calculations show that nearly 60% of the budget is going to pay for past, present, and future wars.

Similarly, students practice arithmetical operations and discuss ways to present the statistics that show that the United States is a welfare state for the rich. They must divide in order to describe tax loophole data, such as "each of the richest 160,000 taxpayers got nine times as much money as the maximum AFDC [Assistance to Families with Dependent Children] grant for a family of four." The students learn about the meaning of large numbers when they use their data to consider the services that the total taxes not paid by the rich ($7.2 billion) could have provided if the money were included in the federal budget.

Other math skills and concepts are learned from applications that challenge the idea that the status quo is natural, good, and just. Operations with decimals center on problems using data from the U.S. Department of Energy, in which students found the costs of the federal subsidy to the nuclear power industry and recognized that without the federal subsidy nuclear power would be twice as costly—and unable to compete with oil-fired electricity, currently the most expensive power.

Applications of percentages occur when students are given information about such matters as the net profits made by 50 of the 32,000 U.S. food-manufacturing corporations and their advertising expenditures, and then are asked to find the percentage of firms that make 75% of the profit. The solution serves several social purposes: changing $50 \div 32,000$ to 0.2% highlights that only a tiny percentage of the firms make most of the profits and leads to political discussions of the agribusiness and corporate monopoly in general, as well as a critique of the advertising industry bringing to bear such facts as 70% of TV food advertising promotes low-nutritious, high-caloric foods; while only 0.7% promotes fresh fruits and vegetables.

Critical Theorists

Critical theorists in education try to affect the way teachers think, talk, and enact curriculum. These theorists typically have common views about knowledge, language, and political power, although each expresses particular concerns under the broad heading of multiculturalism—economic structures that create gaps between rich and poor, mass culture's limiting of personal and group identities, media's blaming of victims, the privileged status of men, discrimination against people of color, and the like.

Knowledge is seen as individually and socially constructed (as described in chapter 3), although critical theorists recognize that official knowledge that serves the interests of politically powerful groups is considered legitimate by schools. Critical theorists focus on the power of language to influence the way students view the world and, as indicated in chapter 4, do try to shape individual and group identities. Critical theorists are advocates for the teaching of new forms of language that offer more possibilities and perspectives to the oppressed. By way of example, traditional classroom discourse features recitation, which is a language form that fosters passive learners, determining who can speak, to whom, when, what can be said, and the like. New forms are needed to give students opportunities to question and transform existing social practices in the school and community.

Critical discourse can start early. For example, Vivian Vasquez has negotiated a critical literacy program with prekindergartners. Her 3- and 4-year-olds engaged in social construction of literacy when given the opportunity to consider what we do with reading and writing and what reading and writing do to us (Vasquez, 2000).

On the first day, Vasquez read a predictable text so that the children could read with her. While reading, children raised questions about illustrations. For example, one child asked whether the pictured animal was a toad or a frog. The question led to the reason frogs and toads are in danger of extinction, to inquiries about the rainforest, ways to save endangered animals and the like which began a curriculum about social justice and the environment that lasted throughout the school year. Issues of marginalization and out-of-school knowledge surfaced. Students entered a contest involving the creation of a bookmark and slogan that represented women's' rights and they won, although only older students had previously entered contests for International Women's Day.

Consequently, the children questioned other ways they had been excluded, leading to their partnering with the PTA and others to fight for the right of kindergartners to have equal access to school events and functions.

The goal of new approaches is to raise student consciousness of social inequalities among advantaged students, to offer marginal students alternatives to official knowledge, and to develop a collective voice against injustice.

One approach to critical discourse in the classroom is to let students compare personal, oppressed, and official accounts or stories related to racism, sexism, political power, or other social issues. Students give their accounts of personal experiences related to one of the issues; they also listen and empathize with an oppressed person's experience with the issue, creating alternatives to the official narrative.

You may be more sensitive to what is missing in the official curriculum after completing Activity 6–1.

Usually students work in groups, each group addressing a different aspect of a larger social issue (e.g., homelessness, joblessness, school failure, single parenting). Students form their own questions and research the topic. They relate the classroom, institutions, and cultural dimensions to the problem so that they can better connect peer particular experiences with the general condition. The

---

ACTIVITY 6–1   FORMING SOLIDARITY WITH
A CHILD

Ten-year old Mike wrote the following for a children's newsletter. Read it and indicate how you would respond to Mike. (A critical reconstructionist would not do something for Mike, keeping him dependent, but would help him do something for himself.)

> In school they never talk about the social worker who comes to see my parents. They never talk about the little neighbor girl who was put in foster care. They never talk about the police who always come around the neighborhood. They never talk about all the men who are ill like my father and can't work anymore. At school it's like a postcard. Everything looks shiny.

report that each group writes from its inquiry is shared and discussed through dialogue with the class. Subsequently, reports are combined as a text to be used by real audiences and to serve as the basis for student action. Classroom dialogues don't demand that all think alike and only begin when students have the confidence to disagree. When the student voices are racist and sexist, they are still affirmed, although underlying assumptions are challenged. Dialogues tend to focus on contradictions in one's views.

A problematic aspect of critical inquiry as outlined above centers on the critical theorists' commitment to a particular social change in the interest of justice. Social reconstructionists in schools have always been sensitive to the charge of indoctrination. Although radical teachers may say that students are not obligated to change their beliefs, critical theory points to the difficulty of the teacher avoiding using power and authority and the improbability of conducting rational dialogue that will result in consensus on deeply controversial issues.

Companion
Website

LA Youth is an independent magazine written by teenagers that distributes bimonthly lesson plans to teachers. The lessons deal with immigrant bashing, homophobia, physical abuse, and other topics from teenagers' lives. Although the lessons elicit opinions and disagreements, students find the classroom debates and discussions serving an educational purpose. To view sample lessons, go to *www.prenhall.com/mcneil* and click on the LA Youth link.

An illustration of the work of critical theorists is provided by Christine E. Sleeter (1996), who emphasizes the social context of learning and recognizes the bifurcation between school knowledge that students perceive as "tasks to do" and real-life knowledge in which students have power to create and participate in life in their own neighborhood. Sleeter has an activist view of multiculturalism, with the teacher giving attention to undervalued forms of knowledge, sharing power with the oppressed community, and encouraging students to impact institutions.

Instead of posting a picture of Martin Luther King Jr. or talking about Harriet Tubman and the underground railroad, a schoolteacher's play at the 93rd Street Elementary School in Los Angeles says more than "We shall overcome." The play engages students with people and events neglected in their textbooks by weaving together elements of black culture from contributions from the countries of Brazil and the United States and Aborigines in Australia. It dramatizes a trial—*NAACP vs. the State*—concerning allegations that African history has been wrongly left out of a state-issued textbook (Texeira, 2001).

Peter McLaren is a provocative scholar and social reconstructionist who critiques capitalism and documents wide-ranging oppressions associated with the economic system. He challenges teachers to form a commitment to recognize and oppose the ways power and privilege shape identities.

McLaren (2001) urges teachers and students to link local issues with the economic struggles of the nation and the world through such activities as interviewing family members, friends, people in the neighborhood about the types of jobs in their community, workplace conditions and terms of employment. Students can communicate through the Internet with those in divergent socioeconomic conditions and the issues that affect the disparity. Why is there a shortage of community centers in some neighborhoods? How can transportation become more accessible? Why is there police repression in one place and a different police presence in gated communities? Why are there so many liquor stores in some neighborhoods and none in others?

bell hooks (who uses a pseudonym in all lowercase letters) calls for understanding human experiences through "the struggle for voice," by which teachers read personal narrative (their own and those of their students) against society's treasured stock of narratives. In telling personal stories, students create a critical language that enables them to break free from those narratives that would limit their possibilities (hooks, 1990).

Sandra Harding seeks a better version of scientific objectivity, which takes into account the cognitive perspectives of women and other groups that have not been featured in Western science. In a recent book, she asks teachers to attend to those who are oppressed by reason of gender, sexual orientation, class, or physical limitations (Harding, 1998b).

Maxine Greene differs from many critical theorists associated with political rhetoric. She is more interested in helping students learn how to see through multiple perspectives, especially in the arts; of learning to make the familiar strange and the strange familiar; and in developing higher levels of consciousness that will contribute to personal emancipation (Greene, 1996).

Activity 6–2 is intended to strengthen one's ability to view a familiar curriculum from a new and critical perspective.

Demystifying the School and Its Curriculum

An underlying conflict is what kind of change should occur in schools and the kind of knowledge that is to be constructed. Should curriculum be differentiated in purpose, content, method, and assessment by social class, or is it sufficient to help students and parents demystify the school and its relation to the larger society? For years analysis of school settings have shown that although all students study the same subjects, working-class schools don't focus on reform and social issues (Anyon, 1983). These students are taught to fit into society as it is, to learn the right way to do something and without conceptual understanding—single textbook, phonics, multiplication tables, and computer drill and practice. Middle-class students have some choice in their learning with an emphasis on understanding. They make literary selections, propose multiple solutions to math problems, engage in numerous projects and activities (plays, expressive writings) related to individual interest.

Students in affluent schools have more experiential activities (investigations, inquiry units) and the production of major undertakings, such as documentaries and original theater. Knowledge in the affluent school is not only conceptual but open to discovery, construction, and the making of meaning. However, increasingly

■ ── ■

ACTIVITY 6–2   CRITICAL ANALYSIS: AN ASPECT OF CURRICULUM

The relation between classroom curriculum and society is of great importance. One way to express this interest is to examine how classroom curriculum might generate particular meanings, restraints, cultural values, and social relationships. Is there any way a particular curriculum can perpetuate social injustice, social class, and economic unfairness?

1. Select an aspect of curriculum from a school or program known to you. You may wish to examine a lesson plan, an instructional unit, a teacher's manual, an examination, a text, a curriculum framework, a course of study, a grading practice, or any other aspect of curriculum.
2. Analyze the aspect of curriculum you have chosen in terms of what it implies about the purpose of schooling, the nature of knowledge, and how learning best takes place.
3. Determine what is omitted from the aspect, and whose interests are and are not served by this aspect.
4. What problem does the material purport to address, and how adequate is the proposed solution? What are possible unanticipated consequences?

■ ── ■

honors and advanced placement courses in these schools valorize the "cultural capital" of the college and university, restricting transformation of what counts as valuable knowledge.

Students in the elite schools are taught decision-making practices with a focus on controlling situations in institutions and systems. The knowledge they construct is academic, intellectual and rigorous with less concern for personal meanings. Opportunities are given for elite students to interact with visiting poets, scientists, and other specialists. Many elite schools today place more emphasis on educating students to be successful global leaders and high achievers in the global workforce than to be only a citizen of a national community. Hence, students of the elite construct knowledge that is valued across cultural and national boundaries.

Critical teachers, students, and parents should examine their own school and classrooms and see what knowledge is being constructed and the life trajectories to which it points.

Activist Teachers' Need for External Support

Teachers who take on the issue of social reform need the support of their professional associates and others in the community. Inasmuch as activist teachers go beyond imparting systematic formal knowledge and the limits set by most schools, the cooperation of consultants, parents, and community agencies (print and television media) is desirable. Social projects are likely to make multidisciplinary and integrative curriculum necessary, replacing a curriculum based on discrete subjects. However, in using academic subject matter as tools for exploring meaningful social issues in a critical way, radical teachers reduce the conflict between rigor and relevance.

Some questions exist about whether public schools will permit curriculum innovations designed to counter the disadvantages of class, race, and gender, and to bring about particular changes in their communities. El Puente United Nations Academy for Peace and Justice, a public school in Brooklyn, New York, is a theme-oriented school whose teachers have developed a curriculum that uses the community as a classroom, with students examining such environmental issues as the proposed construction of an incinerator in the Navy yard and involving themselves in matters of school overcrowding and racial tension.

Pam Chamberlain, who has developed curriculum aimed at social change in the area of homophobia, has found that when the community (especially parent groups) has contributed advice on course content, more information and more controversial topics are included than when the curriculum is designed without parents' advice. She also found that parents with racist and sexist fears are unlikely to challenge homophobia (Chamberlain, 1990). According to Chamberlain, curriculum designed to counter homophobia must go beyond awareness and counseling services. Instead of focusing on gays and lesbians as the "problem," she addresses the institution of homophobia by helping students see how the norms of the school pressure students into sex roles and stereotypes and confirm their fears of differences.

The incorporation of reading materials about community-related nontraditional subjects helps provide a structure for the classroom and can offer a rationale for discussion with other members of the school community. Bringing such materials into the school is a political act: it may involve the teacher in presenting arguments for the curriculum and the specific needs that it will meet, organizing a support network, and organizing a campaign among students and the larger community.

CRITICAL PEDAGOGY AND THE CURRICULUM OF POPULAR CULTURE

Trying to make the familiar strange and the strange familiar, critical pedagogues ask students to look at popular culture in a new light and to question (a) what this culture has to do with the issues of class, gender, and ethnic inequality; and (b) how and what the culture has done to them. The range of popular culture to examine and interpret is great—cereal boxes, rap music, TV soap operas, cartoons, baseball, and many others.

The study of popular culture also can help students develop the intellectual tools for entering the high culture traditionally taught in school, with the promise of finding values that contribute to what students are and perhaps provide images of what students and their culture might be.

The concept of high culture has been associated with the ideal of fusing active and contemplative principles—a means by which one can abstract from, rather than simply respond to, the world. In the past, high culture indicated what was thought to be truly liberalizing and what would open up the riches of civilization (paintings, music, literature, etc.); it represented the most highly developed and complex human expressions and achievements. High culture also emphasized what has been thought and written about for centuries regarding human problems.

Criticism of high culture in education centers on the idea that it promotes the class interest of an elite group and preserves the status quo. Alternative ways of achieving traditional goals of abstract thinking are increasingly found in studies in multicultural contexts. High-level thinking is not dependent on the traditional classroom subjects. Any topic, phenomenon, or activity can become the basis for high-level thinking. It is not the object that defines thinking; it is the nature of the thought that one brings to the subject that makes it intellectual or not. Cooking can become a highly intellectual study, just as the study of a classic can be banal. Recognition of high-level thinking in non-European cultures and among the politically disaffected and economically disadvantaged, among others, has broadened the conception of high culture. High-level thinking is no longer narrowly associated with what occurs in the traditional classrooms of the West.

The cultures that children bring to school can offer alternative educational opportunities. Constructivist approaches indicate how the conceptual maps of students can contribute to more thoughtful, imaginative, and practical ways of understanding the world. The traditional curriculum, however, should be part of their inquiry and construction of knowledge.

The teacher can help students look at particular works from a variety of perspectives—for example, feminist and neocolonial. One way to prepare students for critical reading of traditional works is to develop analytical skills first through study of popular culture.

Film for Criticism

In his illustration of how film can be used to challenge major themes about American culture, Banks (1993) draws on the film *How the West Was Won*. In this film, minorities are almost invisible. Mexicans appear as bandits, African Americans are shunted to the background, and Native Americans are hostile attackers. The film reinforces the notion that the West was won by liberty-loving, hard-working people who purchased freedom for all.

Banks begins his instructional unit on the westward movement by having students share their personal and cultural knowledge of the event; then he screens *How the West Was Won*. The faithfulness of this film to traditional historical frontier theory is made apparent. Then transformative perspectives on the west, which challenge mainstream accounts of what happened, are introduced. Segments from films that offer alternative images—*Honor Lost, Dances with Wolves*—are viewed, and students study newer histories, ones that present transformative perspectives on Native Americans in history and culture. The main goal of this curriculum is to help students see different kinds of knowledge, to understand how knowledge is constructed or how it reflects a given social context, and to make their own knowledge.

Weston (1990) also uses the Hollywood western to awaken critical consciousness, showing how the western reaffirms individualistic, racist, sexist, and imperialistic values. Students see how the western stereotypes women and connects sexism to racism and promotes a domineering attitude toward the wilderness. The degradation or "villainization" of victims—as if to justify their exploitation—is noted. Students learn that, although westerns romanticize conflict and at the same time reaffirm traditional values, behind the myth of the western frontier lies the exploitation of land and workers for profit, together with resistance to the exploitation.

Alternatives in Dealing with Popular Culture

The idea that students are "dupes" of popular culture—that this culture reinforces sexism, racism, and consumerism—often leads to a curriculum that attempts to inoculate young people against its influence. Many teachers offer instructional units on consumerism, for example, using concepts such as supply and demand, economic stability, advertising, and product promotions whereby students critically evaluate TV and newspaper advertisements. Typical activities in such units ask students to do various things:

- Design a survey to show how students are influenced by advertising.
- Analyze the uses, appeals, and effects of advertising.
- Survey and evaluate the contents of a newspaper or network.
- Test several brands of a given product.
- Create advertisements for promoting particular products.

The inoculating approach has been faulted for misunderstanding the relationship of students to popular culture. Many students are sophisticated and critical of this culture. What they tend to lack is an understanding of the importance of popular culture in constructing social relationships and in defining individual and group relations. More than validating the students' existing knowledge, some curricula aim at relating common sense and formal academic knowledge to the study of popular culture.

Shore's (1987) curriculum unit "The Hamburger" is an example of a critical curriculum that relates the academic to the familiar. Studies on the theme of the hamburger begin with the students' immediate sources and move to the hamburger's global relations, drawing on history, geography, economics, and aesthetics. The study illuminates modern capitalism and reveals the consequences of decisions by the industry on the environment, health, and labor. The outlook and style of the fast-food industries have repercussions that extend far beyond food consumption and ultimately make statements about values, attitudes, and beliefs about life. In conducting such studies, students learn how fast-food practices contribute to their entertainment, certainty, and sense of place; perhaps they even learn to see themselves in a new context. At the least, the study gives students a chance to develop a body of knowledge about modern industry, and the culture that created it.

A critical theorist, Henry Giroux, has a pedagogy of the popular, having students critically examine media directed at youth—music, movies, street talk, body language. Students critically analyze the politics of representation in such movies as *Dead Poets Society* and *Stand and Deliver.* Giroux (1994) shows students how such cultural forms and concepts are created, while giving particular attention to how media constructs inequalities and to the idea that images, sounds, and texts don't merely express reality but also help create it. Students are taught how meanings are produced through the use of history, social forms, and modes of address. Students are expected to analyze and reconstruct both their own identity and their representations of others.

Sources for Interpretations of Popular Culture

Critical pedagogy need not seek homogeneous interpretations from students. Indeed, it should welcome diversity and encourage students to negotiate their own meanings, to argue with the interpretations of others, and to make sense of popular culture in terms of their own values. To this end, a wide variety of sources is introduced in the study of popular culture:

- Perspectives from academic scholars (ethnical, historical, economical, anthropological, and sociological studies) that represent political views of both those from the left and the right

- Investigative reports as found in magazines and newspapers (with sources such as *Abstracts of Popular Culture* and *Journal of American Culture* suggesting topics for study and revealing original insights about aspects of popular culture)

- Students' own studies and interpretations of popular culture

Use of these varied sources helps students see that they can deal with culture and challenge traditional notions of what counts as knowledge and culture. This does not mean that student interpretations of culture are necessarily valid but that they should take part in the social and cultural debates. Just as the views of mature scholars reflect their values, prejudices, and stereotypes, the spontaneous and idiosyncratic interpretations of students must be challenged.

Hence, critical pedagogy is associated with practices such as "Others"—an activity that probes students to ask how the situation or discourse could be different: "How would a different gender, social class, historical period, group, sexual preference, or religion alter your interpretation?"

In their language arts curriculum, Livey and Walm (1993) invite students to collect reviews of programs from television, radio, and other media on a variety of subjects from magazines, newspapers and other sources. The students determine commonalities in the reviews and then hypothesize about qualities of a particular form. Next, the students test their hypotheses by studying new reviews and writing their own review of a book, movie, sporting event, concern, recording, or other specific piece of popular culture. Subsequently, the students study several novels treating social issues and then move into the real world to test the authors' ideas against other sources of information—for example, by talking

■ ─── ■

ACTIVITY 6–3   CRITICIZING POPULAR
CULTURE FROM A FEMINIST PERSPECTIVE

1. Select a television program, rap artist, talk show, athletic activity (e.g., as body building), or other popular cultural artifact known to you.
2. Review and analyze segments of the chosen aspect of popular culture using the following questions as guidelines:
   a. How are women involved in this social activity or this cultural medium? What roles do women play and are these roles related to social class and race?
   b. What needs to be changed in this medium? What change should occur?
   c. What role can you play in bringing about the desired change?

■ ─── ■

with people who are directly involved with the situations like those depicted in a novel.

Activity 6–3 is an opportunity for you to engage in critical pedagogy.

SUMMARY

Social constructivists do not view conflicts as undesirable but as opportunities to learn and create something better. Social change, particularly in multicultural contexts, is present. Teachers and students alike are examining their beliefs, texts, institutions, and practices critically. This means reflecting on the categories they use in viewing the world. In classroom practice, everyone can talk about the categories by which they are classifying events, persons, objects (including popular culture) and see how their categories affect their views and their judgments. All can learn how their inferences and imagination impact their perceptions; discover how their memories are coloring their views; and relate how their life histories influenced their practices. In the process, the familiar becomes unfamiliar, and the unfamiliar becomes familiar.

For many teachers, social reconstruction means exploring their own privileged positions and rethinking their ways of working with "disadvantaged" groups.

Some teachers are reluctant to express their own opinions or engage in controversial matters, saying they do not want to indoctrinate their students. Withholding opinions is not education, but there is an obligation to make clear when one is voicing a personal interest and when one is sharing an authoritative perspective and its basis.

Other teachers say they will not engage in critiquing and fomenting social change because they do not want to weaken students' faith in the American dream, believing that focusing on inequities, dominance, and imperfect social situations will replace the students' natural hope with cynicism.

In contrast, some teachers see critical analysis as fulfilling the American ideals of justice and liberty, as well as contributing to the individual's sense of empowerment, intellectual understanding, and vision of a better world.

QUESTIONS FOR DISCUSSION

1. What, if any, responsibility does a teacher have for shaping students' attitudes toward racism and feminism?
2. If you believe that curriculum should help lead society toward change, what is your vision of what that change should be?
3. It is commonly thought that the curriculum best fosters social change when teachers and students work with other constituencies who share their social concerns. Give an example of a desired social change and the popular constituencies that would support it.
4. The curriculum of some teachers aims at helping students recognize the discrepancy between ideals and the status quo, but leaves it up to students themselves to decide what action, if any, is appropriate to take in closing the gap. Should the curriculum stop at intellectual understanding of social problems, or should it include an action phase? State reasons for your opinion.
5. Scholars in all fields are offering alternative views of knowledge—math as socially constructed concepts rather than as universal principles, history from the viewpoints of minorities and commoners, literature that represents a variety of cultures and peoples, science with new views of biological determinism. Whose interests are and are not served by the introduction of this new content (interpretations) in elementary and secondary school curriculum?
6. What are some of the ways popular culture is enlarging or thwarting human possibility? How might your curriculum best relate to popular culture?
7. What is the significance of the following quotation for those who want to promote critical curriculum: "It is easy to pull weeds, but difficult to grow flowers"?

REFERENCES

Anyon, J. (1981). Social class and school knowledge. *Curriculum Inquiry, 11*(1), 3–41.

Banks, J. (1993). The canon debate: Knowledge, construction and mathematical education. *Educational Researcher, 22*(2), 4–15.

Beale, H. K. (1941). *A history of freedom of teaching in American schools.* New York: Scribner.

Bigelow, W. (1989). Discovering Columbus: Rereading the past. *Language Arts, 6*(6), 635–643.

Casey, K. (1993). *I answer with my life: Life histories of women teachers working for social change.* New York: Routledge.

Chamberlain, P. (1990). Homophobia in the schools or what we don't know will hurt us. In S. O'Malley, R. C. Rosen, & L. Vogt (Eds.), *Politics of education: Essays for radical teachers* (pp. 302–312). Albany: State University of New York Press.

Chilcoat, G., & Lignon, J. A. (1994). Developing democratic citizens: The freedom schools as a model. *Theory and Research in Social Studies Education, 22*(2), 128–176.

Frankenstein, M. (1987). Critical mathematics education. In I. Shore (Ed.), *Freire for the classroom* (pp. 180–204). Portsmouth, NH: Heinemann.

Freire, P. (1970). *Pedagogy of the oppressed.* New York: Seabury.

Giroux, H. A. (1994). *Disturbing pleasures: Learning popular culture.* New York: Routledge.

Greene, M. (1996). A constructivist perspective on teaching and learning in the arts. In *Constructivism theory, perspective and practice* (pp. 120–141). New York: Teachers College Press.

Harding, S. G. (1998a). *Is science multicultural?* Bloomington: Indiana University Press.

Harding, S. G. (1998b). *Race, gender, and science.* Bloomington: Indiana University Press.

hooks, b. (1990). *Yearning: Race, gender and cultural politics.* Toronto: Between the Lines.

Ladson-Billings, G. (1994). *The dreamkeepers: Successful teachers of African-American children.* San Francisco: Jossey-Bass.

Livey, R., & Walm, M. (1993). Shifting perspectives. *English Quarterly, 21*(1), 25–27.

McLaren, P. (2001). *Revolutionary multiculturalism: Pedagogies of dissent for the new millennium.* Boulder, CO: Westview.

McLaughlin, D., & Tierney, W. G. (1993). *Naming silenced lives.* New York: Routledge.

Shore, I. (1987). *Critical teaching in everyday life.* Chicago: University of Chicago Press.

Sleeter, C. E. (1996). *Multicultural education as social action.* Albany: State University of New York Press.

Teitelbaum, K. (1993). *Schooling for good rebels: Socialist education for children in the United States, 1900–1920.* Philadelphia: Temple University Press.

Texeira, E. (2001, March 1). Schoolteacher's play more than "We Shall Overcome." *Los Angeles Times,* p. B6.

Vasquez, V. (2000, May). Negotiating a critical literacy curriculum with young children. *Research Bulletin* (Phi Delta Kappa International, Center for Evaluation, Development, and Research), *29,* 7–10.

Weston, J. (1990). Teaching the Hollywood Western. In S. O'Malley, R. C. Rosen, & L. Vogt (Eds.), *Politics of education: Essays for radical teachers* (pp. 177–180). Albany: State University of New York Press.

Windschitl, M., & Joseph, P. (2000). Confronting the dominant order. In P. Joseph, N. Green, S. Bravmann, M. Windschitl, & E. Mikel (Eds.), *Cultures of curriculum* (pp. 137–161). Mahwah, NJ: Erlbaum.

4

Stories of
School Subjects

The academic disciplines are in ferment: the disciplines face new information and new questions, alternative theories, doubts about a problem-solving or scientific method, and fragmentation within individual disciplines together with crossings of disciplinary lines.

Inasmuch as there is a connection between what occurs in the disciplines and what becomes school subject matter, expect changes in what students will learn.

In some cases, the conflicts will become the focus for study, and students will be caught up in the great issues within a field, learning to deal with uncertainty by weighing the arguments and considering the likely consequences. In most cases, teachers will try to put students in touch with ideas, concepts, and theories from the academic domains through classroom activities, inquiries, and projects. The curriculum task of the teacher is to select those ideas and practices that can be linked with work in a discipline, students' daily living, and the strengths and interests of diverse individuals.

Teachers are constrained in their decisions as to what to teach by college entrance examinations, achievement tests, official courses of study, frameworks, textbooks, local board policy, and community attitudes. The issuing of standards for the different subject areas prompted by the federal government and prepared by professional associations is the latest effort to influence what will be taught on a wide scale. These standards give rise to the issue of whether the curriculum should support traditional ideas or respond to new social conditions and intellectual trends. The standards for mathematics and science, for example, favor change and casting in new directions. However, the standards in the arts and the

CHAPTER 7

THE HUMANITIES
AND SOCIAL SCIENCES

Merl: I'll keep much from the Dead White Males, but I need the others to
             know what's missing.

Sara: As the poet said, "Art is long and life is fleeting." How many cultural
             worlds can one expect to enter? Why not invent one of your own?

Merl is alluding to the question of what aesthetic, literary, or historical works should
be included in the curriculum. For example, should United States history focus on
political leaders, military conflicts, and industrial inventors—the privileged group
of society? Sara also is interested in what content to include but seems to be more
concerned about time—whether there is time and place for the arts and humanities
because of the increased emphasis on the "hard" subjects, math and science.

As for time and a crowded curriculum, it is economical for all subjects to have
a humanistic thrust, such as addressing the question, "What does it mean to be
human?" Can you imagine biology classes overlooking this question and not introducing the arts and crafts that are necessary in all disciplines and professions?
(Consider the value of multiple representations in mathematics and the designing
of apparatus in physics as well as the importance of intellectual history in understanding academic disciplines.)

Many teachers in the humanities prefer not to have their subjects considered as
a "tool" but want it taught as a discipline in its own right, and certainly music, theater, and visual arts ought to receive systematic attention. However, there is a trend
toward enriching the general curriculum with the arts and humanities, such as send-
ing artists into schools to coteach in regular classrooms. For instance, the Center for
Academic Achievement (CAA) initiated K–12 school opportunities for teachers and
students to find out what classrooms can look like when the arts are integrated
through coteaching (Werner & Freeman, 2000). Typically, teachers report:

> "I'm learning from my partner artist what is acceptable in presenting the arts and in
> drawing artistic performance out of children."
> "I'm now seeing how I can integrate dance, music, architecture, and sculpture—
> making connections to all subject areas required by the district."

"At first I thought it would be difficult to make connections, but once I saw how connections can be made and tried it, I found it simple."

"It's not just to bring in artists for residency, but to make sure that while they're here, working with students and teachers, something taught will last for years and years."

"It's a different way of teaching but it ultimately makes things easier—an easy way to get concepts across."

"Art experiences allow students to explore concepts and make connections on their own. They're searching for information, they're doing the reading. All I'm doing is providing them with the books that they are interested in."

"Instead of my being the authority at the front of the room, we are a group of people discussing art."

"The arts being a collaborative process, creating and doing with the people around you; you are establishing relationships, which is what the arts can do for a classroom."

"I am still in the book doing it with them, but my partner is the star, which is fun."

The CAA project offers a safe venue for teachers to try different instructional styles without being the expert.

"My partner does things I never dreamed of. She's got imagination, and it's freed me from having to know it all."

"I now feel comfortable using the arts and have some expertise I didn't already have."

"I teach in a different way now. I don't think of myself as an artist. I have limited music experience, but I've found that one of the things that my kids learn best from is music, so I'm willing to do it."

"I've limited drama experience, but we've tried to do little plays and different things to expand their horizons and minds."

"The knowledge we are creating is deeper because the central idea is explored in details that show interconnections and relationships, not fragmented pieces of information."

SHIFTS IN ART CURRICULUM

Freedman (1987) has shown how the study of art in school developed in relation to the purposes of various public interests. She has identified four strands of art education, which parallel social influences:

1. Use of art in developing skills for a labor market
2. Art as cultural education and a leisure activity
3. Art as important in the development of moral character and aesthetic taste
4. Use of art for healthful and creative self-expression

Art in Industry

In the late 1870s, art was taught for industrial purposes. Walter Smith, an art teacher, was brought from England to oversee a design education program that became a model for others in the United States. Traditional design patterns were taught in a procedurally described manner, with industrial design courses following practices in the field, using step-by-step procedures for drawing. Particular manual skills needed for given occupations were taught. For example, the skills of visual perception, manual dexterity, and design were considered necessary for preparing artisans, machinists, drafters, seamstresses, and the like.

In most schools, drawing emphasized the precise copying of illustrations. Children were first taught the parts of shapes, and they then drew individual shapes and finally objects. Initially, students made outlines and followed the teacher as he or she copied outlines from a textbook. Later, the drawings of famous sculptures were studied so that children could copy form and shading. Finally, older children might be allowed to do an entire composition of a pastoral scene. The use of color was controlled to prevent fanciful experimentation. The practice of preparing all public school children for work through art diminished as specialized manual training schools were established.

Art as Culture and Leisure Activity

In the late 19th century, a new middle class sought to show itself as cultured by studying and collecting art objects. At this time, art museums were established for the public (though they were administered by the wealthy elite). Art appreciation courses were introduced into the public schools to support this acculturation of the middle class.

Art as a leisure activity began with decorative needlework classes in private girls' schools. Then, concern in the early 1900s about "unworthy" use of leisure time by citizens resulted in art courses to encourage students to develop an appreciation for beauty and engage in art activities in their spare time.

Art for Morality

Moral education through the arts was also an aim from the 1890s until the 1930s. The study of pictures was introduced to illustrate good character and love of truth and beauty by focusing on the morality of artists' works and "God's handiwork in nature and achievements of men" (Freedman, 1987, p. 71). The pictures used were overly sentimental, such as a "picture of a 'perfect' child with his mother or wild animals tamed by human influence" (Kerry, 1985). Although the moral message was considered more important than the quality of the pictures in the classrooms of those teachers with a moral bent, other teachers sought to help students develop good taste and appreciation of high standards in art by having them study masterpieces.

Art in Everyday Life

During the 1930s, the time of the Great Depression, the elite notion of art was replaced in favor of social realism. Much of the art funded by the Federal Art Project during this period, for example, portrayed the life and work of the laborer. An excellent example of art as related to everyday life is found in Freedman's study of the Owatonna, Minnesota, Project of the 1930s, in which school and community tried to upgrade the aesthetic sensibilities of citizens while enhancing the local environment (Freedman, 1987). Art education centered on the beautification of the family's surroundings. Elementary children made decorative objects for the home, while older children focused on commercial art and industrial design, with lessons on consumer and industrial interests (e.g., posters that would "create a desire for a product") and a unit that taught students the poor state of commercial design in America. Adult classes and community lectures focused on efficient, well-balanced design in architecture, gardening, and other aspects of community life.

Art for Self-Expression

The concept of art education for creative self-expression shaped the art curriculum after 1900. Child study researchers used children's drawings as the basis for illustrating a child's stages of growth and furthering the idea that children's art unfolds naturally. Child researchers opposed technical, segmented drill; instead, they allowed children to begin drawing and painting animals and other things that would appeal to their interests and desires. The teacher's role was to provide materials and show students a variety of mediums. Encouraging original expression in producing objects was associated with the belief that art was therapeutic and could contribute to the child's sense of self-worth.

Franz Cizek, an Austrian art teacher, influenced the American art curriculum by his traveling exhibition of his students' work. He believed that children's art should be free of adult imposition. Victor Lowenfeld, also an Austrian educator, became a very influential art educator in the United States. Lowenfeld (1947) was against imposing adult standards on children and in favor of promoting students' efforts at self-expression, releasing them from pressures of contemporary society and helping them develop as healthy individuals.

Art for Intellectual Development

Contemporary shifts in the art curriculum have been described by Efland (1990). He tells how in the post–World War II era, art education expanded in affluent suburban areas, while the urban poor were denied access to art programs. The art programs for the affluent aimed at helping students interpret the meaning of new forms and styles, such as abstract expressionism, pop art, funk art, minimalism, conceptual art, and performance art.

The art curriculum of the 1960s reflected the trend in science education to pattern school subjects on the ways that specialists in the disciplines structure and derive new knowledge in the field. Other experts advocated that students learn "to make" art less and "to see and understand" art more. Differences in the curricula developed by the various specialists reflected conflicting views of art. Some curricula showed concern for the relevance of aesthetics in personal and social life; others featured the acquisition of art skills as instructional ends so that students could not only construct their own artworks but also analyze and evaluate famous works of art and place them in their appropriate cultural and historical context.

The art curriculum of the 1960s faded as schools digressed from enriching content and began to focus on accountability, preparing instructional objectives and assessment devices. Measurable skills became the focus, not imaginative products and ephemeral appreciations.

In the 1980s, Discipline-Based Art Education (DBAE), supported by the J. Paul Getty Trust, brought renewed interest in strengthening elementary and secondary school study of art through the integration of studio art, production, art history, art criticism, and aesthetics. The DBAE differs from the 1960s curriculum in that it has been designed by art educators, not by studio artists and scholars in the field of art. Yet the authors of DBAE were faulted for making some of the same mistakes as in the past, as well as some new ones:

1. Promoting certain ways of conducting art inquiry and art criticism as if they are the only methods approved by the art community, ignoring the conflicts about purpose and methods that exist in the art community
2. Failing to think through the social consequences of aiming at only providing students with a well-rounded education in art rather than aiming at the highest level of inquiry and understanding as represented by specialists
3. Using works of art to integrate the disciplines rather than using the disciplines to understand the work, a pedagogical formalism emphasizing the structure of the disciplines, not the works of art that the disciplines are striving to understand (Efland, 1990)

Current Trends in the Arts Curriculum

Some teachers have adapted the DBAE curriculum to fit their needs. Child-centered teachers place joy and the emotional growth of the child at the heart of their curriculum. Academicians are now turning to the National Standards for Education in the Arts. These organize dance, music, theater, and the visual arts into three categories: (a) creating and performing, (b) perceiving and analyzing, and (c) understanding cultural and historical concepts. However, there is concern that academicians will not reach beyond their narrowly defined discipline—with its goals of illuminating art history, art criticism, and aesthetics—to relate it to the wider world.

At the same time, multiculturalists are giving attention to non-European, folk, feminist, and ethnic art. Social reconstructionists have broadened their parameters to include the study of the social and contextual connections of art, including the factors of racism and feminism.

The new finding is that teachers are using anthropology, political science, women's studies, and cultural studies to illuminate the meaning of a single piece of work. Similarly, they are designing thematic units that while focusing on art, draw content from social studies, geography, poetry, history, music, science, and math. In these units, students gain knowledge and skills related to the disciplines of art while exploring the human experience from multiple perspectives.

Conflicts about the arts curriculum can be sharpened through role playing. Activity 7–1 presents three roles that are pertinent, although other roles can be added to more fully represent different perspectives (no pun intended).

ACTIVITY 7–1   CREATING DIALOGUE ABOUT THE ARTS CURRICULUM

Form small groups and discuss the question, "What is essential in a good arts program?" For the purpose of furthering discussion, have members of the group take the following roles:

Teacher 1: This teacher has a strong background in gifted children, a field in which careful attention is paid to individual children and their talents. The teacher is worried that schools fail to address children with unique artistic potential.

Teacher 2: This teacher has had many years as an elementary music teacher and believes that arts education is an opportunity for all children and wants all children to have equal access to participation in art experiences.

Teacher 3: This teacher is a trained concert pianist who values professional training, including the development of technique, an emphasis on excellence and hard work, and the tradition of an art form.

ENGLISH AND THE LANGUAGE ARTS

English and language arts as school subjects have had a checkered history caught among demands that teachers (a) transmit particular cultural values, (b) be responsive to new social conditions, and (c) release the creative capacity of individuals.

English as an Imitation of the Classics

There was no "English" in schools in the early 19th century; instead, there was a mishmash of courses in rhetoric, grammar, elocution, penmanship, spelling, declamation, and composition. Then in the late 1800s, college entrance examination requirements shaped the English curriculum in the direction of the study of literature and the study of grammatical and rhetorical principles. These exams demanded that students be familiar with a prescribed list of books representing some period or types of literature, as well as be able to write themes or compositions in given "forms of discourse" and to define and classify sentences grammatically. To compete with the dominant classics—Greek and Latin—and their assumed value to mental discipline, teachers of English built their courses on the model of the dead languages, which resulted in a call for memorization of literary selections and reproduction of the geometry of the story.

Roberts's (1912) account of the teaching of English in the high school at the beginning of the 20th century reveals that most courses were arranged so that the study of literature reflected the work done in composition. Narration, description, exposition, and argumentation formed the basis of the curriculum. In the 1st year, the initial emphasis was narrative, drawing from such authors as Edgar

Allan Poe; Alfred, Lord Tennyson; Elizabeth Barrett Browning; and Robert Louis Stevenson. Composition followed reading of the literature, whereby students wrote narratives according to the principles of literary narrative. In the 2nd year, the curriculum was based on descriptive types, and the writings of Washington Irving, Nathaniel Hawthorne, and George Eliot were often among those included. The essays of Francis Bacon and John Ruskin were the instrument for study of the expository works in the 3rd year. Thomas Macaulay's essay on Addison and Edmund Burke's speech on conciliation generally furnished the principles of argumentation studies during the 4th year.

Other principles on which English courses were based included focusing on the following:

- Materials chosen as representing some literary period—for example, the study of American authors preceding authors more remote in place and time

- Study of the novel in the 1st year, lyrics in the 2nd, the essay in the 3rd, and the epic and drama in the 4th

- Ethical and emotional purposes of literature in the 1st and 2nd years and the intellectual and critical values of literature in the last 2 years

The study of literature in schools in the late 19th century and early part of the 20th century focused on students determining the meaning of the author, comprehending the significance of the whole before examining the parts. Subsequent attention was given to structure, chronology, style, and the life of the author as it related to the work.

Literature was the basis for the teaching of composition. From the literary works, students were introduced to the principles of composition. Units, mass, and coherence were examined and applied in the students' own compositions. Composition varied from the daily theme to weekly exercises. Before writing their themes, students made outlines. These outlines were critiqued and revised. When students finished their themes, the teacher would select two or three papers for class criticism and later read and correct portions of the compositions turned in by the other students. Noteworthy in view of today's "new" assessment procedures was the practice more that 100 years ago of using portfolios that contained a student's compositions and other written work to submit as evidence that a student was prepared for college.

Oral work was also common. Public speaking included declamation, debate, oration, simple plays, and the reading aloud of themes and compositions. Usually, the content related to the books read in class in order to deepen student understanding of the literature.

The Elementary Language Curriculum in the Early 1900s

The elementary language curriculum at the beginning of the 20th century was criticized in professional journals for putting too much emphasis on the memorization of spelling words and grammar without student understanding. The literature studied in schools was beyond the reach of many children: *The Christmas Carol,*

The Courtship of Miles Standish, The Lady of the Lake, The Legend of Sleepy Hollow, Rip Van Winkle, Snowbound, Tales from Shakespeare, The Great Stone Face, The Man without a Country, and *Heidi.* Mechanical mastery of reading—phonics—was incidental to oral reading and the study of literary selections. In the lower grades, much of the literature study was by means of stories told by the teacher. Oral and written work focused on reproduction of, and reactions to, what was read, including producing riddles, anecdotes, stories, and simple dramatizations, thus allowing for some personal interpretation of the text. Students did do some original oral and written work. Capitalization and fundamentals were taught in the lower grades, but formal grammar was left for the sixth and seventh grades.

The following is an illustration of aspects of language taught in elementary schools in the early 1900s:

- *Grade 1*—capital letters at the beginning of the sentence, periods at the end

- *Grade 2*—capitals for the days of the week and month; use of question marks

- *Grade 3*—exclamation points; contractions; capitals in names of places; indention of paragraphs; homonyms

- *Grade 4*—apostrophes; commas in a series; writing from an outline

- *Grade 5*—divided and undivided quotations; use of comma; the three-paragraph form for a composition

- *Grade 6*—subject and predicate; adjective and adverbial phrases; parts of speech

- *Grade 7*—complements; modifiers; compound and complex sentences

An Experience Curriculum

Between 1929 and 1935, 175 members of the National Council of Teachers of English engaged in a large-scale curriculum-making endeavor that resulted in the production of a guide for the teaching of English, kindergarten through 12th grade, called *An Experience Curriculum in English* (National Council of Teachers of English, 1935). The term *experience* set the direction for the curriculum. By "experience," the teachers meant many things:

- Meeting real language situations of life—communicating with others in and out of school

- Making decisions, taking action, and showing responsibility for the consequences of actions

- Reliving vicariously lives and events presented through literature

- Expressing personal thoughts and feelings through written and oral language

Students were encouraged to interact with many sources: films, drama, poetry, newspapers, books, and social activities. However, the experience curriculum excluded materials the teacher thought would be harmful, such as those depicting horrors, sex, sentimentality, and the contravention of natural laws. Grammar (usage) and the technical skills of reading and writing were taught in use, not for use. Teachers assumed that when students do interesting things with language, they are in the best frame of mind for a vigorous and self-motivated attack on their own errors.

The experience curriculum featured units of instruction, each occupying 5 to 15 days throughout the K–12 program. Each unit consisted of a major purpose, or social objective, indicating the activity that would take place—for example, to write an account of a sports event or other school function for the newspaper. In addition, the unit had an enabling objective that stipulated the academic and other prerequisites for successful attainment of the social objective—for example, to write headlines or leads to secure economy and exactness, using verbal nouns; to give the reader the impression of observing action by using varied sentence structure, concrete details, and specific nouns. Units were ordered by "experience strands" of literature, reading, creative expression, speech, and writing.

An Experience Curriculum in English moved school "English" away from literary analysis and history and toward the study of varied types of language activities— conversation, letter writing, telling stories, dramatizing, reporting, and speaking to large groups. Creative expression differed from the other strands in that it was "done primarily for its own sake," not for external or utilitarian motives.

English as a Response to Personal and Social Problems

Beginning in the 1940s, personal and social problems were at the center of the English curriculum for many teachers. For example, Roody's (1947) curriculum for the adolescent introduced "true to life" literature and drew from psychology as a way to reach the new goal of developing student personalities. Roody gave psychoanalytic explanations for facing reality, confronting life problems, and achieving maturity. Typically, literature was selected for its contribution to understanding problems of the family, American culture, prejudice, and oneself. Important works, such as *The Diary of Anne Frank* and *Catcher in the Rye*, entered the curriculum at this time.

Some concern was expressed about the suitability of introducing popular materials. For example, popular novels were faulted for the way they solved the problems they posed and the generalizations readers might derive:

- Immaturity equates with isolation from the group.
- All problems can be solved successfully.
- Adults often are not much help.
- Solutions are discovered by chance.
- Maturity means conformity.

The Academic Tripod as English

Language, composition, and literature composed colleges' definition of English in the 1960s. In an effort to make English a discipline in competition with the sciences, curriculum scholars gave a greater role to linguistics in the teaching of language. Teachers attended workshops at which scholars told them to emphasize syntax rather than the parts of speech and to teach usage and the history of language. They also heard that no dialect was more logical or functional than any other.

The teaching of literature reflected the influence of the "new critics," in that teachers taught students to ask questions about the text:

- *Its form*—How are all parts related?

- *Its rhetoric*—Who is the audience?

- *About meaning*—What is the intention and how is it made apparent?

- *About values*—This calls for both personal response and judgments of excellence (Commission on English, 1965).

Close reading was related to students' development of composition and language. The academic point of view was that English should be studied for its own sake, not for a presumed utilitarian purpose or personal value. That approach led to reading of standard literary selections. Many major 20th-century works were omitted because of the pressures of censorship.

English for Growth versus English for Efficiency

From the 1970s through the 1980s, two competing views of English confronted teachers. Some teachers favored the idea of language as an instrument for personal and social growth, whereby students used language and literature in their attempt to define and express themselves. Other teachers valued efficiency and the direct teaching of skills thought to be important to reading and writing.

Teachers in the first category, usually in affluent schools, followed a curriculum that provided students opportunities for reading, speaking, writing, listening through dialogue, and responding to literature and the world at large. Storytelling, drama, and discussion, as well as writing, were seen as ways for students to make sense of their lives. Elementary school teachers of the growth orientation created "open classrooms," which offered opportunities for student collaboration and choice. Typically, in the open classrooms, several activities occurred at once. Some students read self-selected materials, others worked at a writing corner expressing their feelings about a picture, and still others listened to recordings of poetry.

In the secondary school, teachers with personal growth as an aim favored minicourses designed in response to students' interests and the passion of the teacher. Various electives were offered—for example, a genre elective: "The Modern American Novel"; a literary history elective: "English Literature"; a thematic elective: "Oedipus Rock Opera" (rock music on a sexual theme); a classics elective: "The Great Books"; an author elective: "Mark Twain"; an individualized elective: "Paperback Power." Nonprint media, especially films, became the stimuli for classroom discussion and writing. Writing as composition was broadened to include filmmaking and journal writing, and the composition activities were done for a range of purposes. All called for a sense of audience, point of view, and awareness of what students wanted to communicate.

In opposition to teachers who favored the curriculum of growth, teachers who were efficiency oriented saw English as a subject to be studied, manipulated, and mastered. The English curriculum consisted of skills in reading and writing organized into a hierarchy of objectives. Each objective was presented by example or by rule, followed by guided practice, usually in the form of worksheets, and a criterion-referenced test for students to show evidence of mastery of the objectives. The efficiency curriculum required students to attain competency on particular reading and writing tasks. The specified competencies tended to be minimal and related to daily living—for example, locating the time for a favorite TV program or writing a three-paragraph essay with few spelling and grammatical mistakes.

Current Directions in English Literacy and Writing

From a social constructivist position, reciprocal teaching is an excellent way to promote high-level reading. This approach allows learners to work together in clarifying text both from the perspective of the author and from the perspective of the reader, making inferences and predictions about consequences. Reciprocal teaching is adaptable to learners at all ages and all contexts. This approach together with the student-centered model for lessons entailing connect, organize, reflect and extend (CORE) are described in detail in chapter 12.

"Balanced reading" was offered as a truce whereby explicit phonics, word identification, spelling, and writing were to be taught followed by experience with authentic tasks and comprehension of texts. Now, however, the "truce" is being broken. Scholars are faulting the political influences of corporations in setting federal, state, and school bureaucratic policies for the teaching of reading (Strauss, 2001). Specifically, these policies are calling for (a) explicit teaching of phonics to beginners instead of giving opportunities for students to interact meaningfully with printed materials and (b) the expectation that older learners accept literal meanings of texts rather than encouraging them to make multiple interpretations.

Until recently, whole-language instruction was popular in the primary schools. Basic to whole language are the practices of focusing on meaning of an entire text, teaching skills in the context of reading and writing, exposing children to good literature, offering individual choices in what to read and write, and getting children to write early and often.

By century's end, however, teachers were expected to put more emphasis on the teaching of skills that could be measured, such as those featuring the alphabetic principle—beginning with phonetic awareness of separate sounds and patterns that relate to words, especially decodable or "regularly" spelled words. The policy initiatives that mandated the teaching of the English sound system in each grade level gave rise to the "reading wars." This war was between those who saw reading as integrating, interpreting, and critically analyzing text and those who wanted reading to be the literal acceptance of texts.

The writing workshop has become an important structure for enacting curriculum. Workshops include an opening meeting for about 5 to 10 minutes, during which the teacher presents some aspect of the writing process or shares his or her own writing. The second part is writing time, a nearly 30-minute period in which children write stories or comment about topics of interest to them and engage peers and teacher in helping them with their work and the problems they have faced in writing. Children are free to go to peers and teacher for ideas about revision, brainstorming, drafting, editing, and "publishing" of the text. The selecting of a real audience for the text is important at the beginning of the writing process.

There is a generalization that literacy in the interests of the state differs from literacy for social and individual empowerment. Activity 7–2 may show the validity of the generalization.

Many teachers are relating various language activities to a common theme. By way of illustration, a first-grade teacher might fill the classroom with books about bears. The teacher and children sing songs and read poems and stories giving facts and fantasies about bears. Writing "bear facts" gives practice in writing factual pieces. Children bring their teddy bears to school and later write their own bear stories, poems, and articles. This new activity curriculum gives support to individual and group purposes. Drafts of student writings are shared, and students are encouraged both to make individual responses to literature and to develop common meanings from their experiences with literature and language.

Multiculturists want students to acquire the social understandings of literacy, not merely to express their own feelings and opinions. They want students to see how literacy operates in different settings by studying what is read and what is not read in different places by different people and the kinds of meanings that are constructed by texts. Students might, for instance, determine the meanings implied by standardized tests in the school context or contrast the way meanings are conveyed by advertisements and the way cartoons use satire and other devices to create meaning.

Today's educational journals feature the conflict between (a) conservatives who emphasize correctness in language—spelling, writing, and reading—and the

ACTIVITY 7–2   RELATING LANGUAGE ARTS CURRICULUM TO SOCIAL CLASS

Do the following to see how curriculum can relate to one's social class:

1. On a slip of paper, write the social class you think you belong to: affluent/ executive, middle/white collar, working/blue collar. Then write what comes closest to representing the kind of English language program you were offered in school: efficiency (skill emphasis); academic (disciplinary value, close reading); experience (personal growth and social problems).
2. Collect and make a graph on the board showing the relation between social class and the curriculum received.

imposition of classical models from without on the student—and (b) the new romantics who see growth in literacy from within as children learn to read and write in order to make sense of their world and to express their concerns and interests and who see the teacher's role as being sensitive to the child's intentions for reading and writing before introducing the appropriate techniques.

This conflict is associated with issues of the teacher's responsibility for imparting a cultural literacy and of the student's right to participate in his or her own culture and to use the cultural resources of the home and local community as the basis for learning a literacy that will connect the student to a larger world and culture.

It is a good idea to let students study the literacies that vary with gender, social class, and ethnicity; to contrast these literacies and their functions (to see what literacies are good for); and then to extend the boundaries of their own literacy to other times and places.

The following is an illustration of how a teacher can help students see the historical and political nature of literacy and develop the capacity to express their own experiences and creativity by acquiring prestigious cultural forms and turning them toward their own purposes.

In one of his programs, Willinsky (1990) awakened students in the fourth and sixth grades to the importance of literacy in context through a curriculum that sampled 3,000 years of publishing. During a 9-day period, students "published" their poetry, using both historical and contemporary techniques. The students began with Homer and the oral tradition to learn the value of reciting a work that is both fresh and familiar. Next, the students experienced the early days of drama when prop and action told the story and the classroom became the amphitheater. The scriptorium of the medieval monk followed as students created illustrated manuscripts and framed their poetry with intricate borders. Then the students matched Gutenberg's movable type and printing presses with their own printer's marks to designate their poster-sized broadsides of poetry, flooding the school with their poetry in imitation of what took place in Reformation Europe. Before each of these activities, a short history lesson described how the transmitting and publishing of ideas changed over time to meet the events of the day. Finally, after a visit to a local print shop, Willinsky's students leaped ahead to desktop publishing, issuing their own small magazine modeled on such literary innovations as *The Dial*. (*The Dial* was a literary magazine of the 1920s that featured stories by writers who later became famous.)

Willinsky said the program was a harried one, with every day given to a different type of historical publication method, with students writing new works and preparing them for publication and delivery to the school and community. Writing was seen as a form of public expression, involving a production process to make the work available for sharing.

Literature is once again central in the English curriculum, but there is conflict about what literature to select. Teachers who are cultural conservatives favor a core of works that they say mirror Western values and transcend time, such as the Bible and works by Shakespeare. They also want American literature included, as represented by Mark Twain, Henry Thoreau, and William Faulkner. Teachers sensitive to the contributions of minorities give greater emphasis to literature that reflects the diversity of America's cultural heritage—Ralph Ellison, Diego Rivera, N. Scott Momaday. Teachers with a concern for social justice select works that honor the value of the female perspective and the working class.

Furthermore, the idea that literature must be print is being challenged. Films, videotapes, and recordings are entering the classroom as literature and not merely as supplementary to the written text. Moss's (1985) curriculum is an example of how films such as *King Kong*, *The Godfather*, and *One Flew over the Cuckoo's Nest* represent genres worthy of study, as well as providing a springboard to writing. Teachers and students alike are seeking the connection between literary works and other arts—dance, music, painting, and the way all act on the development of the human being.

Among the current organizational trends in English curriculum are thematic, genre, and student choice. Thematic organization, whereby several texts and activities are focused on a given theme (e.g., prejudice, family ties, or personal dignity), is popular. The danger with this organization is that the theme may "preinterpret" the texts for students and lead to bland generalizations. Although genre is an old way to organize the curriculum, it does allow for the introduction of a wide range of forms, authors, periods, and styles. Teachers on the leading edge let students themselves decide what they are to read and what the theme, if any, will be.

TABLE 7–1 Literacy for the masses	Period	1600 Oral	1776 Visual	1864 Recitation
	Purpose	Maintaining tradition	Keeping records, contracts	Nation cohesion
		Keeping records orally	Visual design	Recording communication
			Handwriting an art	
	Action	Memorizing the Bible	Copying text	Recitals
		Listening—oral exchange	Meaning from reading the Bible	Orations
		Interpreting body movements	Keeping records	Memorizing secular works
	Interaction	Face to face	Copier	Impersonal
			Listener	Copier reactor

Aspects of deconstruction are a new fashion in English study. Students don't look for a theme but search for the displacement of meaning: reading to find what has been repressed in the process of writing, what is omitted because of social, political, and historical constraints. Students are expected to learn how language defines social relations, positioning people and determining their prospects for the future. Students are taught to look for unexpressed and socially unacceptable ideas, and to search for contradictions and aberrant meanings, particularly in footnotes and parentheses. Similarly, students are encouraged to write without the pressure of perfect clarity, knowing that writing is a never-finished process. In brief, the aim of the new English is for students to respond to texts in light of their own experience and yet learn to see the world anew in their pursuit of meaning and social justice.

As seen in Table 7–1, literacy for the masses has focused on maintaining social hierarchies, preparing students for their roles as workers and consumers and enabling them to receive official information and conform to rules and regulations. Although literacy as transformation may be gaining because of the availability of unsanctioned literacy through technologies, government and school bureaucracies are attempting through the accountability movement to exercise a holding action whereby literacy is decoding and translation.

1916 Decoding	1980 Translation	2000 Transformation
Communicating	Comprehending many texts	Critical collation
Accessing information from text	Aesthetic appreciation	Broader concepts of texts
Academic skills		Making visible the invisible— intratextual reading
		Awareness of how text is defining identities
Decode unfamiliar text	Functional reading	Rewriting texts for own purposes— show what's missing, excluded
Silent analyzing	Translating text— reader responses	
Studying forms; finding author's intent	Translator	Critical reader/viewer
	Responder	Interpreter Collaborator
Writing to others		
Analyzer		
Decoder		

HISTORY

Conflicting views of history and its use have been present for centuries. In ancient Greece, Herodotus relegated history to the describing of events, while Thucydides argued that it should guide one's actions. Greeks and Romans used stories of heroes to develop character and patriotism. In the medieval period, study of the saints and popes perpetuated religious doctrine; but during the Reformation, history was used to justify reformed religious beliefs. Comenius, in the 17th century, wanted world history taught in the interest of international understanding; and Rousseau, in the 18th century, valued the teaching of facts about common life and depreciated history's focus on kings and the elite. After the Napoleonic Wars of 1800, history was taught in the self-interests of nations.

In the United States, answers to the question of why study history have followed two viewpoints:

1. *Traditionalists*, who are interested in transmitting a cultural heritage and developing a national loyalty through the study of history
2. *Functionalists*, who would draw on history and social sciences for their contributions to the understanding of contemporary social and individual problems

Activity 7–3 may promote reflection on the value of humanistic study for everyone.

Evolution of the Traditional Curriculum in History: The Memoriter System

In the 1800s, separate courses in geography, government, and history were taught in a chronological and structured way to shape student values and behavior. Geography for primary students consisted of local geography taught through object lessons and descriptions of the Earth as a whole. Intermediate geography emphasized the study of geographical features and locations, using maps and atlases. High school courses featured both descriptions and physical geography. In

---

ACTIVITY 7–3   IDENTIFYING CENTRAL CONTENT IN A SUBJECT RELATED TO THE HUMANITIES (ART, MUSIC, LITERATURE, AND HISTORY)

Select one of the humanities that has been important in your life. Identify one or more of the key concepts, important perspectives, or functions associated with this subject that you want all students to acquire.

---

all instances, students were expected to answer a variety of questions and to memorize facts about given localities. The curriculum in government focused on the U.S. Constitution, the rights and duties of a people in a republic, the obligations of public laws, and civil and religious beliefs.

The history curriculum varied with the age of the students. In the early grades, children were told about the history of the United States and about heroes of the world. In the higher grades, students were given accounts of the principal events of American history. In the academies or high schools, there was considerable variation. College-bound students studied Greek or Roman history; other students studied American history or English history.

The Memoriter System relied on the use of a textbook from which students were expected to reproduce the exact words of the text. The practice of allowing students to sum up passages in their own words evolved in an effort to help "weaklings" who could not recall the text. Textbooks often featured guidance questions and outlines that highlighted the essentials to be memorized. Students wrote and rewrote these essentials and said them backward and forward; the essentials were the basis for grouping what one remembered of books, sources, and classroom talk (Johnson, 1915).

The following are typical examination questions of the period ("Examination Questions," 1872, p. 38):

1. What river basin does the great central plain of North America include?
2. Name the three great currents of the ocean, and tell how they modify the climate of the earth.
3. What was the general order of creation?
4. What parts of the Earth are inhabited principally by the Caucasian race?
5. What was the design of the 15th Amendment to the Constitution, and when was it adopted?
6. What was the Louisiana Purchase? When was it made, and what territory did it embrace?
7. What did England and the colonies gain by the French and Indian War?

Circumscribed Inquiry

In the late 19th century, Mary Sheldon Barnes, a noted teacher, teacher educator, and author of materials for the teaching of history, was scathingly critical of the Memoriter System and offered—as an alternative to the imparting of information—curriculum aimed at awakening a spirit of inquiry (Barnes, 1883). Instead of viewing students as passive vessels to be filled with historical knowledge, Barnes wanted students to be active learners who, with the guidance of the teacher and the curriculum materials, would draw their own conclusions from rigorous inquiry. Barnes's curriculum relied heavily on selected primary source documents and illustrations of historical artifacts. Students were to develop proper historical and civic perspectives by extracting general truths from the study of "the special fact" embedded in the historical document or artifact.

Barnes (1893) advocated the use of skillfully designed questions to help students work with historical materials. Her teaching manual encouraged teachers to arrange situations where students collected, discussed, and critiqued interpretations drawn from their studies of documents or artifacts. Individual interpretations were expected to be reported in an atmosphere of freedom and honesty, and the conclusions of the class were recorded in simple tabular arrangements convenient for review and examination. A variety of questions were included:

- *Analytical* questions to guide the extracting of information from primary sources and the summaries provided

- *Synthetic* questions that led students to draw the information together into a coherent image of the past society

- *Evaluative* questions that asked students to reflect on the ideals, character, and moral qualities of the historical personages and society

Barnes believed that through the use of her curriculum, students would learn how to judge and interpret what they saw in their own country and help make America the strongest, noblest, and finest nation in the world.

In his recent study of Mary Sheldon Barnes and her work, Anniel (1990) makes clear that Barnes circumscribed student inquiry by her acceptance of certain fundamental truths about American democracy. There was, for example, a faith in the supremacy of democratic principles in political and social life. She represented the constitutional form of government as allowing for political stability and moral progress and ensuring maximum personal freedom of action. None of her questions, documents, or artifacts took into account the predicament faced by African Americans, the working class, or other groups that often did not share in national progress or experience personal freedom of action.

One source, for instance, was an article written by an African American academic who attributed the cause of racial prejudice against African Americans to their poverty and ignorance, rather than their color, and who offered hard work and education as the way for African Americans to win the respect of whites and a share in the prosperity of the South. This piece was published at a time when disfranchisement of African Americans, lynchings, and other terrorist acts aimed at African American communities were common in the South (Anniel, 1990). Barnes's treatment of the subject ignored the violence and suppression of rights. The question that followed such excerpts asked students, "Who is to blame if the southern black is 'poor and has a bad time now'?" The answer most likely to occur to students was that the fault lies with a black population unable to take advantage of a rapidly growing economy, an answer consistent with the excerpts and the viewpoints found in the newspapers and books of the time.

In brief, Barnes's curriculum did not help students learn to detect and evaluate the kinds of ideological premises that underlined the histories they read. It reinforced uncritical acceptance of the assumption that national progress and democracy remedied racial discrimination and other injustices. Barnes unintentionally made injustice invisible and absolved students from having to give personal attention to, or to take action toward, resolving national problems not directly touching their lives.

Current Trends: History Wars in the 1990s

The Bradley Commission on History in Schools, which represented scholars in the field of history, focused on studies indicating that many students were unfamiliar with historical and geographical facts and knowledge believed necessary for understanding complex social and political questions (Gagnon & the Bradley Commission, 1989). The commission's recommendation called for more courses in history at all levels.

Also, the staff at the National Center for History in the Schools defined the historical understandings they thought students should acquire before graduating from high school (National Center for History in the Schools, 1992). Teacher associates at the center created teaching materials—units of instruction—in accordance with the center's criteria for use in the schools. The resulting curriculum emphasized knowledge of historical facts, significant historical documents, historical chronology, democratic heritage, and the nation's political institutions.

This curriculum contrasted with a new social studies curriculum that centered on social issues and problems. The new curriculum included courses in history, geography, and government aimed at developing history's "habits of the mind" such as these:

- Connecting the past to the present

- Perceiving past events as they were experienced by people at the time

- Comprehending the diversity of culture, while acquiring a sense of a shared humanity

- Grasping the complexity of historical causality

- Recognizing the importance of individuals who have made a difference in history

Although this new curriculum had many similarities to the old traditional curriculum, there were some differences. Memorization of names, dates, and places were out; case studies and narratives were in. In preparing their units, teachers looked for engaging stories from each era of history. The units presented specific "dramatic moments" that illuminated landmark events. Students would examine a crucial turning point in history and learn that choices had to be made and that there were consequences. The dramatic moments were based on primary sources—documents, artifacts, journals, diaries, newspapers, and literature from the period under study. The unit tried to re-create for students a sense of "being there," while giving them opportunity to practice the role of historians, analyzing the sources, making interpretations, and constructing narratives that relate relevant factors. Units were selected for distribution by the center on the basis of their historical interest, liveliness, use of primary sources, and contribution to the students' historical and cultural literacy.

Authors of the new curriculum said their curriculum differed from the curriculum of Mary Barnes because they made a conscious effort to introduce the role played by people at many levels of society, in many regions, from different backgrounds—women, minorities, and the common people. They also addressed tensions in conflicting national values—aspirations for freedom versus security, liberty versus equality, and unity versus diversity. The authors attempted to counter older histories that suggested the inevitability of progress and destiny by giving more emphasis to the importance of human agency. Nevertheless, the themes and units of the new curriculum, such as the development of society, institutions, culture, and democracy, implied progress and a common purpose.

In 1994, the Center for History in the Schools published the *National Standards for United States History* along with a companion volume setting standards for world history study. These history standards reflected history as historians understand it. They gave examples of student achievement, showing how students can read and write narratives and use documents, maps, and charts in constructing sound historical arguments. American history was not presented as the story of an exceptional nation, and the history incorporated the experiences of slaves, minorities, women, and the poor.

Lynne V. Cheney, a former head of the National Endowment for the Humanities, one of the initiators for the development of the standards, and the wife of the vice president of the United States, attacked the standards set by the scholars, saying that the proposed standards were "politically correct" and had an overdue emphasis on the kingdom of West Africa and on the bad side of men like John D. Rockefeller by criticizing their "unethical and amoral business practices." Cheney counted the references to groups, individuals, and events that show the American past in a negative light, indicating the 17 times that the Ku Klux Klan was referred to and the omission of Paul Revere, the Wright brothers, and Thomas Edison. After listening to Cheney and other critics, the U.S. Senate condemned the National History Standards by a vote of 99–1 (the person with the dissenting vote thought he was voting no as well). Subsequently, the authors of the standards defended their position and defined the controversy as important because history defines a society and shows what that society wants to be (Nash, Crabtree, & Dunn, 1997). New history textbooks written since the debate over the National History Standards show that these standards have been used in creating the new editions of the books but that they are not a dominant influence on the finished product.

Teachers in Oakland, California; Portland, Oregon; Milwaukee, Wisconsin's Immersion Schools; and in other places where members of ethnic groups are concerned about unfavorable treatment of certain groups in the history taught in schools have rejected official curricula. Instead, these teachers and parents have developed their own curricula, which present the heritage of groups in their own way. These curricula aim at increasing students' self-concept and countering historical interpretations that favor dominant interests and that fail to present a history that gives students from various ethnic groups a sense of hope for the future.

CHANGES IN SOCIAL STUDIES

Generally, school history reflects an academic thrust with separation of subjects—history, political science, geography—while social studies draws from many social sciences in the interest of addressing social problems.

Social Function Curriculum

In the early 1930s, thousands of teachers throughout the United States constructed units of instruction aimed at preparing students to perform major social functions. The particular functions were identified by a state or local curriculum authority. In Virginia, for example, hundreds of teachers working in committees developed units of instruction dealing with nine functions:

1. Protection and conservation of life, property, and national resources
2. Production and consumption of foods and services
3. Recreation
4. Expression of aesthetic impulses
5. Transportation and communication
6. Exchange of goods and services
7. Expression of religious impulses
8. Education
9. Extension of freedom and distribution of rewards of production

With few exceptions, activities in each grade addressed these functions. For example, first-graders who learned to cross a street properly were achieving something related to the protection and conservation of life. Centers of interest for sequencing the activities in each category were these:

■ *Grade 1*—home and school life

■ *Grade 2*—community life

■ *Grade 3*—adaptation of life to environmental forces of nature

■ *Grade 4*—adaptation of life to advancing physical frontiers

■ *Grade 5*—effects of discovery on human living, effects of the machine on human living

■ *Grade 6*—provision for cooperative living

For example, in the fifth grade, the function of expressing aesthetic impulses in conjunction with the center of interest—the effect of discovery on human living—resulted in one teacher posing the question "How was recreation influenced by frontier living?" This, in turn, suggested a detailed activity "designing a sampler."

Life Adjustment

Learner concerns about everyday life and persistent life situations became the foci for social studies curriculum in the 1940s. Persistent life situations were defined as those that recur in different ways as one grows from infancy to maturity, situations involving health, personal relations, natural phenomena, moral choices, and political structures (Stratemeyer, Forkner, & McKim, 1957). Activities and content were selected as they contributed to an individual's ability to deal with situations typically confronted by students of different ages.

In the elementary school, life adjustment curriculum often took the form of an area or culture study or a social project through which students contrasted their own responses to persistent situations with those of other people in other places. At the secondary school level, life adjustment meant teaching whatever was useful to students, such as applying and qualifying for a job; critically reading newspapers, advertisements, and the fine print in contracts; and learning to use community resources in solving personal problems.

Generalizations as the Basis for Social Studies

Harold Rugg and his teacher associates in the 1920s created social studies materials aimed at helping students understand a changing civilization and its programs. Rugg set a precedent in his attempt to identify the problems of modern society and the key generalizations for dealing with these problems through analysis of the works of leading "frontier thinkers" in science, literature, economics, and social sciences. In Rugg's curriculum, problems and issues such as socialism, unions, corporate wealth, corruption, world interdependence, ecology, and immigration were the foci for study. Generalizations were grouped by the category of problems to which they related. In the category of "war," for instance, were generalizations regarding the influence of climate and conquest, political coordination, alternatives for gaining access to resources, psychological factors leading to war, and the consequences of accepting a common purpose for humankind (Billings, 1927). The use of generalizations showed the commonalities among problems and interconnections of economic, social, and political movements.

Rugg's texts contained extensive bibliographies, dramatic episodes to show how people are living and have lived, autobiographies, travel and personal diaries (both actual and fictional); and suggested research projects and discussion topics. Typically, students were given data such as maps and the history of trade routes for an area and then presented with a problem such as determining the best location for a city in the area. Later, the actual location would be revealed and discussed.

As with circumscribed inquiry, the generalizations approach can be faulted for bias on the part of the curriculum developers. Although Rugg opposed nationalism in the social studies, he was biased toward democratic principles in his selection of content and his presentation of the problems of contemporary life.

Social Science as Social Studies

University scholars in the 1960s fragmented the social studies program by developing materials that isolated the social sciences—economics, anthropology, political science, geography, sociology. Teachers were uncertain about which discipline to teach and concerned about the limitations of relying on the contributions of any one discipline to understand social problems. The content of each discipline was organized to advance knowledge in that subject, not to address problems that covered multiple subject areas. Soon people became disillusioned with a curriculum that featured competing structures of disciplines and that seemed more appropriate for future academic specialists than for all citizens.

Problem Solving in Social Science

By the 1970s, another social studies curriculum emerged, one called by its critics "The Smorgasbord" curriculum and by its proponents "The Relevant" curriculum. Topics such as race, poverty, civil rights, and environmental contaminants became the foci. Ethnic awareness and student activism were encouraged. The mini-course, a brief course on a limited topic of importance to crucial issues, appeared in many secondary schools. The issues curriculum was justified as contributing to the decision-making ability of students, preparing them for participation in a democratic society. Accordingly, students identified aspects of problems, gathered and analyzed relevant data, reached conclusions, and sometimes took action to ameliorate the situation. Critics faulted the curriculum for its lack of continuity, its localism, and its departure from academic and cultural traditions.

Current Social Studies Programs

Historical literacy has regained its prominence in the school curriculum. The trend in elementary schools is toward integrated units built around a historical period. An interdisciplinary unit, such as "Life in Colonial New England," encourages children to draw, paint, read, write, and role-play aspects of life in the past. Geography and historical narratives are central. Lessons throughout the unit are connected by major concepts or themes such as change, traditions, or values. Attempts are made to have children not only experience the lives of those in the past but also see how some of these experiences are part of their lives today.

The trend in secondary schools also is toward inculcation of a set of traditional beliefs and values, drawing on history, government, institutions, and culture to illustrate fundamental ideas. Not all teachers are following the trend to historical literacy. Some secondary school teachers follow the social science approach and provide scientific explanations for aspects of social life. The systematic study of economics, sociology, or political science characterizes their courses. Other teachers keep to a problem-solving curriculum, placing world, national, and local problems of the day—ecology, AIDS, homelessness, gender, trade, terrorism, community—to the forefront. Their curriculum draws from a wide range of subjects to focus on one or more of the problems that entail students' taking action consistent with their findings and conclusions. Teachers with a predisposition to social reconstruction sometimes subvert the official historical literacy curriculum so that students center on key issues such as treatment of minorities and women as they compare the past and present. The issue becomes the filter for the study of history.

Activity 7–4 is best conducted by brainstorming with others, sharing what comes to mind by the term *social studies*.

As the new millennium began, the National Council for the Social Studies proposed thematic strands for planning social studies curriculum at every school level. These themes as paraphrased are

■ understanding culture;

■ knowing what things were like in the past and how things change;

■ understanding the relationship between humans and their environment;

■ examining how personal identity is shaped by culture (groups and institutions);

■ knowing how institutions are formed and controlled and how institutions control individuals and culture;

■ understanding the historical development and current functions of structure of power, authority, and government;

■ understanding the interdependency of the world economy and the role of technology in economic decision making;

■ understanding science teaching and society;

ACTIVITY 7–4   DEFINING A FIELD OF KNOWLEDGE

It is unlikely that teachers of the arts and social sciences have a common concept of these fields, yet a teacher's "cognitive map" of a field indicates that is a key factor in how that teacher constructs curriculum in that field. Use the following questions in defining your own definition of a field of interest to you.

1. What do you think it means for someone to know X? If someone is an expert in this field, what would you expect the person to know and do?
2. What are some of the major areas that make up X as a field or discipline?
3. How are the areas related to each other?

Your responses might be compared with the definitions given by colleagues.

- understanding the realities of global interdependency; and

- understanding the ideals and the practices of citizenship.

Companion
Website

> For more information on language arts, the Arts, multiculturalism, or history, go to *www.prenhall.com/mcneil* and click on Chapter 7 links.

SUMMARY

Most teachers need help in integrating the arts and humanities into their curriculum. Artists as partners is one way of getting this help.

Many aspects from the history of the arts curriculum still hang on, creating tensions as well as opportunities for something different. This chapter reviewed art curricula aimed at technical proficiency, creative expression through engagement, sustained attention and problem finding, and the knowledge structure of the arts when they are seriously pursued. Authentic practice in studio classrooms, museums, critiques, performances, and artist residencies suggest the nature of future arts curriculum. Invention, verification, and experience rather than teaching isolated skills are ways art contributes to ways of learning.

Multiculturalism in the arts has gone beyond the introduction of the arts of diverse groups devoid of context. The new shift is to find meaning in the aesthetic objects of previously overlooked cultures by placing them in their ongoing social, political, and community life.

The roots of the English language arts curriculum have also endured. English as a study of language as a formal system and as part of a social and cultural heritage reflects a classical past. Curriculum based on the tripod of language, literature, and composition is a response to the search for a body of learning, which the field lacks. Literature is still taught as the basis for moral and historical studies and for studies of structure and style. The current popularity of thematic approaches to literature together with an emphasis on creating multiple interpretations through reader response, whole language, and studies of popular culture are viable alternatives for teachers as they develop curriculum for English.

Balanced reading, as a basis for a peace accord to the "reading wars," is questionable. Underlying the conflict regarding the teaching of reading is the central question, "What should constitute literacy—an uncritical acceptance of literal communication in support of existing social structures or a powerful tool for transforming society and its institutions?"

Different curricula for teaching history were described: the Memoriter system, circumscribed inquiry, and the new history curriculum, which was generated by historians to develop history's habits of the mind. The political fallout from a proposed multicultural history curriculum attests to the political power of dominant groups in deciding what counts as knowledge.

Social studies curricula were shown to be responses to public and social agendas of officials, interest groups, and members of local communities. At the same time, these curricula have attempted to represent the knowledge of academic scholars. Variation among social studies curricula corresponds to the different motivations of teachers: those who see its purpose as promoting certain values; those who want students to know history, geography, and economics; and those who want students to acquire knowledge and values for improving the society and dealing with world conditions rather than focusing only on national interests.

QUESTIONS FOR DISCUSSION

Arts

1. Which of the following goals are appropriate for a school's arts curriculum?
   a. *Personal development:* Arts, such as painting, music, dance, drama, and clay modeling, should center on students' expressing feelings, releasing tensions, and overcoming frustrations.
   b. *Aesthetic judgment:* The arts curriculum should aim at the development of aesthetic sensibilities, harmonizing art with ideals of character and conduct.
   c. *Realism:* Students should learn to produce an excellence in art that is measured by faithfulness in representation of actual things.
2. Should school art courses include more material from art history and criticism rather than the hands-on activities that now characterize many arts classes? Why or why not?
3. How should the arts curriculum be related to the ordinary concerns of people and to their everyday activities?

English and Language Arts

1. Should English programs inculcate ideals and values? If so, which ones and on what bases are they to be selected?
2. How can the language curriculum address the personal nature of language and the individual as the unit of meaning while serving the social enterprise of language and the need for shared meanings?
3. Consider your own experiences in the study of English and the language arts. What trends in the field have you encountered? What was valuable and what was missing in each?

History and Social Studies

1. Much curriculum work in the field of history rests on the belief that understanding the past and the present world will motivate individuals to transform society into some improved form. Is this a valid assumption? Give reasons for your answer.

2. Which of the following social studies traditions are most appropriate for today's curriculum?
   a. *Citizenship transmission:* A set of beliefs and fundamental ideas should be perpetuated through study of history, government, and institutions of the society.
   b. *Social sciences:* The methods of knowing and knowledge gained by the social sciences—economics, sociology, political science, and anthropology—should make up the content of social studies as a school subject.
   c. *Social problems:* The social problems identified by students should become the basis for reflective inquiry, including data collection, analysis, interpretation, drawing conclusions, and taking action.
3. Which aims would you promote through a curriculum in history?
   a. To develop historical empathy
   b. To comprehend the interplay of change and continuity
   c. To understand the significance of the past for our own lives
   d. To recognize there are multiple interpretations of historical events
   How can these aims best be achieved?

REFERENCES

Anniel, S. A. (1990). The educational theory of Mary Sheldon Barnes: Inquiry learning as indoctrination in history education. *Educational Theory, 40,* 45–52.

Barnes, M. S. (1883). General history in the high school. *The Academy, 4,* 286–288.

Barnes, M. S. (1893). *Teachers manual.* Boston: Heath.

Billings, N. A. (1927). *Determination of generalizations basic to the social studies curriculum.* Baltimore, MD: Warwick.

Commission on English. (1965). *Freedom and discipline in English.* New York: College Entrance Examination Board.

Efland, A. (1990). Curricular fictions and the discipline orientation in art education. *Journal of Aesthetic Education, 24*(3), 67–81.

Examination questions. (1872, August). *The California Teacher, 10*(2), 37–39.

Freedman, K. (1987). Art education as social products in the cultural society and politics in the formation of curriculum. In T. Popkewitz (Ed.), *The formation of school subjects* (pp. 63–85). Philadelphia: Palmer.

Gagnon, P. (Ed.), & the Bradley Commission on History in Schools. (1989). *The case for history in the schools.* New York: Macmillan.

Johnson, H. (1915). *Teaching of history in elementary and secondary schools.* New York: Macmillan.

Kerry, E. J. (1985, November). *The purpose of art education in the United States from 1870 to 1980.* Paper presented at the History of Art Education Symposium, State College, PA.

Lowenfeld, V. (1947). *Creative and mental growth.* New York: Macmillan.

Moss, R. F. (1985). English composition and the feature file. *Journal of General Education, 37*(2), 122–143.

Nash, G., Crabtree, C., & Dunn, R. E. (1997). *Culture wars and the teaching of the past.* New York: Knopf.

National Center for History in the Schools. (1992). *Essential understandings and historical perspectives all students should acquire.* Los Angeles: University of California Press.

National Council of Teachers of English. (1935). *An experience curriculum in English.* New York: Appleton-Century.

Roberts, A. E. (1912). The teaching of English in the high schools of the United States. *The School World, 14*(159), 81–83.

Roody, S. (1947). Developing personality through literature. *English Journal, 36*(6), 299–304.

Stratemeyer, F. B., Forkner, H. L., & McKim, M. G. (1957). *Developing a curriculum for modern living* (3rd ed.). New York: Columbia University, Teachers College Press.

Strauss, S. (2001, June/July). *Educational Research*, *30*(5), 21–26.

Werner, L., & Freeman, C. (2001, April). Arts integration: A vehicle for changing teacher practice. Paper presented at the annual meeting of the American Educational Research Association, Seattle, WA.

Willinsky, J. (1990). *The new literacy: Redefining reading and writing in the schools*. New York: Routledge.

CHAPTER 8

MATHEMATICS AND SCIENCE
IN THE SCHOOL CURRICULUM

Sara: I can't teach what I don't know, so why should I encourage students to ask questions that I might not be able to answer?

Merl: You know how to learn, so why not model how to learn? Join your students in finding answers. Unload your burden of being the only knowledgeable source. Kids themselves, other teachers (like me), parents, community people—all make good consultants. And what about on-line consultants via electronic mail?

Constructivist pedagogy in math and science with students inventing their own algorithms and applying math to other subject matters places new demands on teachers. Ma's (1999) study showing the superiority of Chinese teachers of mathematics has drawn attention to U.S. teachers' need for deeper mathematical knowledge and ways to acquire that knowledge.

Ma contrasted the teaching of topics in elementary mathematics such as subtraction, multiplication, and fractions. By way of illustration, when asked how they would teach the division with the fraction problem 1 3/4 divided by 1/2 to make it meaningful to students, about half of the U.S. teachers could apply the rule to reverse and multiply to get the correct answer, but they failed to come up with ways to represent dividing by fractions. Most of the Chinese teachers knew different approaches to solving division with fractions using decimals, applying the distributive law, and multiplying reciprocals, and they could create numerous stories to illustrate the meaning of the operation:

Measurement

"How many 1/2-foot lengths are there in something that is 1 3/4 feet long?"

"If workers construct 1/2 kilometer of road each day, how many days would it take to build a road that is 1 3/4 kilometers long?"

"How many times 1 3/4 is 1/2?"

"We planned to spend 1 3/4 months to build a bridge; it only took 1/2 month. How many times is the original time more than the time taken?"

Partition

"Find a number if 1/2 of the number is 1 3/4."

"Mom bought a box of candy. She gave half of it, which weighed 1 3/4 kilograms, to Grandma. How much did the original box of candy weigh?"

Product

"Find the factor that multiplied by 1/2 will make 1 3/4."

"We know that the area of a rectangle is the product of length and width. If the area of a board is 1 3/4 square feet and its width is 1/2 feet, what is the length?"

In trying to think of representations, U.S. teachers tended to use a concrete whole (pies and pizza) to represent a whole and fractions, often confusing division by 1/2 with division by 2, failing to recognize that dividing 10 apples between two people is division by 2, not by 1/2. Most of the difficulty lies in language. Most U.S. teachers and students would know how much they should receive if told that $1.75 is 1/2 of what they are owed.

The NCTM's 1989 Curriculum Evaluation Standards for School Mathematics and the 2000 update of these standards provide the rationale for new content (e.g., statistics) and new emphases that call for using technology in mathematics, investigating, drawing graphics, and estimating as well as constructivist approaches to achieving new goals and competencies.

HOW TEACHERS ACQUIRE NEW LEARNING ABOUT MATH

Materials

The availability of on-line resources—sample units and updates as given in this chapter—are added tools for teachers. Also, other publications (e.g., magazines and yearbooks from professional organizations) are a source for learning.

Replacement units on particular topics—place value, fractions, geometry, measurement—are one of the very best ways for teachers to acquire new teaching strategies, expanding their own content knowledge and learning how to elicit and extend their students' thinking. Replacement units overcome the weaknesses of traditional textbooks—too many topics and too many repetitions—although wide differences are evident among math textbooks.

The American Association for the Advancement of Science (1989) has rated math textbooks using these criteria: identifying a sense of purpose, building on student ideas, promoting student thinking about math, assessing student progress, and enhancing the mathematics learning environment.

Colleagues

Some teachers meet weekly for an hour to reflect on student work, sharing ideas about math concepts and their plans for teaching. The key is to have a school environment where teachers feel free to seek clarification from colleagues: "What does X mean? How would you teach it?"

Useful practices include videotaping lessons, coteaching in which math is integrated into other content areas, drawing on the strengths of particular teachers, and opportunities to teach at different grade levels.

Students

"His way was much simpler than my way. I had never even thought of this smart way, but I understood it immediately. However, the other students were puzzled, and I needed to help them understand how it would work." Listening to students giving explanations to their peers when they are working in small groups reveals both good ideas and misconceptions that have to be addressed.

Companion
Website

To view descriptions of five exemplary and five promising math programs from the U.S. Department of Education (DOE), Math and Science Education Expert Panel, including curriculum materials and professional development resources, go to *www.prenhall.com/mcneil* and click on the ENC or U.S. DOE links.

THE MATH WAR

Reforms in the teaching of math have given rise to conflict between traditional and reform views. Generally the traditionalists believe that not all students need to engage in understanding math and high-level thinking, but all must be able to perform basic skills; and that understanding mathematics, if it is to occur, follows one's ability to perform the fundamental algorithms, fractions, formulas, equations, and other concepts almost by second nature. Accordingly, it is wasteful to spend time as the reformers recommend on activities in which students invent their own algorithms and try to use math in making sense of real-world situations. The reformers argue that their ideal is to bolster student understanding while giving weight to the basic skills. They want students to compute but also understand why the calculations work and what the answer represents. The views of traditionalists and reformers are shown in Table 8–1.

After adopting big math standards that favor a social constructivist approach, many states and districts returned to little standards geared to the basics and the testing of specific skills. Among the reasons for return to the traditional was fear that students were using calculators and failing to memorize computational skills. Also, many parents did not know how to assist their children in the integrated mathematics curriculum whereby algebra, geometry, and trigonometry might be used in the context of real-world problem solving.

TABLE 8–1
Traditional and reform views of math

Traditional	Reform
Core Ideas	
Math is a fixed body of knowledge involving numbers and their manipulations.	Math is a set of conceptual relations between quantities and symbols.
One must know and apply rules.	One must construct relationships.
There is one correct answer.	There are many ways to construct an answer.
Lessons	
Specific objectives, skills, or concepts	Extended projects involving more than one big math idea
Instruction on how to solve problems	
Tests for speed and accuracy	
Practice exercises and applications	
Review of lessons before semester ends	
Assignments	
Drawn from textbook	Challenging assignments extending over several days
Individuals do own work.	Broad complex problems with peers working on common projects
Drill and practice	Homework shared and clarified
Learning	
Students listen.	Attend to peer explanations.
Attend to teacher.	Time for reflection, student questioning
Teacher corrects misconceptions.	Students confront misconceptions.
Students speak when called upon.	Encourage alternative solutions.
Student Interaction	
Students expected to work alone, perhaps grouped by ability	Small heterogeneous groups
	All encouraged to interact with each other
Assessment	
Tests match skill and assignments.	Evaluate work, not the student.
Questions have one right answer.	Many forms of assessment
	Students explain their thinking.
	Revision expected

There were cultural overtones to the math war as well. Traditional math has had a negative impact on the poor, whereas blacks and Latinos tend to close their achievement gap with Asians and whites when taught integrated math and when assessed by multiple measures rather than only by standardized tests (Moses, 2000).

Moses (2000), an ex–civil rights activist, has introduced an algebra project, for example, that has been successful in helping African Americans make connections among algebra, other mathematics, and their own lives. His approach involves five steps: physical experience with the concepts, pictorial representation, student explanations in their own words, students talking about the concepts in proper English and math terms, and symbolic representation.

Recently, the National Academy of Science (2001) issued a report offering a truce in the math war. "We want to move past the debates over skills versus understanding." The report stresses the importance of real-world problems, thinking logically, and seeing math as useful. Students are to master more than disconnected facts and procedures. Beginning in preschool, students should have opportunity to extend their comprehension of numbers; in subsequent years, the curriculum should link calculations to everyday life. Numbers and operations should be illustrated in different ways. Teachers should teach concepts in depth rather than to "cover" a multitude of topics superficially. Exams should be carefully designed to test student progress on a range of mathematical proficiencies—conceptual understanding, procedural fluency, strategic competency, adaptive reasoning, and productive dispositions.

MATH CURRICULUM

Just as with the arts and social studies, the curriculum of mathematics and science has changed greatly throughout the past 100 years. All of the subject areas follow a common pattern, swinging from a practical orientation (centered on the world of work and response to social developments) to an academic and intellectual orientation (whereby college and university scholars influence the content of the elementary and secondary curriculum) to a humanistic orientation (concerned with individual expression and participation in the construction of knowledge). The pattern has repeated itself at ever more frequent intervals. As the practical curriculum loses its connection to the state of knowledge as conceived by academic scholars, the stage is set for the introduction of the intellectual orientation. However, the abstract curriculum that results from this influence, in turn, is associated with loss of student motivation or with declining enrollments, and a corrective shift to a curriculum with a humanistic orientation follows.

The Beginnings of Math Instruction in the United States

The United States was the first country to establish arithmetic as a special subject. Kamens and Benavot (1991) attribute this early commitment to numeracy as part of the new nation's ideal of progress and political freedom. The ability to count was related to making the community aware of social problems. Statistics was the basis for national action on a wide range of issues.

Inasmuch as numbers were thought to be objective and value-free, they were more persuasive than opinion in political debates—the beginning of America's scoreboard mentality. In the 1840s, for example, numerical reasoning was used to assess the value and effects of slavery. Throughout the 18th and 19th centuries, calculating was seen as a way to both produce and measure progress. The counting of population and exports was part of American political life. Statistics were used to draw attention to the need for morality by showing the number of crime and social abuses and to assess the efficacy of social practices such as inoculation against smallpox. Throughout U.S. history, tension has existed between those who wanted mathematics taught for its disciplinary value in developing students' ability to reason carefully and logically and those who wanted it taught as a useful tool in daily life and in particular occupations.

Prior to the 19th century, little emphasis was placed on the teaching of mathematics in colleges or in the Latin Grammar School. The academies and private teachers gave instruction in arithmetic and other practical mathematics. The developing need for mathematics in commerce, surveying, and navigation was met through the academies, apprenticeships, and self-study. Textbooks of the time featured examples appropriate for given occupations, which students were to follow, similar to today's vocational manuals.

Arithmetic was not a requirement for entrance into Harvard until 1802. At that time students were expected to have knowledge of the four operations with integers, tables of measures, fractions, and the "rule of three" (ratio and proportion as "A is to B as is C to the unknown"). In 1820, algebra became a required subject for entrance to Harvard, and applicants were to have an understanding of simple equations, comprehending also the doctrine of roots and powers and arithmetical and geometrical proportions. Little change occurred until 1872, at which time the following requirements were established: arithmetic, algebra, and plane geometry. These requirements and the textbooks written by college professors shaped the mathematics curriculum for the secondary and elementary schools of the period. In general, the same courses and textbooks that had been offered in colleges were the curriculum of high schools and academies.

It was thought unfeasible to teach arithmetic to primary students until Pestalozzi illustrated how to present it concretely and in an interesting fashion. Influenced by Pestalozzi, Warren Colburn in 1826 introduced lessons that featured a sequence of questions and exercises of increasing difficulty and that differed from former materials in putting more emphasis on explanation than on rules to be memorized. Colburn also prepared materials for introducing students to algebra through a series of problems requiring reasoning and simple intuitive use of equations.

Arithmetic was taught incidentally in the primary grades: basic arithmetic in grades 2 through 6, intuitive algebra and written work in grades 7 through 8, algebra in grade 9, and plane geometry in grade 10.

The math curriculum for the elementary and secondary schools reflected the logic of adults more than the learning perspective of students. It followed the traditional classification of subjects that divided the content of mathematics into arithmetic, algebra, and geometry instead of equations, ratio, measurement, similarity, functional dependence, scale, variation, and the like, making it difficult for students to see that these concepts were involved in each subject. This practice also made it difficult for students to find connections and realize that they could use the same concepts in different ways and contexts.

Practical Uses of Math

In the early 20th century, the mathematics curriculum in the elementary and secondary schools centered on practical and vocational goals. Social factors influencing this change included a larger population of non-college-bound students, concern about the large numbers of students who failed disciplinary courses, and the growing influence of psychologists who discredited the mathematicians' claim that mathematics would improve one's thinking faculty, especially the ability to reason in all situations.

The arithmetic curriculum of elementary grades at this time focused on the four operations, fractions, common tables of measures, the decimal point, decimal fractions, and percentages. Instruction in the seventh and eighth grades centered on percentage and its applications such as business arithmetic.

A variety of approaches—such as drill work and exercises in actual measuring and computing—were used to teach arithmetic in the primary grades. Children sometimes did the purchasing of food for the day's luncheon, using current prices that they had obtained. For part of the day, children solved problems that appealed to them or played games involving numbers. The use of splints or tongue depressors in learning place values and the addition of three-digit numbers was popular (Smith, 1917). Children in the upper elementary grades confronted different kinds of applied problems: application of a rule, narrative problems, grouped problems, problems without numbers, oral problems, and problems in real situations. In rural areas, they might learn laying out and measuring fields, finding the value of crops, putting up fences and buildings, and farm economics. In the city, an equally broad range of real-life problems were drawn from industry, home economics, and civic expenditures.

At the beginning of the 20th century, the traditional course in algebra was modified by reducing manipulations, postponing difficult topics, and increasing the application of algebra and the solving of equations. Similarly, courses in geometry were made less difficult by eliminating materials on limits and incommensurables and adding informal proofs and graded theorems for students to prove in place of the required theorems to be memorized.

From the 1920s through the 1950s, conflict existed in the secondary school between those who wanted to teach traditional mathematics to all and those who wanted to vary the content according to future roles, making the subject chiefly an elective (Stanic, 1987). Those of the social efficacy persuasion won the day. The number of secondary school students who took algebra and geometry declined during the period. Many teachers did not believe that all students should study mathematics throughout the secondary school years and opposed the teaching of mathematics as a discipline—the logical organizing of subject matter as defined by university scholars—to future laborers. Accordingly, a variety of courses were developed to meet the different "needs" of those preparing for the following:

- General education

- Certain trades

- Engineering

- Specialized studies in math

The prevailing view was that after finishing a junior high course teaching the general nature and use of arithmetic, intuitive geometry, practical algebra, and the meaning of demonstration in geometry, only those students who had ability and interest in mathematics or who expected to enter a college or technical school were required to pursue the subject.

Paradoxically, as the place of mathematics in the school curriculum declined, the contributions from researchers in mathematics within the colleges and universities were unparalleled. This widening gap between the mathematics taught in schools and the knowledge of specialists set the stage for reform and attempts by mathematicians to change the school mathematics curriculum.

Preparation of the Elementary and Secondary Mathematics Curriculum by University Scholars

Mathematicians in the 1960s gained the upper hand in shaping elementary and secondary mathematics in the direction of disciplinary and cultural aims at the expense of utilitarian aims. University curriculum projects in mathematics funded by the National Science Foundation gave as their rationale the importance of mathematics in science and technology and the need to modernize the curriculum to reflect newer developments in the mathematical sciences—statistics and pure and applied mathematics (University of Illinois, 1959).

Changes in the elementary curriculum included the introduction of new topics: probability, geometry of physical space, positive and negative numbers, graphs, sets, Venn diagrams, and numeration systems other than the decimal. Instead of a focus on the processes (algorithms) of arithmetic and the authenticity of the grocery store, the curriculum of mathematics centered on the properties of numbers by introducing mathematical sentences such as: "What number for N will make this sentence true: $56 + 28 = N + 56$?" The curriculum of the junior high school lost application to social situations; instead, study was directed toward the structure of mathematics and the interconnections of the various branches. New activities were created to help students discover concepts for themselves, similar to Colburn's (1826) inductive method; students were engaged in working with Cuisenaire rods, multibase blocks, geoboards, and abaci for learning the various numeration systems. Some teachers encouraged group activities in constructing models, writing computer programs, and planning exhibitions showing probability and growth patterns.

In the high school, first-year algebra became more abstract and featured generalizations about equalities and solution sets. An emphasis was given on the concept of function and graphical representations of function theory, showing how changes in one variable resulted in or were caused by changes in another. Geometry was revised to allow students to use their knowledge of algebra in proving theories by coordinating methods. More attention was given to proofs that are unacceptable because they rest on unproven incidence relationships, as a way to show how difficult it is to prove "obvious" statements and reject false statements.

The curriculum of math scholars was faulted for introducing too many mathematical details and lack of applications to real-life problems. Many parents did not see the reasons for introducing the structure of mathematics in place of arithmetic. Reports of a decline in basic math skills as measured by conventional tests also contributed to a return to teaching minimal mathematical skills in the elementary schools and reserving algebra and geometry instruction for the college-bound students in the secondary schools. Some teachers, however, maintained aspects of the reform: the notion of sets and the use of sets of objects to explain the various operations, the use of "big ideas" in mathematics such as patterns and graphing, and activities that encouraged students to solve problems rather than to follow a set of rules or steps to get a correct answer.

Current Trends in the Mathematics Curriculum: Problem Solving and Practicality

Under the auspices of the National Council of Teachers of Mathematics, a cross section of mathematicians, teachers, and teacher educators developed a framework to guide reform in school mathematics throughout the 1990s (Commission on Standards for School Mathematics, 1991). The framework encourages the teaching of a broad range of math topics: number concepts, computation, estimation, data analysis, model building, discrete math, function, algebra, statistics, probability, geometry, and measurement. However, these topics are not taught in isolation but in ways to show their connections. It is suggested, for example, that number theory be used in grades 5 through 8 as the basis for bonding many individual facets of the curriculum into a whole, such as the commonalities among various arithmetics.

The current direction in mathematics curriculum differs from the traditional curriculum in three essential ways:

1. The presentation is problem oriented. Instruction revolves on concrete and real-world problems, whereas the traditional curriculum proceeded from concept to concept.
2. Classes are conducted to encourage active participation of each student. A constructive view of learning dominates, one that holds that individuals must construct their own understanding of math principles and concepts. Hence, children are encouraged to rely more on one another and less on the teacher in judging whether and why their answers are right. The teacher tries

to find out what individuals are thinking and then helps them refine their ideas and encourages them to invent ways to solve problems.

3. In contrast with the traditional division of math into algebra, geometry, algebra II, trigonometry, and calculus, the curriculum is organized around five or six major problems per year. Each time a problem comes up, new tools and concepts (regardless of whether they are from algebra or geometry) are introduced until the problem is solved.

Teachers are expected to develop learning opportunities in accordance with the following goals:

■ *Valuing of mathematics.* The goal is a combination of the old cultural appreciation of mathematics for its beauty and power and the importance of mathematics to the present scientific and technological world.

■ *Confidence in one's own math ability.* There should be opportunities for students to be successful in using math in their own situations.

■ *Problem solving.* Students should explore individually and in groups both classroom and real-world problems.

■ *Communication.* Students should read, write, and discuss ideas, using the signs, symbols, and terms of mathematics.

■ *Reasoning.* Students should make conjectures, gather evidence, and build arguments about the validity of a conjecture.

Current issues of both *Teaching Children Mathematics* and *The Mathematics Teacher* describe the curriculum developed by individual teachers in accordance with the guidelines. By way of example, a 4-week unit called "Beyond the Surface" helps middle-grade students relate many mathematical concepts and tools to one another, to other subject areas, and to personal growth (Brutlag & Maples, 1992). This unit deals with surface area–volume relationships and was built around four general principles that promote the making of connections by students:

1. Math is related to student interest.   The teacher selected ideas from the student world that involved relationships among scale, similarity, surface area, and volume. Popular literature and movies suggested that students were familiar with scaled-up or scaled-down versions of animals, plants, and people. Hence, the unit began by asking whether such fantastic things as killer bees as large as airplanes are possible. Could there really be blimp-sized bananas? Can human beings be shrunk to the size of grasshoppers? Are these things possible, or will they exist forever only in the movies? The answer to the questions lies in the mathematical relationship between surface area and volume. To comprehend biological information about the relative effects of size (and hence biological possibilities), students needed to have a sophisticated understanding of the mathematical concepts of similarity, scale, surface area, and volume.

2. Students construct their own concepts through concrete, active tasks.   Accordingly, students explored several tasks at the beginning of the unit to answer the questions "What is surface area?" and "What is volume?" They built objects out of Cuisenaire rods held together by putty. Because the rods were centimeter rods, the volume and surface area could be found by counting. Gradually students devised their own algorithms and formulas to make the counting easier. In one of the tasks, students worked in groups to build different objects all having a volume of 22 cubic centimeters and to find the minimum and maximum possible surface area for objects built with six rods. After looking at the class data, students wrote their conclusions and gave the reasons for these conclusions.

To answer the question of how surface area and volume change as objects are scaled up in size, students were assigned to two group tasks. In the first task, students built a "rod dog" out of centimeter rods and then built a similar dog with dimensions twice those of the original. The surface areas and volumes for the two dogs were counted and compared. In the second task, each group was assigned particular scale facts. Each group used these facts to build an enlargement of the original dog out of centimeter-grid paper, found the surface area and volume for their dog, and recorded their data on a table to be used with an overhead projector.

3. A mathematical relationship should be represented using several mathematical tools.   In the "Beyond the Surface" unit, students represented the same information using models, diagrams, tables, graphs, and formulas. It is assumed that students who are able to apply and translate among different representations of the same problem situation or of the same concept will have both a powerful set of tools for solving problems and an appreciation of the consistency and beauty of mathematics.

4. Students should reflect on the connections of their mathematical experiences by writing in journals, making presentations, discussing in seminars, and working on projects.   Throughout the unit, students wrote about their experiences and understandings. At the end of the unit, each student completed an individual project rather than taking a traditional chapter test for assessment. To complete the project, students had to reflect on the ideas learned and show what they learned in a creative, open-ended way. Options for projects included (a) building models of three similar houses, finding the scale factor, surface area, and volume of each, and to comment about the relationships; and (b) inventing a new friend about half the student's height, to devise a method to find the surface area and volume of the student and half-sized friend, and to comment about the relationships.

Controversy About the Present Math Curriculum

Not all teachers are committed to a math curriculum that offers the same topics to all students. The early 20th-century approach of differentiating the math curriculum on the basis of career aspirations is alive. The mathematics curriculum proposed by Burke (1990), for instance, offers one required course for all high school students followed by elective courses that would offer mathematical topics appropriate for the preprofessional training of scientists and engineers. The required course would be of a practical nature and center on such topics as percentages, logic, and statistics. The study of percentage would include compound interest received on savings or paid on credit cards and mortgages, the unemployment

---

ACTIVITY 8–1   DESCRIBING THE "MATHEMATICAL VISION" OF TEACHERS

1. Interview one or more teachers about the mathematical visions they hold.
2. Consider asking these questions:
    a. What are their goals for their mathematics program? What kinds of mathematics learning do they hope their students will experience?
    b. What do they see as worthwhile mathematical tasks or important mathematical ideas?
    c. Do their programs emphasize problem solving, communication, reasoning, conjecturing, and making connections among mathematical ideas? Are there commonalities in their thinking?

---

rate, inflation rate, growth rate of cells, and special cases that confuse many people (e.g., tenths of a percent and figures over 100%). Logic would be broadly conceived with examples from all fields in hopes that knowledge would transfer; arguments by counterexamples, definition of terms, and induction would be included. Statistics would include the reading of complex graphs and tables, with data coming from newspapers, almanacs, and other reference materials; the strengths and biases of surveys, polls, and lists of best-sellers would be noted; the concepts of average, weighted averages, median, and percentiles would be analyzed and applied to real-world situations. The strengths and weaknesses of regression equations would be shown through study of such questions as the relation between education and income. The use of standard deviations and confidence intervals would be applied to real-life situations.

Activity 8–1 will reveal the widely different views of what "math" should be in the curriculum.

SCIENCE IN THE SCHOOLS

Science in the elementary schools cycles its foci on nature, scientific process, and transmission of scientific facts; while science in the secondary schools is identified by discrete subject matters.

Introduction

Science education has long been an area of contention. Throughout much of the 19th century, many people viewed science as of little use to the average citizen, something easily forgotten; some thought science inferior to Latin and Greek in developing the reasoning faculties of students; and others saw science as hostile to organized religions, undermining religious beliefs and authority. Layton (1973) tells how in 1840 a "science of common things" was introduced in primary schools in England as a way to relate science to people's lives. He tells of the short-lived duration of this program and how it was followed by science in an abstract form—a textbook-based discipline entailing laboratory work aimed at confirming knowledge found in the text rather than a science addressing the personal interests of students and the social needs of society.

A review of the elementary and secondary science curriculum in the United States in the 19th and 20th centuries shows a continuous debate about the primary goal of science education—for knowledge or for a better life.

Science in the Elementary Schools

Many teachers in the elementary school are uncertain about teaching science. This uncertainty stems from doubts about what students are capable of learning, as well as from the teacher's own limited preparation and weak scientific background.

Object Lessons   Science made its appearance in the elementary school about 1850 as object teaching. Objects were taken from the wide range of phenomena of nature, such as dew, frost, hail, and wind. Animals and inanimate objects—all that could fall within sense observation—were the materials for study, not models or pictures. Students were encouraged to differentiate among the objects seen and touched—the shades of color or the variations in surfaces. The role of the teacher was to draw the student to correct observations and exact inferences through suggestions and questions, not by telling or making direct statements. The purposes of object lessons for students were these:

■ To gain knowledge of common things

■ To cultivate the capacity to observe

■ To develop reasoning ability

Unfortunately, many teachers had difficulty adjusting lessons to individual variations of students' interests and abilities within the large classes they commonly had to teach. Sometimes the lesson tended to be highly formal and to neglect the interpretation and understanding of events and phenomena. Objects (animals, plants) were placed before students who were asked to name them, describe their parts, and state the relationships among the parts. From the observation of single objects, students were led to compare them with others, taking the first step toward classification.

Nature Study   By 1870, object teaching had evolved into nature study. By contrast with science in the secondary schools of the time, which was directed toward the acquisition of knowledge of scientific principles, nature study in the elementary school dealt with natural things and processes as they related to daily life.

The exact shape that nature study took depended on the season of the year and the locality of the school. Common themes, however, were these:

■ *Studies of the weather*. Daily systematic readings and chartings of the thermometer and barometer, wind direction, and other meteorological observations

■ *Celestial studies*. Finding the altitude midday of the sun throughout the year

■ *Physical geography.* River courses, hills, valleys, sand, stratification of rocks

■ *Study of plants and animals.* Structure and germination of seeds, influence of light on green plants. These concepts were usually taught through a class garden that served as a laboratory for illustrating the fundamental condition of growth. Insects, worms, frogs, and domestic animals offered abundant sources of study about how animals move, feed, breathe, grow, and care for offspring.

An important aspect of the nature study curriculum was that the same materials and phenomena could be studied by students of different ages. The students' continued and growing interest in the phenomena was considered more educational than introducing new and unrelated subject matter by grade level.

Nature study's goals were to develop students' interest in objects and processes of nature, to give them training in accurate observation and in classifying facts, and to provide them with useful knowledge of nature as it affects human life. Nature study was used to correlate learning in many areas. Modes of expression—drawing, dancing, acting, constructing, writing, and composing music—were featured as students responded to the emotional stimulation of a field trip or other experience with nature.

Physiology and hygiene were correlated with nature study in such activities as comparing form and uses of human body parts with those of animals. The industrial and physical aspects of geography were introduced through nature study, and, of course, the mathematics applications were both necessary and numerous. For example, one group of students took as their inquiry the problem of determining the rate at which plants multiply as indicated by the seed production at a vacant city block covered with wild verbenas. Students measured the area as one-quarter acre and calculated the average number of plants per square yard. They then found out how many seeds were contained in each plant and the number that failed to mature, indicating an average of 1,700 seeds available for growth. Based on the proper distribution of good seeds and the assumption that each would produce a plant, students determined that the plants from the quarter-acre, assuming continuous reproduction, could provide enough seeds to furnish plants as thickly as those found on that quarter-acre for an area equal to sixteen times that of the entire earth (Jackman, 1904).

By the 1920s, enthusiasm for nature study began to wane. There were criticisms that the nature study curriculum lacked organization, that students tended to study a disconnected series of object lessons, that a chaotic array of goals— aesthetic, ethical, intellectual, and civic—was pursued. Nature study was faulted for expecting the teacher to be an expert naturalist and for failing to introduce vital elements of scientific method and content: the teacher gave lists of flowers, birds, or constellations to study each month but no suggestions for the meanings that might be developed from the study.

Generalizations   The study of science tended to replace nature study in the 1920s. This change in orientation is seen in the curriculum developed by Gerald Craig (1927) and his coworkers at the Horace Mann Elementary School within Teachers College, Columbia University, New York. The process for developing this curriculum is itself of interest to curriculum makers. Craig first prepared a list of specific objectives for elementary school science that conformed to scientific generalizations fundamental to modern life; contributed to health, economy, and safety; and were considered essential for understanding phenomena of interest to children. These objectives were submitted to parents and other educated laypeople for ranking as to importance. These judgments were supplemented by the judgments of scientists and foremost thinkers of the time, as found in authoritative source books of science. In addition, Craig and his fellow teachers tried to find out from children what questions in nature and science interested them most. The generalizations from science that best answered the children's questions were included. Assignment of the objectives to grade level was based on the assumed order of complexity. There were specific topics and major generalizations for each grade level:

- *Grade 1*—change of seasons; effects of cold weather; where plants and animals live; plants and seeds; sun, moon, and stars

- *Grade 2*—plants and seasonal changes; animals and seasonal changes; water, ice, steam, air, and weather; heat and light from the sun; magnetism; plants as food; ways electricity helps

- *Grade 3*—how animals protect themselves and care for their young; how seeds are scattered; the sun and moon; cause of day and night; food of animals

- *Grade 4*—the Earth; economic value of animals; social life of animals; air, soil, gardening; molds and bacteria; electric wiring; fossils, importance of water

- *Grade 5*—hibernation and migration; causes of fogs and clouds; metamorphosis; the moon and its movement; conservation of nature; balance of nature; protective coloration; how plants grow

- *Grade 6*—the story of the Earth; the solar system; reproduction; methods of adaptation

The topics were interrelated from grades 1 to 6 by certain themes. Migration, hibernation, metamorphosis, parental care, and community life, for example, all relate to the theme of adaptation. Examples of the kinds of generalizations that compose the course objectives and essential meanings to be taught were these:

- Nature's laws are invariable.

- Humans' conception of truth changes.

- The Earth is one of a number of bodies that revolve around the sun.

- The Earth rotates on its axis once every 24 hours, causing day and night.

- All life depends on vegetation, and vegetation languishes outside the temperature range of 55 to 10 degrees centigrade.

- All life has evolved from very simple forms.

In the 1950s, some scientists faulted the social utility approach to elementary science education, saying it was not science but only bits of information about favorite topics such as weather, nature study, magnets, and other 'Gee Whiz' topics. Other weaknesses in the generalization-oriented curriculum included the following:

■ Topics were presented as results to be accepted on faith with little experimentation.

■ There was a failure to show how scientific conclusions are derived by induction and deduction.

■ The connections between all natural phenomena were not revealed to students.

Processes and Concepts   Federal support for elementary school science began in 1961. The curriculum projects undertaken with this money were conducted by academic scientists and used a variety of approaches. The leaders of the American Association for the Advancement of Science project "Science—A Process Approach" (Gagné, 1966) held that science consisted of the processes scientists used, not the concepts with which they worked. Hence, this curriculum was designed to teach the scientific processes of classifying, measuring, observing, and inferring. Materials were made available for these purposes. Students were encouraged to question and hypothesize about the phenomena presented and to conduct experiments using numbers and making inferences in testing their hypotheses. They were taught how to summarize and communicate their findings.

Other scientists, notably the developers of the Science Curriculum Study (SCIS) at the University of California at Berkeley, centered their efforts on producing materials and ways of teaching fundamental science concepts (Karplus & Thier, 1967). Two major categories of concepts were chosen: description ("What happens?") and an explanatory or interpretive concept ("Why does it happen?"). Concepts were arranged in a hierarchy by degree of abstraction. Major ideas from both biological and physical science were drawn upon. The major concepts by grade level were these:

■ *Grade 1*—organisms and material objects

■ *Grade 2*—life cycles and interaction of systems

■ *Grade 3*—population and subsystems

■ *Grade 4*—environment and relating of positions and motion

■ *Grade 5*—community and energy sources

■ *Grade 6*—ecosystems and models of electric and magnetic interaction

Boxes of equipment and materials together with instructional units were part of the program. Three different kinds of lessons were featured:

1. Students are left on their own to explore and discover while playing with collections of objects.
2. Students are helped to invent a concept that is new to them and to find meaning from the exploratory experiences. (The invention lesson also provides guided practice in using new labels and categories.)
3. Students discover the usefulness of the new concepts by applying them in their own situations.

Only about 30% of elementary schools used any of the curriculum developed by the scientists, and by 1980, evidence indicated that teachers were not providing hands-on experiences so that students could get greater insights into the basic concepts of science. Instead, a return to the textbook approach and an emphasis on the memorization of scientific facts had occurred (Harms & Yager, 1981). Increased control by state authorities through testing that demanded selection of "right" answers to fragmented questions contributed to the decrease in student's having hands-on practice and experience with scientific processes and inquiry using concepts from several subject areas. Nevertheless, some elementary school teachers developed science curriculum to meet local needs, moving away from science as a discipline to the social significance of science, and some teachers followed ecological approaches centered on human interests and called on interdisciplinary sources.

Current Directions   Among the goals for science in the new century are the prior generation's goals of developing student skills for scientific investigation and facilitating students' acquisition of concepts that approximate those of scientists. Other goals, however, are getting equal attention: to prepare students for technological problem solving, to equip students to make decisions about science-related social issues, and to help them be independent, life-long learners of science.

Science for All America, the report issued by Project 2061 sponsored by the American Association for the Advancement of Science (1989), envisions an ideal elementary curriculum that demonstrates the connections that exist among the different disciplines and helps students understand their changing world. Accordingly, elementary school teachers might develop their classroom science experiences around major themes such as energy, evolution, patterns of change, scale and structure, stability and interaction. The theme "evolution," for example, is treated in grades 1 through 3 by the study of the diversity among living things and in grades 3 through 6 by the study of how living things adapt to their environment in order to survive and how the various adaptations of living things help them keep alive and grow. Activities in physical, earth, and life sciences are related to the themes, and students try to draw connections from concepts being studied to daily experiences and previously learned ideas. In many schools, science is used as a vehicle to enhance reading, math, and the arts, much like the science curriculum of the 1920s.

Under a grant from the Packard Foundation, nearly 300 elementary teachers developed themes for a school year to relate the different subjects and to incorporate firsthand, real-world science activities (Greene, 1991). Under this curriculum, students read and write about science. Working in groups, they investigate and solve problems requiring measurement and computation, and they express their understanding through art, music, and movement. One first-grade class (using the theme "Over in the Meadow") experimented, drew conclusions, and recorded their observations on such topics as the senses, weather, rocks, and soils, birds of prey, and metamorphosis.

Activity 8–2 is a group activity that allows for selecting the most defensible goals for science education in the elementary schools and the best corresponding approach for reaching these goals.

ACTIVITY 8–2 CREATING A FUTURE SCIENCE CURRICULUM BY JIGSAWING

The task is to come up with a science curriculum for the future derived from "puzzle pieces."

1. Each small group selects one puzzle piece for a desired science education goal from the sets given here, as well as a puzzle piece from an approach that best matches the selected goal.
2. Reports from each group are given and the reasons for their selection are discussed.

Puzzle Pieces: Goals

- Generate scientific ideas from experience.
- Change students' conceptions.
- Relate to the scientific community and its questions.
- Understand natural phenomena.
- Continue learning in science.
- Prepare for the changing world of work.
- Use science in personal and social decision making.
- Recognize the limitations of science and technology.
- Judge reliability of knowledge.

Puzzle Pieces: Approaches

- *Everyday coping*—learning to understand objects and events
- *Disciplinary*—approximating the way scientists question and proceed in investigating and determining validity
- *Process*—emphasizing the acts of observing, experimenting, classifying, and learning subject matter
- *Educational*—learning subject matter
- *Student search*—searching for answers with other students

Communities of Learners

The late Ann Brown and Joseph Campiones's *Fostering Communities of Learners* (FCL) is a glimpse of the future elementary science curriculum and offers insights into the decision making necessary for its construction (Brown & Campiones, 1996). The problem, for example, of teachers not having the scientific knowledge required for handling student queries is addressed. This innovative curriculum is being implemented in inner-city schools for grades K–8.

FCL is designed to promote children's critical thinking through research, reading, writing, and designing tasks. Central to an FCL classroom is discourse involving student negotiation and definition of ideas, so that a common voice (meaning) and a common knowledge base evolves. Individuals, however, own more than the common voice because within the classroom each learner decides in which aspect of the problem he or she wants to specialize—similar to what takes place among scientists in an academic discipline.

Biology is the discipline from which children draw their questions and form their learning community. The biological underpinning of environmental science was the central focus because the curriculum planners knew something about the theories about biology held by children. They wanted to better understand children's emergent theories about biology and to lead them toward principles of the discipline: interdependence, biodiversity, evolution, and adaption. The curriculum places children in the world of 19th-century naturalist study, instead of contemporary biology that requires familiarity with biochemistry and genetics, beyond the grasp of young children. The curriculum developers elected not to water down content to a strange mixture of the biological and biochemical, as is done in many textbooks for young children.

However, by the time students are introduced to contemporary disciplinary knowledge, they will want—and be ready for—that knowledge just as scientists did as the discipline evolved. The fact that by age 6 children can investigate the concept of living things, but that it is not until age 10 that they are likely to place plants within this category, influenced the decision about the content.

In the FCL curriculum, by second grade, students address the connection between animals and habitat, exploring the concepts of mutuality and interdependence; sixth-graders examine biodiversity and the effect of the space that animals need on endangerment; and eighth-graders study the effect of variations in the gene pool on adaptation and survival. Similarly, curriculum designers expect different kinds of student reasoning at different levels. Teleological theories and reliance on causality in general is expected with young children along with attributing human qualities to animals. Older learners are encouraged to reason using the ideas of cause and effect, chance, probability, and randomness.

Second-graders might research the survival mechanisms of animals by beginning with an "anchor event," such as reading *Tree of Life* by Barbara Bash, with its theme of animal and habitat interdependence. Individuals then adopt an animal or plant mentioned in the book; with help from one another, they write and illustrate a paragraph on why their animal is dependent on the tree of life and why the tree is dependent on the animal or plant.

The research expands as students build on their emerging knowledge by exploring subtopics that surface, such as food chains and defense mechanisms. However, the "big idea" underlying their research is animal and habitat interdependence. Six research groups are formed: food chains, predators, defense mechanics, protection from the elements, animal communication, and reproductive strategies. Children in each group write and illustrate booklets about their subtopic. They share information both within their group and across groups; and as a integrated design task, they create an animal of the future that shows a solution to the six research questions.

Design groups display illustrated text about the animal of the future to their classmates and to others. When exhibiting before a variety of real audiences, children learn to respond to the audience's demand for coherence and clarity; students need to push for high levels of understanding, satisfactory explanations, and clarification. In subsequent years, children delve more deeply into the underlying principles of the domain.

The curriculum has a carefully organized plan for using peer and cross-age tutors, reciprocal teaching, jigsaw activity, and guided writing. In carrying out their research, students first rely on what they learn from a jigsaw activity, as well as from independent study. In jigsaw activities, each group of students studies part of an overall question. Later, the groups come together to share information and to create a complete answer to the problem. However, this is not enough. They need someone to help them with misunderstandings and to push them into higher levels of understanding. As a result, there are provisions for students to have access to consultants, both face to face and through electronic mail.

Inasmuch as elementary classroom teachers are not usually steeped in an academic discipline, subject matter specialists work with teachers to develop units and subtopics, to select resource materials and artifacts, and to teach occasional lessons. Subsequently, classroom teachers take over the responsibility for these lessons.

The consultants are especially helpful in introducing the "big ideas" and principles that are to be studied and in leading children to more advanced concepts—from discussions of the notion of energy related to amount of food eaten, the expert might introduce the concept of metabolic rate. Consultants also model thinking and self-reflection.

Experts coaching via electronic mail is an FCL essential resource, freeing teachers from the sole burden as knowledge source. Expertise from the local community is also drawn upon. The use of older students as discussion leaders guiding the reciprocal teaching and jigsaw activities of younger children is beneficial to everyone.

Science in the Secondary Schools

Changes in Secondary School Science   The traditional curriculum divisions of physics, chemistry, and biology have evolved from other subjects and have experienced periodic swings in content and direction, from that which is useful in daily life to that which prepares one to enter the scientific community. When the lag between what scientists know and what schools teach becomes acute, the curriculum is bent toward the disciplines. The abstractions of the discipline, in turn, invite student and public dissatisfaction and a return to a more personal and society-relevant science curriculum.

Chemistry   The early academies and public high schools taught a practical chemistry that could be applied in the home and in agriculture. These courses largely involved lecture and demonstration. After the Civil War, laboratory work in chemistry was offered in most schools. The period 1872 to 1900 saw domination of the chemistry curriculum by colleges, as was the case with the physics curriculum. Chemistry texts were organized by the logic of the subject. An issue at the time was whether laboratory work that consisted of observation and the introduction of generalizations should only affirm the textbook. Formalism, as opposed to inductive method, increased under the influence of college teachers of chemistry, and as formalism increased, the percentage of students enrolled in chemistry declined from 11% in 1890 to 7% in 1905.

After World War I, industrial chemistry became more important for the nation. High school chemistry courses became more applied and taught such information as how to remove stains and how to test for adulteration in foods. At least 14 different types of chemistry courses of an applied nature (e.g., technical chemistry, textile chemistry, dairy chemistry) were offered.

In the 1960s, the federal government, through the National Science Foundation, funded programs such as the Chemical Education Material Study. The outcome was a curriculum that followed an inquiry approach and introduced both laboratory work and theoretical concepts (e.g., rates and mechanisms of reactions, chemical bonding, structural ideas, the systematization of chemistry in terms of the periodic table). The goal was to have students attain a highly mathematical and logical form of science. The program succeeded in revising the teaching of chemistry so that courses reflected modern knowledge of the subject. However, the disciplinary approach to chemistry did not increase student interest, as indicated by falling enrollments.

Currently, the teaching of chemistry has a constant stream of new curricula. In some of the new courses, chemistry is taught as part of a general science course. In other courses, it is combined with biology, geology, physics, and other subjects. In general, much attention is given to the application of chemistry to everyday life and to industrial uses through the study of plastics, detergents, medicines, insecticides, and other products.

Biology   Biology teachers today differ among themselves about biology as a school subject. Some follow an evolutionary approach, with an emphasis on adaptation and change; others take a functional approach, highlighting physiology. Many favor an environmental approach with a focus on ecology and conservation, and a few have a genetic and molecular approach. The latest approach is an applied biology approach that uses biology to solve human problems. In part, these differences in orientation reflect the 100-year history of the field.

Biology as Natural History   In the early 1800s, the academies and prep schools offered courses in natural history in which students studied plants, animals, and nature and acquired medical information, especially as related to herbs and botany. In their courses, students described and classified living things and were taught to view the "wonderful harmony of nature and its relation to moral behavior" (Rosen, 1959, p. 480). Specialized courses in zoology and botany also had a natural history approach, with an emphasis on the classification of animals and plants. Human physiology became part of the curriculum in 1839. Because many of the authors of physiology texts were physicians, the courses stressed anatomy and body functions.

Biology as a Mental Discipline   After the Civil War, biology shifted its aim to mental discipline and introduced the laboratory method as an appropriate instrument for attaining this goal. Botany, the morphology of plants, became a focus. Similarly, under the influence of Louis Agazzi, who taught high school classes and brought other teachers to his laboratory, the focus of zoology changed from natural history to comparative anatomy and the classification of animal life from man to protozoa, with mental discipline as the major aim. After 1865, the temperance movement succeeded in having physiology textbooks devote pages to the evils of alcohol and tobacco, which diluted the mental discipline emphasis and adversely affected the popularity of physiology.

Integrated Biology   In the 1870s, the concept of a general biology course that would integrate botany, zoology, and human physiology was promoted. Huxley and Martin (1876), for instance, held that study of living bodies, plants, and animals is really one discipline. As the result of problems in organizing an integrated course, for many years teachers followed a "fern and worm" method (in which those two organisms were studied as prototypes of their respective kingdoms). Until the 1900s, biology courses were highly academic, demanding attention to structural details and following laboratory instructions to confirm prespecified observations.

Practical Biology   The academic and disciplinary orientation for biology lost ground through the first half of the 20th century. Instead, the subject was regarded as useful for both college-bound and non-college-bound students. Knowledge of biology was seen as helping citizens deal with problems of health, hygiene, food preparation, sanitation, and conservation of natural resources. Where laboratory work had formerly been justified as promoting the faculties of observation and willpower, psychological evidence cast doubt on the possibility of training students' powers of observation and denied the existence of a general faculty of observation. Teachers responded by justifying such work as developing thinking skills and the scientific method.

Courses of the times were often organized around projects and problems involving field trips and study of the local environment. Textbooks introduced a number of generalizations derived from scholarly studies: micro-organisms are the immediate cause of disease; all life came from preexisting life and reproduces its own kind; food, oxygen, and certain optimal conditions are essential for the life of living things.

Biology Updated   By 1960, the disparity between what was taught in high schools as biology and what scientists thought essential was great enough to warrant a change in the curriculum. The Biological Science Curriculum Study (BSCS), a committee of high school teachers, administrators, and research biologists, expressed its concern about the failure of biology courses to deal with such issues as organic evolution, the nature of individual and racial differences, sex and reproduction in the human species, and the problem of population growth and control. The committee also faulted courses for not developing understanding of biological concepts and organizational ideas such as the genetic continuity of life and for not accurately portraying scientific activity. The committee created three versions of the same course (Glass, 1962):

1. A molecular approach, including genetic evolution
2. A community approach, with attention to ecological problems
3. A cellular approach, with emphasis on physiological functions

In all instances, supplementary materials—such as films to stimulate original investigations and articles to assist students in their inquiries—were available.

By the end of the 1970s, nearly half of the school districts in the United States were using the BSCS materials. The social atmosphere of the 1970s supported the teaching of biological education as relevant for a broad range of students, not just for those planning careers in science. Many teachers adopted an ecological perspective combined with the aim of developing decision-making skills for citizenship. They taught biology in relation to important aspects of contemporary life—in the context of population growth and need for family planning, stress and mental health, proper food preparation and use, and other such issues.

Current Biology Curriculum   Currently biology teachers are asked to develop curriculum in accordance with the recommendations of Project 2061 of the American Association for the Advancement of Science (1989). Its widely encompassing recommendations aim at helping students become familiar with the natural world in its diversity and its unity, understand key concepts of biology, and apply biological knowledge to connections among the sciences. It recommends such practices as showing how the transformation of energy occurs in physical, biological, and chemical systems and how evolutionary changes appear in stars, organisms, and rocks.

Activity 8–3 will help bridge the divide between knowledge of science and how to teach it—the connection between the teacher's content knowledge and the teacher's pedagogical knowledge.

ACTIVITY 8–3   RELATING A SCIENTIFIC DISCIPLINE TO A SCHOOL SUBJECT

A school subject differs from a discipline in that a school subject should be consistent with the purposes of the school and the reasons for teaching the subject, including social and personal relevance. Mastery of an organized field of knowledge may be necessary for an expert, but the general education of a citizen may not require the same degree of specialized knowledge.

Consider a class you might teach. What are some of the reasons students in the class should study X (an aspect of science)? What areas would you want students to experience? What makes X difficult for students? What can be done to make the study of X more satisfying for students and to enhance their success with the subjects? Compare your answers to the curriculum in X at different historical period.

For more information on math or science, go to *www.prenhall.com/mcneil* and click on Chapter 8 links.

SUMMARY

Teachers may resist constructivist pedagogy because they are unsure of their knowledge of math and science. This chapter challenged the notion that teachers must be experts in these subjects instead of facilitators of learning whereby teachers and students draw from a range of resources. Suggestions were made for getting the necessary collegial support and help in understanding the big ideas of math and science. Although traditional and reform curriculum were contrasted, it may not have been clear that at times explicit instruction is needed, particularly for students to acquire the skills and rules for engaging in inquiry and exploiting technology—including how to collaborate, respect one another, and share information.

A basic skill curriculum oriented to computational procedures alone is generally agreed to be inappropriate for today's world. Computational procedures and scientific facts are important but should not dominate the elementary school curriculum in terms of textbook coverage and class time. Similarly, a danger persists that the drive for accountability and standardized testing will hinder reform. Too many math and science lessons lack focus and are cluttered with unrelated activities. On the other hand, there are numerous descriptions by teachers showing how they have made their curriculum coherent and aligned with big math and science goals and ideas while engaging in real-world problem solving, confirming that social constructivism can be effective in various contexts.

QUESTIONS FOR DISCUSSION

Math

1. Which of the following ideas should guide curriculum development of mathematics?
   a. *Empiricism.* Math has been derived from studies of physical objects; hence, the math curriculum should include manipulation of objects and the application of math concepts to problems of the real world.
   b. *Reasoning.* Math is not bound to statements that respond to the way things really are but only to conclusions that follow by logical necessity from the premises defining given mathematical systems. Hence, the teaching of mathematics should aim at understanding the intellectual rigor and logic of abstract mathematics.
2. How can newer topics such as probability, statistics, and estimation best be related to other topics of arithmetic, algebra, and geometry?

Science

1. What knowledge from the domains of science and technology are central to citizens' decisions about such matters as toxic waste, life support systems, conservation of natural resources, and AIDS?
2. Give reasons for or against the science curriculum concentrating on each of the following:
   a. More scientific theories and concepts, less on facts
   b. The cutting edges of science and technology
   c. Methods of scientific inquiry
3. The science curriculum has been faulted for presenting ordered pieces of someone else's knowledge rather than helping students develop their own knowledge by exploring a repertoire of phenomena in the physical and natural world. Should the science curriculum consist of ways of engaging students in a wide range of engaging phenomena, giving less attention to scientific views and focusing more on the processes students use to make sense of the phenomena? Why? Why not?

REFERENCES

American Association for the Advancement of Science. *Science for all America: Project 2061.* Washington, DC: Author.

Bash, B. *The tree of life.* (1987). Boston: Little, Brown.

Brown, A., & Campiones, J. (1996). Psychological theory and the design of innovative learning environments: On procedures, principles and systems. In L. Schauble & R. Glaser (Eds.), *Innovations in learning: New environments for education* (pp. 289–326). Mahwah, NJ: Erlbaum.

Brutlag, D., & Maples, C. (1992). Making connections: Beyond the surface. *The Mathematics Teacher, 85*(3), 231–234.

Burke, P. (1990). Should we stop force-feeding math in high school? *Virginia Journal of Education, 84,* 14–15.

Colburn, W. (1826). *Colburn's first lesson: Intellectual arithmetic upon the inductive method of instruction.* Boston: Hilliard Gray, Little & Walker.

Commission on Standards for School Mathematics of the National Council of Teachers of Mathematics. (1991). *Curriculum and evaluation standards for school mathematics.* Reston, VA: National Council of Teachers of Mathematics.

Craig, G. (1927). *Certain techniques used in developing a course of study in sciences for the Horace Mann Elementary School.* New York: Columbia University Teachers College, Bureau of Publications.

Gagné, R. M. (1966). Elementary science: A new scheme of instruction. *Science, 151*(3706), 49–53.

Glass, B. (1962). Renascent biology: A report on the AIBS Biological Sciences Curriculum Study. *The School Review, 701,* 1–43.

Greene, L. C. (1991). Science-centered curriculum in elementary school. *Educational Leadership, 49*(2), 42–46.

Harms, N. C., & Yager, R. (1981). *What research says to the science teacher* (Vol. 3). Washington, DC: National Science Teachers Association.

Huxley, T. A., & Martin, H. D. (1876). *A course of practical instruction in elementary biology.* New York: Macmillan.

Jackman, W. S. (Ed.). (1904). *Nature study: National Society for the Study of Education: The third yearbook.* Chicago: University of Chicago Press.

Kamens, D. H., & Benavot, A. (1991). Knowledge for the masses: The origins and spread of mathematics and science education in national curriculum. *American Journal of Education, 99*(2), 137–180.

Karplus, R., & Thier, H. *A new look at elementary school science.* Chicago: Rand McNally, 1967.

Layton, D. (1973). *Science for the people.* London: Allen & Unwin.

Ma, L. (1999). *Knowing and teaching elementary mathematics: Teachers' understanding of fundamental mathematics in China and the United States*. Mahwah, NJ: Erlbaum.

Moses, R. (2000). *Radical equations*. Boston, MA: Beacon Press.

National Academy of Science (2001). *Adding it up: Helping children learn mathematics*. Washington, DC: National Academy of Science.

Rosen, S. (1959). Origins of high school general biology. *School Science and Mathematics, 59*(60), 473–489.

Seaborg, G. (1960). New currents in chemical education. *Chemical and Engineering News, 38*(49), 97–105.

Smith, D. E. (1917). Arithmetic. In L. Rapeer (Ed.), *Teaching elementary school subjects* (pp. 207–252). New York: Scribner.

Stanic, G. M. (1987). Mathematics education in the United States at the beginning of the twentieth century. In T. S. Popkewitz (Ed.), *The formation of the school subjects* (pp. 145–176). New York: Falmer.

University of Illinois Committee on School Mathematics and the Advisory Committee of the School Study Group. (1959). Chicago: University of Chicago.

5

Creating Curriculum in the Classroom

Hollywood films show the teacher as a hero/heroine combating tough kids and bureaucratic principals. The two chapters in this part depict the teacher more like a modern novelist who chooses a theme and situation and then lets the characters write the book. Accordingly, curriculum planning by the teacher involves (a) selecting a problem that warrants deep inquiry and relates to an important theme and (b) finding ways students can pose their own questions about the problem and determine what they need to know in answering them. Of course, that means that the teacher doesn't control the information, expertise, or experience that students draw upon as they try to answer their questions, and, like characters in the novel, they have their own trajectories.

Similarly, assessment is concerned with student thinking, feeling, and acting in real-world contexts as they carry out the deeper inquiry—a far cry from memorizing information from a text in order to pass a test.

Assessment is considered in relation to teachers' and students' decision making—the new ways teachers are uncovering student thinking and finding out what students already know and what processes will help them construct knowledge. Assessment that is integral to informed instruction and learning should not be confused with assessment that merely ranks and sorts students or is the basis for comparing schools, states, and individuals.

CHAPTER **9**

CURRICULUM AND PLANNING

Sara: How can you tell a dead curriculum from a live one?

Merl: One tries to cover a subject; the other, to uncover a person. Also, the dead one is all skeleton and no meat. And for you, when is less more?

Sara: When investigating one problem and incidentally learning many new things versus being exposed to many topics but learning nothing.

Constructivist planners are less concerned with ensuring that the teacher control what is to be learned and more interested in how best to help students form and pursue their own questions. Planning involves bringing more of the world into the classroom—ideas, views, facts—through technology, experts, and original sources. It also means using what is learned to help others in the school and the wider community.

Success of teaching and learning from this viewpoint depends on how well the teacher can establish a learning community whereby individuals and small groups work on aspects of a common problem and the efforts of all are shared yet recognizing that individuals and groups may have different levels of understanding. A learning community is committed to a dialogue that aims at increasing personal understanding, not consensus or grudging assent. Questions are framed so that evidence can be brought to bear in supporting or refuting ideas and practices, seeking facts and ideas that are beyond what they already have, and students show a willingness to listen to others as well as to challenge and dissent.

Curricula are initiated as teachers visualize what might occur in a classroom, tentatively answering their own questions about content, materials, student learning activities, time allocation, and other aspects of a framework to guide future action. Curricula are created as plans are revised and implemented. When the interactions among students and teachers result in new content, interpretations, ways of working, and purposes, curricula are created. The feelings and meanings generated from classroom experiences may make up a curriculum; indeed, curriculum may continue to form as the meanings of classroom experiences unfold throughout a lifetime.

LONG-RANGE, DAILY, AND UNIT PLANNING

Although teachers engage in long-range planning as well as daily planning, they regard course and daily plans as less important than the planning of instructional units. Long-range planning, which is typically done during the summer months, usually consists of reviewing materials to be used during the coming year, rearranging topics from school curricula and previous teaching experiences, and adding and deleting content to be taught. A broad outline of instruction, together with ideas for how the content is to be taught, is formed as teachers do a mental review of the events of the past year and of newer materials and ideas. Detailed long-range planning tends to be counterproductive because of unpredictable changes in schedules, students and student needs, and interruptions.

Daily plans are usually nested within the unit plan and depend on the progress of a class in that unit. Most teachers' daily plan consists of a mental picture of the content to be taught and the sequence of activities that might occur, supported by notes and lists of important points that the teacher wants to be sure to remember. Daily plans are likely only to be written in detail and in a prescribed form when the teacher has to comply with administrative requirements for turning in plans on a regular basis or when the plan is to be used by a replacement or substitute teacher.

The planning of an instructional unit offers the teacher an opportunity to initiate a curriculum that is responsive to a local situation, individual students, and the teacher's own passion. Unlike curricula presented in textbooks that isolate knowledge into subject matter compartments, a teacher's unit plan may forge connections among subject matters, as well as connect to life in a particular community.

Planning as Mapping

One notion of curriculum has been associated with the idea of movement toward a destination, a set of experiences, a stream of activities, a journey involving increasingly wider ranges in modes of thinking. Hence, the metaphor of the map is sometimes used by teachers in creating their instructional unit plans. Accordingly, the plan specifies the steps for reaching a predetermined goal. However, maps are seldom complete, and they require frequent revision. Travelers using the map may decide to change their original destination and route for reasons of feasibility and interest. They may seek a new map or make their own.

In their planning or curriculum mapping, teachers vary in attitudes about flexibility of the plan and their relative concerns about the quality of the learning experience or about the attainment of a goal. Units of instruction take on the characteristics of open and closed maps:

■ *Thematic units* are open maps of broad focus that allow for many subthemes and encourage unexpected outcomes.

■ *Subject matter units* are closed maps that focus on prespecified topics with less opportunity for students to determine the central questions, subtopics, and the sequence in which content is presented.

■ *Inquiry and problem-based units* are focused on a central question or problem to be solved. Usually the question or problem has been chosen or defined by students, although the teacher may have provoked the inquiry. Inquiry and problem-based units give task responsibility to students for planning and completing the work required in addressing the common problem; they allow for individual students to study subtopics of personal interest when they are pertinent to the inquiry.

The Organizing Center as a Vehicle for Learning: More Than Meets the Eye

Much has been made of the theme, the topic, and the problem as bases for organizing instructional units. In the language of curriculum, these focal points are called *organizing centers* or *instructional foci*. Generally, if you ask students what they are studying, they reply by naming the organizing center. Organizing centers can be contrasted with organizing elements. A *center* is the direct object of study—topic, question, event, or phenomenon. An *organizing element* is the intellectual, moral, or physical attribute that learners may develop as they pursue their study of the center. For example, a center titled "Computer Science in Society" allows a teacher to draw curriculum elements from many sources:

1. From mathematics: calculus and algorithms
2. From computer science: computer programming and use of software
3. From social sciences: computer ethics, including whistle-blowing, improper use of data, invasion of privacy, and censorship

Organizing elements are important generalizations, values, principles, and the like that are continuously constructed through a semester, year, or years as one purpose or study. Also, curriculum elements serve as schoolwide themes by which all teachers contribute to the construction of big ideas and values, having a cumulative effect on student learning—writing (writing across the curriculum), social relations (conflict resolution in all classes), conservation (saving the Earth through science, math, and the humanities).

Teachers, however, know that centers are chiefly vehicles for learners' intellectual and emotional development. Although the study of a noteworthy event, work of art, problem, or other phenomenon is valuable in its own right, it is of more worth when it leads students to the construction of concepts, attitudes, skills, and concerns—elements of educational importance.

Different organizing centers can serve the same educational goals. Teachers have much to do in influencing the kind of development that occurs as learners pursue the immediate focus of their study. Young children may believe they are learning to build birdhouses (the organizing center), but the teacher may view the activity as an opportunity to form new concepts and skills in measurement, to improve motor dexterity, or to learn how to use tools (the organizing element). Another teacher may see the activity as a way to build the learners' self-confidence or to foster students' concern about wildlife (other elements).

FIGURE 9–1
Example of a teacher relating an activity (center) to organizing element and an educational goal

Center	Creating crossword puzzles
Element	Learning to read and write
Goal	Developing citizens

Although organizing centers should be broad enough so that students can find an area of personal interest, they shouldn't be so broad that the study becomes unmanageable or meaningless. Nevertheless, in the hands of a good teacher, nearly any center can lead to powerful ideas from science, math, social studies, psychology, English, and more. Furthermore, the activities carried out under the rubric of the center can contribute to long-term educational goals. Mathematical modeling or consumer mathematics, for example, can be taught through such centers as population growth, the stock market, credit cards, and taxation.

As students engage in activities related to centers, they reiterate or extend organizing elements throughout other units, courses, and experiences, culminating in long-term goals.

Figure 9–1 illustrates a teacher's long look ahead while engaging in a classroom activity.

Activities can integrate the arts, science, math, and social studies. The activities in some units call for imaginary solutions, such as simulations, mock trials, straw votes, and the building of model communities. The units of other teachers will feature academic solutions to real problems, and the activities will involve real experiences in which students make use of the information they obtained in situations relating to civic responsibility and quality of life in their community.

THEMATIC UNITS

The broad focus of thematic instructional units and how they can be related to subject matter areas can be seen in the brief descriptions of several such units: "The Circus," "Humanitas," "Hudson River Valley," and "The Vietnam War."

"The Circus"

Kohl (1976) tells how he went about creating a thematic unit for young children in preparation for the school year. He chose the theme "The Circus" because it combined danger and discipline, farce and high seriousness, and because few students can be indifferent to the many aspects of life and fantasy embodied in the circus. Kohl began by going to the circus to remind himself of what it was all about. Then he analyzed what he saw and speculated about what could be studied through the circus. His general map of the circus looked something like the illustration in Figure 9–2.

Next Kohl developed subthemes, matching them with activities for the classroom. For example, the subtheme "Tightrope Walking" was turned into "Balancing," which brought forth such content ideas as vertigo and balancing games,

FIGURE 9–2
General map of the circus

	Animals	
Jugglers		Clowns
Tightrope walkers		Freaks
Pitching tents		Parades
Movers	Posters	
	Art	
	Music	

floating and sinking, gymnastics, center of gravity (equilibrium and the ear), balancing a checkbook, and associated weights and balances (scales and measures). Classroom activities included making balancing toys; making a seesaw and balancing things on it; building balanced structures with blocks; walking a straight line on the floor, then on blocks, and then on chairs and then talking about fear of heights and how feelings affect performance; writing about confidence; imagining walking the wire 100 feet up; and measuring actual heights.

Kohl thought about the best time to introduce the unit—before or after a circus would come to town—and the resources available. He was lucky in that a former student who had attended Ringling Brothers Clown College could come to class and show his clown faces and tricks, which, in turn, led to the children's evolving their own clown characters, listening to the opera *Pagliacci*, making masks, and creating short plays with masked superheroes.

All teachers would have their own ideas about what activities might go on under the circus theme. Instead of circus performers coming to the class, volunteers from local theater groups could visit and make theater real for the children. Other teachers might have the students decorate the class with old circus posters or record other aspects of what they remember about a circus. At one time, Kohl brainstormed the circus theme with his first-graders, producing a map that looked like Figure 9–3.

From the map, groups studied the different aspects of the circus and then performed part of a class circus. Some classes may create a circus with students as performers, or perhaps train their own pets to do tricks, or dress up for a parade, or play music to accompany the performers; other classes may prefer to build a model circus with balancing toys and clowns, papier-mâché animals, and carts. The students' circus act can be performed for other classes or demonstrated in them. In brief, the possible curricular responses to a circus or other themes are varied.

FIGURE 9–3
Circus theme map

	Clowns	
People on stilts		Trapeze artists
Midgets	Circus	Beautiful costumes and parades
Trick animals		Elephants

Themes also lend themselves to the planning of interdisciplinary units at the secondary level in which teachers from several fields organize their courses around five or six common conceptual themes likely to evoke intellectual and emotional responses from students, such as those of "Women, Race, Social Protest" or "The Protestant Ethic and the Spirit of Capitalism." Students may answer a question such as "Is war ever justified?" from the perspectives of history, literature, and science.

Seventh and eighth grade teachers' integrated and interdisciplinary curricula are described by Hargraves (2000) who shows that teachers use three kinds of relevance through their planning—relevance to work, personal relationships, and social and political contexts. The descriptions illustrate how teachers make learning more applied, critical, inventive, and meaningful for students.

"Humanitas"

In the program "Humanitas," more than 267 Los Angeles secondary school teachers have formed individual school teams for the purpose of developing interdisciplinary units around central concepts and producing their own curricular materials. Typically, members of a team represent English, social studies, and art. Materials related to a theme come from a variety of sources—primary sources, novels, newspaper articles, plays, videos, and art exhibits. "Humanitas" teachers may use a final examination as a planning technique in order to identify significant issues to discuss, clarify their objectives, and guide their selection of materials and activities. The teams develop cooperatively early in the planning process an end-of-unit essay. This essay requires students to synthesize what they will be learning in all their "Humanitas" classes. The following is a typical essay question that serves as a basis for planning a unit on "Culture and Traditional Societies" taught in a ninth-grade class:

> The cosmology of a traditional culture permeates every aspect of that culture. This is illustrated in the following three culture groups: the Eskimo, the Southwest Indian, and the Meso-American. Specifically discuss the spirit world that each group believed in, and explain how it influenced their culture and values. Include examples from your reading in art history, literature, and social institutions to illustrate and substantiate your analysis. Finally, to what extent, if any, does the spirit world affect us today?

"Hudson River Valley"

Working solo, teachers can make their curriculum more interdisciplinary by realigning the subjects they are already teaching. For example, one teacher in Pelham Middle School in New York focused on a theme of great local importance, the Hudson River Valley. She encouraged students to examine maps of the valley (geography), to read about the valley's past (history), to read legends of the Hudson River (literature), and to write their own legends (writing). Students also studied the geometry of the river's bridges (math), examined the river's water purification (science), and became familiar with Hudson River artists. The culminating activity was a trip on the river and the preparation of essays on the relationships between the river and the people, in which students drew on everything they had learned in class.

"The Vietnam War"

Some teachers prefer to integrate the content of their course within a subject matter or academic discipline. For example, Meadows (1990) has developed a 4-week unit, "The Vietnam War," for high school social studies that relates geography, political science, ethics, history, and other social sciences. Meadows's unit begins with an introduction stating the reasons for the study. He points out the need for students to understand the history and culture of Vietnam, as well as the roots of U.S. involvement, so they can draw lessons from that war. He then presents the major goals, concepts, and student activities for the unit. An example of a goal is "that students will learn to think objectively and critically about conflict and its resolution in international relations." An example of a concept is "the geography of Vietnam has had a fundamental impact on its history and development." Examples of activities are these: role playing, group discussions, and written reports to foster critical thinking; readings, library research, guest speakers, and video presentations to inform students about the history and culture of Vietnam; map construction and readings to learn about geography and its role in Vietnamese history.

"The Vietnam War" unit also features a preliminary reaction guide for establishing baseline beliefs of the students, such as these:

- "Only when a nation is invaded does it have the right to go to war."

- "Even though some Americans may oppose war with another country, once war is declared, each person should give the government full support."

This unit also includes a study guide; semantic maps for major concepts; copies of historical documents; such as the Gulf of Tonkin Resolution; a bibliography; and a listing of art sources, drama, poetry, films/videos, documents, and community resources.

Designing Thematic Units

Four steps are involved in designing thematic units: (a) selecting a theme and generating subthemes, (b) selecting content, (c) planning learning opportunities, and (d) selecting resources.

Selecting a Theme and Generating Subthemes   Many teachers begin their design with a theme. There is an unlimited list of possible themes for a unit—phenomena, concepts, persons, events, places, or problems. Teachers often narrow their choice to a theme of local importance, one relevant to the concerns of students and with potential for illuminating content related to the teacher's educational goals. A teacher is unlikely to suggest a theme if relevant materials and human resources are not readily available. Although the teacher may propose a theme, students should be encouraged to suggest in turn their own questions and concerns as possible themes or at least participate in brainstorming to identify possible subthemes and questions to pursue.

Kohl's (1976) planning process shows how his own values, concerns for student interests, and sense of educational purpose influenced his selection of a theme and how brainstorming by children of that theme created subthemes worthy of study. The theme and subthemes organized as a map suggest materials and activities. The map generally groups ideas together, and ideas may be arranged in a variety of organizational patterns, such as hierarchy, sequence, cause and effect, problem solution. The language arts map suggested by the unit "Journeys," for example, lends itself to compare-and-contrast patterns (see Table 9–1). This pattern is useful in helping students differentiate the schemata in different literary genres (Walmsley & Walp, 1990).

Selecting Content   The selection of content or organizing elements—values, processes, concepts, skills, generalizations, and forms of perception—should reflect the teacher's educational goals. Often these goals and the content they imply are similar to those set by state and local policy boards and promulgated through curricular frameworks and official courses of study. Another source of content is found in the standards and other publications by professional organizations that represent the content fields. Teachers are asked to regard the content of these documents as representing the sinews or overarching ideas that are to be extended through the educational program—a formal curriculum rather than a cluster of topics.

In the "Journeys" unit, the teacher regarded the strategies for reading and writing in different genres as important curriculum content to be developed by learners throughout the unit. The notion of the writing process as prewriting, composing, revising, and editing was to be central in all activities related to the organizing centers or themes. Knowledge of reading as comprehending a complexity of literary styles and plots was also to be attained by students through the learning activities.

TABLE 9–1
Language arts map

Journeys				
Factual Journeys			*Fictional Journeys*	
Symbolic journeys (e.g., Smith's visit to USSR)	Children's own journeys Journeys to improve technology (e.g., shuttle)	Journeys that challenge—personal endurance, adventure Migration (e.g., birds, whales, butterflies)	Science fiction journey (e.g., *The Time Traveler*)	Imaginary journeys (e.g., *Alice in Wonderland*, *Wizard of Oz*) Realistic journey (e.g., Laura Ingalls Wilder stories)

Planning Learning Opportunities   Three general principles guide the planning of learning activities:

1. *There should be varied ways for students to engage in the content of the unit.* In addition to reading and writing, ideally the content would also be represented in visual and auditory mediums and expressed through movement and narration. The unit "Journeys" gave students opportunity to respond to a variety of types of literature and to express themselves in writing and discussing, and the verbal mode dominated. Other teachers using the principle of variation might have included activities in drama, music, dance, painting, film, and the like, in developing reading and writing; or have taken advantage of the wide choices in literature to help students find their connections to science, history, geography, and other subject areas.

2. *The activities should be within the range of possibility for the students, consistent with their present attainments and predispositions.* This principle, implying that students should have success in the activities, is met when teachers and peers provide the scaffolding (assistance, support, modeling) by which learners develop capacities for performing the activities independently. Also, the principle has a corollary: the activity should allow students to reach new levels of accomplishment.

3. *The activities should be satisfying to the learners.* Although learners differ in what they find satisfying, depending on age and prior experience, general features characterize satisfying activities, such as opportunities to make choices; to interact with significant others; to combine thinking, feeling, and acting; and to confront novel and puzzling situations or events that can be resolved through problem solving.

Selecting Resources   The map for a thematic unit suggests many of the resources that will be needed. The map for "Journeys" identified appropriate fictional and nonfictional selections. Books, literature, poetry, magazines, newspapers, articles, extracts from larger works, documents, diaries, and official records were included (and the absence of films, videos, and other sources has been previously noted).

Teachers may feel constraints in their selection of resources, both human and material. Many teachers have a traditional orientation that favors an idealistic philosophy, which holds that selection of resource persons, literature, art, and other cultural products be of recognized worth by a dominant class. Other teachers with a pragmatic philosophy are more open to including representation for popular and diverse cultures, seeking resources that are representative of the lives of real people and that make a difference in the lives of students. The broad, unexpected areas of learning that are opened by thematic units are likely to exceed any teacher's knowledge. Accordingly, adult (teachers, parents, community persons) and student resources should be sought. A great strength of the thematic unit is that it is likely to draw on many community materials, records, collections, and sites.

To visit some Web sites that are available to help teachers plan units, go to *www.prenhall.com/mcneil* and click on Unit Plans.

INQUIRY UNITS

Inquiry units can take the form of social projects in which students make a difference in the real world or in which they try to answer questions and problems that they themselves generate from classroom materials.

Foxfire Projects

More than 2,000 teachers following Foxfire principles are developing social projects of inquiry, as mentioned in chapter 5. The Foxfire network of teachers sprang from the experiences of a teacher whose students in English classes for more than 20 years examined the culture, traditions, and history of their Appalachian community and then documented and published what they found in issues of *Foxfire Magazine*. Among the Foxfire community's principles are those stating that students should solve real problems or create real products that the community values and applauds. If, for example, students research national and world issues such as change in climatic patterns, prejudice, or AIDS, students must "bring them home" by suggesting how their findings can help the community respond to general problems.

All the work that the Foxfire teachers and students do flows from student desire; students choose, design, revise, execute, reflect on, and evaluate their projects. Problems that arise during the project are solved by the class itself. Every student in the room is included and needed in the project, and all students are expected to operate on the edge of their confidence, not doing what they already know how to do. There must be an audience beyond the teacher for student work—another individual, small group, or the community. This audience, in turn, must affirm that the work is important, needed, and worth doing. Students indicate to the teacher the ways they will prove at the end of the project that they have mastered the objectives the project is designed to serve. They also say what they would like to know about the subject of inquiry and what they will be able to do at the end of the project that they cannot do at the beginning. Students are helped to monitor their own progress and develop their own remediation plans. Each student's progress is the concern of every student in the room.

Hands On, Foxfire's journal for teachers, carries accounts by teachers as they apply the principles. For example, Amy Rodger's second-grade class voted down her original suggestion for a project and instead decided to make a half-hour videotape about environmental pollution in the county. The finished tape included four short plays written and performed by students depicting environmental dangers in the community and possible ways of responding to the dangers, a song related to the topic, and interviews with community residents and managers of a local landfill. The tape won a state environmental award.

Barbara Lewis, a teacher in Jackson Elementary School in Salt Lake, has promoted social projects at her school and among teachers throughout the nation (Lewis, 1991). Sixth-grade students in her class discovered a hazardous waste site near their school. Students began their inquiry with the question "How can we find out whether our water supply is contaminated?" The students' initial efforts to answer the question by contacting the health department were fruitless, and their efforts to interest residents in the possible dangers of hazardous wastes brought only "I don't care" responses. Nevertheless, the students sought more information about hazardous waste sites that had exploded and created toxic clouds. They also visited the local site where they were told there were no problems. However, the children were unconvinced.

After further reading about hazardous wastes, the students invited an environmental specialists to their classroom. Armed with new information, the students formed a new solution, calling on a national environmental hotline to ask for help. They also wrote to the Environmental Protection Agency's regional office, called the local power company who owned the site, and asked TV, radio stations, and newspapers to cover the story. The students visited the mayor and secured his support. Under public pressure, personnel of the Environmental Protection Agency tested the site and found that harmful substances had polluted the soil and the groundwater, threatening over 477,000 people.

The students mailed letters to business and environmental groups, asking for donations for a cleanup. They raised about $2,700 for their contribution to the task. However, a state law impeded the use of funds for this purpose. So the stage was set for further inquiry and action. The new question became "How do we change the law?" After reading about the national Superfund, which is used for cleaning up abandoned toxic waste sites, the students wrote a resolution proposing a state Superfund. Legislators turned the resolution into a bill, and the students lobbied for it. They testified before a committee and spoke to the state senate. They also passed out flyers (trimmed in red crayon) to all the legislators. As the bill was passed, one lawmaker said, "No one has more effectively lobbied us than those young kids—and they didn't even have to buy us dinner."

"In Search of Our Mothers' Gardens"

As an inquiry unit in literature, a junior high English class sought answers to such questions as these:

- What is the state of mind that is most favorable to the act of creation?

- What are the circumstances that obstruct or silence that state of mind?

- Why have so many women (in history, literature, life) been silenced? (Donovan & Walsh, 1991).

The resulting unit, "Silence," drew on life stories. For example, students were awakened to the way culture constructed gender and silenced women as they read Virginia Woolf's *A Room of One's Own*. This text also helped students see the importance of each student's own life story and family story and indicated the service students could do by recording the memories of their own mothers and grandmothers, memories that otherwise might be lost.

In their reading of Carolyn Heilbron's *Writing a Woman's Life*, students learned how many women have been deprived of narratives by which they might have assumed control over their own lives by not inquiring about the lives of their parents and grandparents or in cases where elders were reluctant to reveal their past or were physically missing. Alice Walker's *In Search of Our Mother's Gardens* taught students what it meant for a black woman to be an artist in their great-grandmothers' time and how biography reclaims silences, allowing women of the past to continue their presence among us.

After reading these and other biographies, the students realized that they must become their mothers' and grandmothers' biographers. The writing of a biography of a female relative or friend became an independent project in the class. Students chose someone they could research through interviews, diaries, letters, photographs, scrapbooks, genealogies, and other records. First, they wrote a preliminary description of the person with a brief explanation of why they chose that person and the sources available. Then they completed an initial five- to seven-page biography, which was later rewritten using the course material to pattern their stories in manner of the exemplary pieces they had read. Finally, they composed a two- to three-page explanation of how the form and content of the course material influenced the revision.

One student wrote her mother's biography, a less tragic version of Ibsen's *Doll House*. Several students echoed Walker's sentences, "In search of my mother's garden, I found my own" and "Why hasn't the world realized that we can learn from them and in the process discover our own selves?" A representative comment is this: "I gained an incredible respect for and knowledge of my grandmother. Even though I believe it would be easier to write a fairy tale account of her life, I feel strongly about her silence and want her voice to be heard" (Donovan & Walsh, 1991, p. 39).

PROJECTS

Projects for both young and older learners offer opportunities for self-direction and personal involvement in learning, complementing formal instruction.

Projects for Younger Learners

The inquiries of young children are likely to touch on a range of subject matters. In their description of projects for children ages 4 to 8, Katz and Chard (1996) show how children investigate, record, and report their findings as they study real phenomena in their own environments. Projects are investigations, and the title of the project indicates the direction of effort ("How Are Houses Built?" or "Who Measures What Is in Our Town?"); these are unlike the titles of thematic units, which merely indicate subjects ("Houses" and "Measurement"). The question form helps young children in their planning, giving focus to their investigations.

In projects, children actively negotiate the questions to be answered, the experiments to be conducted, and other features of the effort. In the project "How Water Comes to Our House," children determine the data to be collected, such as where the water comes from; how it is treated, stored, and pumped to households; its uses; quantities used; its properties at different temperatures; and how the findings are to be reported. Children are encouraged to raise questions of personal interest and to take responsibility for the learning tasks.

Selecting an Issue or Topic   Suitable issues or topics for possible projects by young children are those that fill these criteria:

■ Topics are partially familiar so that all of the students will be able to generate questions, and some of the students will be able to serve as expert resource persons during the inquiry.

■ Topics provide opportunity for students to apply and develop a range of subject matter and basic skills—reading, writing, measuring, drawing, mapping, and making music.

■ They give opportunity for students to collaborate and cooperate through such activities as model building, construction, dramatic play, making posters and graphs, creating diagrams, developing questions, interviewing, recording, and tallying surveys.

■ They take advantage of local resources—sites, experts, and historical and currently critical events.

Planning and Conducting the Project   Projects are generally planned and conducted in three phases, after the teacher has selected the general issue or topic.

Phase 1: Getting started   The teacher encourages students to express their associations, knowledge and interest in the topic area. Children raise questions about the topic and begin to explore how these questions might be answered. They are encouraged to take the initiative in exploring the topic, finding resources, and suggesting activities.

Planning in this phase includes identifying the information needed and means for collecting it. Students also decide about an audience for their work (parents, other students, or others) and begin to accept responsibility for the different tasks related to the undertaking.

Phase 2: Collecting information   When the students know what information they want from different sources and how this information will help answer their central questions, they prepare interview questions, observation forms, and consider the use of cameras, videos, and other equipment for data collection. Although secondary sources (texts, films, articles, reference works) are consulted, primary sources (interviews, field trips, and other firsthand experiences) are more characteristic of the project. In the preparation of field trips, teacher responsibilities include adherence to school policy as well as clarifying the questions to be asked, people to be interviewed, observations to be made, and ways to record the data. Classroom rehearsal of the methodology is important.

After returning to the classroom, students discuss their findings. Conflicts in interpreting the data collected by different teams may require repeated visits to the site. As the work progresses, students give more attention to how they will present their findings to the intended audience.

Phase 3: Culminating the project   In the primary grades, dramatic play using what the students have constructed is a common culmination activity. Students assume roles associated with the setting they have studied. Older children often present the findings to an audience through publications, panel discussions, displays, demonstrations, and other public presentations.

The culmination is an opportunity for students to review their work and to indicate what they know and can do now that they didn't know when they started. Culminations are also beginnings in that students indicate how they will use what they have learned in some new area of inquiry. A good study is known for the questions it generates.

Instructional units and projects can be judged by the extent to which they satisfy selected criteria. Activity 9–1 encourages you to determine essential criteria.

Projects for Older Learners

Secondary school teachers think of projects as related to school subjects. Either they select a subject matter topic that is taught in the course and together with students create a project around a topic, or they start with an idea for a project and then see how the content of the course can be related to the project.

The projects involve students in taking appropriate action to improve, change, serve, or otherwise influence some public matter constructively. Students deal with real situations as opposed to imaginary or speculative ones and with issues that are significant to them.

In planning the project, teacher and students analyze what needs to be done, what can be done, and what the possible hurdles are. Students must be informed about the issues with which they propose to deal. In addition to general information from texts, essential information for a project is individualized in character. Usually students gain their information from local communities by consulting records, individuals, and organizations. When the students have worked out many of the details, they must get cooperation from school administrators and other adults with whom they may be working on the project. Steps to ensure community understanding are also a part of the planning process.

Students must be clear about the purpose of the project and weigh the difficulty of the concept and its likely demands on time and effort. There are variations

ACTIVITY 9–1   SELECTING CRITERIA FOR DESIGNING ACTIVITIES FOR INSTRUCTIONAL UNITS

Criteria are useful as heuristics. In making planning decisions in accordance with criteria, teachers take into account many more possibilities than when planning without stated criteria. The use of criteria will contribute to a more balanced and coherent curriculum plan. Whenever two or more people are to engage in curriculum planning and desire consistency in their plans, they should first agree on the criteria that will guide their efforts and then frequently check each other's work against these criteria.

What criteria would guide your curriculum development?

1. Rank the following criteria as essential, useful, less useful, not useful, or inappropriate. Select the *five* most essential criteria that you would want to guide the planning of activities by a group of teachers.
2. Compare the criteria you rank as essential with what significant others (administrators, fellow teachers, students) consider essential. Try to account for differences through a discussion that will clarify the meaning of the statements, reveal possible consequences from applying the criteria, and identify reasons for the different views regarding what is essential.

	Essential	Useful	Less Useful	Not Useful	Inappropriate
The activity should:					
1. Relate to large curriculum goals—critical thinking, problem solving, self-confidence, or other valued ability and dispositions.					
2. Put students in touch with a powerful idea or form of perception.					
3. Be scaffolded so that students are not confused or frustrated.					
4. Challenge students so they will extend their present status.					
5. Allow for individualism so that those with different backgrounds and levels of development can contribute and progress.					

(continued)

ACTIVITY 9–1 *continued*

	Essential	Useful	Less Useful	Not Useful	Inappropriate

6. Fit within existing constraints of time, space, resources, and student characteristics.

7. Provoke emotional and physical as well as intellectual responses.

8. Offer multiple perspectives on a topic, issue, or problem.

9. Help students make connections to what they are learning in other subject fields.

10. Contribute to the quality of life outside school (i.e., be real).

11. Contribute to multiple goals and outcomes.

12. Allow students to choose, design, revise, carry out, and evaluate the activity.

13. Offer students many ways to construct knowledge—through movement, manipulation, visuals— not just through text and number.

14. Conform to official mandates regarding the content to be taught.

15. Give students the opportunity to see how the activity fits within the bigger curriculum picture.

16. Draw on community resource people, sites, records, and other documents.

17. Integrate skills in larger natural tasks rather than in isolated skill exercises.

for scheduling projects—a fixed block of time (e.g., a 5-week project); a project in which the class devotes 1 hour a week over an extended period of time; or a "seminar in the round," in which students meet at a scheduled time to plan and review progress and to build connections between the project and their formal course work.

Some teachers prefer projects that draw on two subjects. For instance, in New Richmond, Wisconsin, a math teacher and a teacher of economics made it possible for students to conduct a study regarding a proposed community golf course. The study called for statistical application (math) and market research (economics). After the data were gathered and analyzed, the final products consisted of videotaped documented statements from community members and experts; these statements influenced the community's decision not to build the golf course (Beck et al., 1991). The ideal in curriculum integration is that students will advance in several subject areas.

THE PROBLEM-BASED APPROACH

Newer problem-based units reflect three curricular perspectives:

1. The *academic perspective* and its concern that an authentic view of the subject matter and its methods be represented
2. The *utilitarian perspective* that holds that the unit should be relevant to everyday life
3. The *student-centered perspective,* with its concern that the study trigger interests among students and prepare them for further learning

In contrast with the thematic approach, the problem-based approach focuses on the concrete by introducing the idea of a problem platform, a "physical" context. The teachers in one school selected a question related to a nearby drainage pond: "Why is life as it is in the pond?" Students used library sources to identify their *questions—not answers—*that might be fertile paths of investigation, coming up with these questions: "What is the effect of light on the pond?" "What nutrients control life on the pond?" "What are the relationships among different kinds of life in the pond?"

Once students chose their questions, their activities included observing and describing microscopic pond life; collecting samples and maintaining them in tanks in a lab; and initiating experiments and manipulating the tank's chemistry, light, and temperature. In so doing, students dealt with essential content of subject matter in support of their experiments (Eggebrecht, Dagenais, & Dosch, 1996).

The problem-based unit begins with an orientation showing the connection between a specific subject matter domain and the context of everyday life—how the knowledge is helpful in using technology, making a consumer decision, or understanding a social or scientific issue. This relationship is cast as a central question that sets the scene for the unit. This question also functions as the basis for selecting the content and skills that students study in the unit and gives rise to a variety of suitable student-generated activities.

The orientation is followed by direct teaching of basic information and skills necessary for pursuing the question. For example, in one science unit on weather change, the central questions were these:

■ Which factors determine the weather picture?

■ How do these factors influence weather change?

■ How can a reliable weather forecast be based on such information?

In this unit, students are first taught methods for measuring temperature, air pressure, humidity, wind velocity, and direction, and then they learn how to interpret single weather charts and satellite photographs (Lijnse, Kortland, Eijkelot, Van Genderen, & Hooymayers, 1990). In addition, to access common basic information, students work on different options in parallel groups. The essential information from all groups is required in subsequent phases of the unit. Hence, there is a reporting session for various groups to exchange ideas—for example, with one group reporting on clouds and cloud formation, another on precipitation, and another on fronts and high/low pressure areas.

After students have the basic information and skills and the learning that takes place in studying the optional parts, they are ready to pose their own questions related to the central questions, such as which method to use in forecasting, how to interpret forecasts, and what to expect from their reliability. In pursuing the answers to these questions, students engage in a variety of activities, some of which involve contacts with out-of-school sources. Although these activities allow for differences in interests, working styles, and capabilities, students are responsible for their own learning and for the learning of fellow students.

In trying to answer their own questions, students make and test their predictions (hypotheses), seek solutions for problems, test solutions, design their own procedures, and formulate new questions based on the outcomes. They also act as members of an academic community by discussing the assumptions underlying the activity and sharing predictions, procedures, and solutions. Problem-solving units encourage students to use their own backgrounds of experience in the activities, linking their views of the situation (and the world) to the views of a larger scientific community.

In brief, problem-based units have these characteristics:

1. Problem-based units begin with a real problem related to the student's world.
2. Working on a unit, students have the major responsibility for shaping and directing their own learning through inquiry that is organized by investigating in order to answer the students' driving question ("need to know").
3. Small collaborative teams address their own questions, but later teams synthesize their findings as they create a culminating solution, product, or performance.

Activity 9–2 calls for a mental rehearsal for a problem-based unit.

ACTIVITY 9–2   SELECTING A PROBLEM FOR A UNIT

Consider a problem close to you or your students. Imagine some of the questions students might think they need to know before the problem could be addressed, such as, "What do we know?" and "What do we need to know?" Then think of how students might find answers to their questions (e.g., using experts, library resources, experiments, data collection).

LEARNER-GENERATED UNITS

In view of current dissatisfaction with elementary science programs that rely on textbooks, it may be that in the future, science units will follow students' efforts to make sense of particular phenomena. For example, Henriques (1990) has given a glimpse of a future science curriculum, which is not unlike Meriam's old activity curriculum described in chapter 3. She is not interested in presenting on encyclopedic recitation of scientific facts, or in giving out well-organized information, or in having students carry out guided experiments to confirm present conclusions. Instead, her unit encourages students to find problems, make hypotheses, and carry out their own experiments. The goal of the unit is construction of knowledge by students.

The teacher has three things to do in Henriques's curriculum:

1. *Assemble a wide variety of objects that might be related to a theme.*   Possible physical science themes are "Water," "Weight," "Mixing and Mixtures," and "Motion." The objects assembled for the unit "Mixing and Mixtures" might include liquids (water, oil, vinegar, methylated spirits), powders (flour, sugar, salt, sodium bicarbonate, dyes), and grains (lentils, wheat, etc.). In addition, newspaper, waxed paper, rags, cottonwood, straws, plastic spoons, and immersion coils for heating water might be provided.

2. *Observe students as they freely interact with the material.*   The teacher makes notes of the problems students encounter as they attempt to do things with the material. The teacher also interviews children during the free-activity sessions, asking, "What are you doing?" "Can you explain that to me again?" or "Tell me more." The teacher refrains from giving information and explanations. Students' responses are analyzed to reveal the mental activity in which they a engaging.

3. *Conduct synthesis sessions with students in which they focus on problems encountered in the free sessions.*   In the synthesis sessions, students discuss difficulties, confront points of view, question assertions, and propose other activities. New experiments may be designed by the whole class and entrusted to one or two groups to carry out.

In interpreting the student's activity during both the free spontaneous sessions and the synthesis sessions, the teacher identifies the following:

- Activities in which the student focuses on acting on objects, trying to get a certain result and trying to understand how something works

- Activities through which the student seeks to single out the factors that have contributed to a particular result, considering steps taken and the role different objects played in getting the results

- Activities that are experimental in which the student wants to reproduce a result, planning a sequence of logical steps for an experiment that will support an assertion that the child believes to be true

Learner-generated curriculum casts the teacher as facilitator whose function is to keep students on a stable course pursuing their own discoveries. Consider, for example, a kindergarten project on shoes (Katz & Chard, 2000). The goals for the project were set by the teacher but developed over time through the children's interests. Unlike planning where a goal and objectives drive the planners, goals emerged after the project was under way.

The project began as a result of discussion of new shoes worn by some of the children. Students asked numerous questions about shoes and shoes in everyday life, which the teacher as facilitator or listed. Special interests were identified, such as responsibilities of the salesperson and how shoes are displayed. A trip to a store was followed by the students' developing their own shoe store in the classroom. It was the students rather than the teacher who chose the direction, set the goals, and determined efforts. Such a project can be regarded as the foundation for the development of practical, aesthetic, historical and scientific ways of thinking and learning.

In the past, criticisms were directed toward child-centered curriculum— "Teacher, do we have to do what we want to do again today?" As indicated in chapter 1, in planning constructivist curriculum, four interests are reconciled:

1. Teacher and students' preferences (questions and answers are meaningful to students)
2. Institutional (the curriculum supports the school's legitimacy)
3. Professional (the curriculum requires original thinking, interpretations and allows for the social construction of knowledge thorough small groups and whole-class discussion.)
4. Critical (students, teacher, and others regularly judge their work against criteria jointly developed)

As facilitators, teachers have responsibility for eliciting student ideas—probing, interviewing, concept mapping and designing semistructured activities that allow students to incorporate their own experiences and backgrounds. Furthermore, they must negotiate with students regarding the inquiry, questions, activities, and methods that will lead to learning.

Activity 9–3 is a guide to preparing an instructional unit that can serve as evidence of a curriculum competency. The resulting document can be part of a teacher's professional portfolio and a basis for classroom instruction.

ACTIVITY 9–3   CONSTRUCTING AN INSTRUCTIONAL UNIT AS A DOCUMENT

As you know, there is not a single procedure for designing units of instruction. Some teachers begin by thinking about the intended learners, content, and time frame, others won't decide about the unit until they meet their students. Traditional teachers commence with purposes and objectives. In this activity, you may follow any approach. Prior activities and illustrations and guidelines found in the chapter have suggested different types of units and techniques for designing them.

This activity is an opportunity to organize your plan as a document that can be presented to others. The format suggested is a common one. However, feel free to modify the form to suit your own purposes. Your unit may be a thematic, subject matter, inquiry, problem-based, or learner-generated type.

1. Give a title to the unit.
2. Make a statement identifying those for whom the unit is designed.
3. Present a rationale or justification for this unit. How might the unit enrich the lives of the students? How might it contribute to educational goals and values? Does the unit fit into the overall curriculum?
4. State possible outcomes from this plan.
5. Indicate the content in the unit. What are the overarching ideas, generalizations, central questions, concepts, processes, skills, perspectives, or other values that student might attain or construct through this unit?
6. Illustrate the nature of learning activities within the unit:
   a. Describe the introductory activities that motivate and set the stage for initial inquiry. Indicate the degree of students' choice and ways for activating background knowledge.
   b. Describe or illustrate implementing activities: getting students to ask "need to know questions" and providing ways for students to collect and analyze information related to their questions and the "central questions" of the unit. You may wish to state the criteria that might be used in planning learning activities or the principles that underlie your teaching strategies.

(continued)

ACTIVITY 9–3 *continued*

7. Indicate possible resources for the unit. Include both primary sources (local resource persons, sites, materials) and secondary sources (texts, references).
8. Indicate the ways you and your students might evaluate the unit, including ways to collect evidence related to both intended and unintended outcomes—observations, self-reports, products, presentations to audiences.

SUMMARY

Units of instruction differ in their flexibility. Some are fixed in purpose; others are designed to promote multiple outcomes. Thematic units have a broad focus that allows student participation in organizing subthemes and alternate routes to common ends. Subject matter units typically focus on prespecified topics, and the logic of the subject matter determines the organizational plan. Inquiry units have a central question or problem but invite students to generate and pursue related tasks and subquestions, individually and in groups. In problem-based units, students address problems in their everyday world using academic subject matter. Learner-generated units grasp the "teachable moment" and are more spontaneous in their design. Illustrations of each type of unit have been presented.

Unit planning rests on the distinction between the focal point or organizing center of the unit (theme, topic, problem, or central question) and the content or organizing elements (ideas, values, skills, concepts, perspectives, etc.) likely to be constructed by learners as they pursue the focus of their study. Teachers and students have wide latitude in what to propose as an organizing center and in choices for activities related to the center. Although the center or focus may be significant in its own right, it is chiefly a vehicle for engaging students in activities that will elicit content consistent with educational goals. The fact that there are widely diverse ways to help students create socially desired knowledge and preferences supports the practice of selecting foci and activities that respond to school community, student, and teacher interests.

Although a recognized format exists for public presentation of the unit as a document, the process for creating the unit need not occur in any particular order. Resources, content, purpose, centers, activities, and the like, are important design factors that are used when planning and implementing units. Guidelines for making decisions about these factors were presented, and different approaches to the planning of units were illustrated. Variation in the procedures and the principles applied is accounted for by both the types of units and the value orientation of the teachers.

In considering units which integrate subject matters, we recognized the importance of trying to extend students' knowledge in several subjects rather than exploiting one field in the interest of another. Throughout the chapter, an emphasis was placed on the autonomy of the teacher and students in curriculum development without ignoring the problematic issue of the establishment of an appropriate relationship between the knowledge students construct through their experiences with an instructional unit and the official course of study or professional standards in a subject area.

QUESTIONS FOR DISCUSSION

1. Should knowledge constructed by students always conform to what the state or district prescribed, or should the students challenge these prescriptions? What is your position on this issue?
2. It is sometimes charged that instructional units tend to center on current and local interests and thus are tainted by "presentism" and "localism." How can immediate concern go beyond to the development of multiple perspectives and interest in other times and other places?
3. Children can learn mathematical measurement by engaging in the performing arts, building sets, plotting the path of a turtle using Logo software, and many other ways. Educational goals in other areas can also be attained through varied experiences. What is the significance of this finding for teachers and policymakers?
4. The explosion of knowledge and the growing heterogeneity with the academic disciplines makes it difficult to identify essential content for organizational elements. Should we abandon the idea of curriculum coherence across units and courses?
5. What would you say to a teacher whose instructional unit plan is based on the idea that the curriculum should provide a break from everyday experience rather than build on it?
6. If curriculum is grounded in the events that students and teachers jointly construct in the classroom, then how can preplanning of units be anything more than setting the stage for learning?
7. Which of the following metaphors best describes you as a unit planner?
   a. An explorer who searches with others to determine new places and routes
   b. An architect who wants to build an edifice of knowledge
   c. Something else
8. As students participate in planning and implementing a unit, should they also participate in discourse about the nature and purpose of education? Give your reasons.
9. What are the advantages and disadvantages of projects where students deal with real situations in the school or community as opposed to projects that treat imaginary or speculative situations?
10. How can a teacher best deal with student-initiated questions and activities that require an expertise the teacher does not have?

REFERENCES

Beck, R. H., et al. (1991). Vocational and academic teachers work together. *Educational Leadership, 49*(2), 24–31.

Donovan, M. A., & Walsh, M. (1991). In search of our mother's garden we found our own. *English Journal, 80*(4), 38–43.

Eggebrecht, J., Dagenais, R., & Dosch, D. (1996, May), How can a sustainable habitat be created? *Educational Leadership, 53*(8) (Reconnecting the Sciences issue), 410.

Hargraves, A. (Ed.). (2000). *Learning to change: Teaching beyond subject and standards*. New York: Jossey-Bass.

Henriques, A. (1990). Experiments in teaching. In E. Duckworth, J. Easley, D. Hawkins, & A. Henriques (Eds.), *Science education: A mind's on approach for elementary years* (pp. 141–186). Hillsdale, NJ: Erlbaum.

Katz, L. G., & Chard, S. C. (1996). The project approach. In J. E. Johnson (Ed.), *Approach to early childhood education* (2nd ed., pp. 30–43). New York: Macmillan.

Kohl, H. (1976). *On teaching*. New York: Schoeken.

Lewis, B. A. (1991). *The kids' guide to social action*. Minneapolis, MN: Free Spirit.

Lijnse, P. L., Kortland, K., Eijkelot, H. M. C., Van Genderen, D., & Hooymayers, H. P. (1990). A thematic physics curriculum: A balance between contradictory curricular forces. *Science Education, 94*(1), 95–103.

Meadows, D. (1990). *The Vietnam War: A four week instructional unit*. St. Louis: University of Missouri Press.

Walmsley, S. A., & Walp, T. T. (1990). Interpreting literature and composing in the language arts curriculum, philosophy and practice. *Elementary School Journal, 90*(3), 251–274.

CHAPTER 10

ASSESSMENT IN THE CONTEXT OF CONSTRUCTIVISM

Sara: I present concepts clearly and clarify if necessary. I give tests so that students can practice what I have taught. If kids aren't successful, it means they aren't doing their part or are just not cut out of the right stuff.

Merl: Have you thought about having your kids listen to one another and work collaboratively as they learn concepts, or having individual students explain the concepts to you and the others revealing their understanding and confusion?

Assessment in the constructivist classrooms has for its primary purpose student learning—focusing on what students say, do, think, and feel as they attempt to make sense of the world around them and try to achieve their goals. The key problem for the teacher is not only how to elicit student predispositions, concepts, strategies, ways of writing, attitudes, and the like, but how to interpret what is observed and how best to respond.

Indeed, teachers spend nearly 30% of their time on assessment-related activities, and teachers' judgments are better than judgments formed on the basis of standardized tests (Webb, 1992). As the strongest assets of the educational system, teachers have far-reaching knowledge of the ideas likely to surface in class; they use their informal assessments to direct the activities of learners, to reallocate time to a topic or question, to recognize patterns in idiosyncratic thinking, and to challenge students and students' interpretations. Teachers with a constructivist persuasion regard assessments as revealing the learner. Hence, they give increased opportunities for learners to experience intellectual problems, to voice perplexities, to give personal interpretations, and to explore their thinking. Constructivist teachers want students to consider whatever is to be learned from their own perspectives and to relate the new knowledge to their daily lives.

In this chapter, assessments in the constructivist context and the emphasis on finding out what learners know is contrasted with traditional assessment and its interest in finding out what students don't know. (Standardized test makers throw out all well learned test items in their effort to spread students out along a "normal" curve.) Readers might begin this chapter by giving thought to the discussion questions at the end as a way to explore the issue of assessment for the purpose of control versus assessment for the purpose of learning.

The National Research Council's Committee on the Foundations of Assessment (2001) has called for an overhaul of testing, asking that states and districts sample a broader range of competence and understanding by using a variety of techniques or multiple measures of student performance. The committee is pushing more coordinated systems of assessment, including alternative measures, such as portfolios and tasks that students complete during ongoing classroom instruction and moving from high-stakes large-scale exams. Most tests were faulted by the committee for being mired in the past and reflecting earlier theories of learning characterized as the step by step accumulation of facts, procedures, and definitions, providing very limited information that teachers can use to identify why students do not perform well or how teachers can better modify their teaching. New assessments probe how students reflect on their own thinking (metacognition) and examine the strategies that students use to solve problems.

It is true, however, that the public doesn't realize the weaknesses of standardized testing:

■ Inadequate measures of what is learned (limited sampling of content)

■ Poor assessment of the student's depth of knowledge (no allowance for multiple ways to represent one's knowledge)

■ Invalidity (inferences based on test results are not justified)

■ Unreliability (insufficient evidence that the results are reproducible on different occasions and with different questions)

TRADITIONAL VERSUS ALTERNATIVE OR AUTHENTIC ASSESSMENTS

Basic to the discussion are three orientations to assessment, each reflecting a different view of learning:

1. *The technical*—a positivist orientation found in standardized testing and in many classroom exams. This orientation is tied to the transmission theory of learning and the assessing of the student's ability to reproduce and apply particular knowledge and information.
2. *The interpretive*—aims at understanding the student's point of view through the use of such devices as portfolios, concept mapping, and interviews. This orientation helps the student reconcile perturbations brought about by conflicts between the student's present thinking and new curriculum experiences, concepts, and world-views.
3. *The critical social constructivist*—assesses students in collaborative group activities in which students observe how others reason and get feedback on their own efforts, taking into account social and contextual factors of learning. In the process, students dimystify the status of knowledge (how knowledge is developed) and the factors that influence practice.

In an article describing the invalidity of traditional standardized tests for measuring mathematics achievement, Stake (1997) tells how standardized tests indicate very little about how much mathematics a student knows and how such tests do not identify the structure of children's thinking. Standardized test scores are of little diagnostic value and contribute little to redirected teaching, although they cause some teachers to attend to the most elementary knowledge and skills at the expense of fostering deep understanding on the part of the students of even a few topics. Traditional standardized tests function to sort individuals, schools, and school systems and are used to control or coerce students into reproducing particular information and knowledge.

Traditional tests are used to show which students are better than others on the types of items included in the test. Traditional tests are not, however, a sound basis for determining who is mastering a particular subject matter. Test content is always too narrow and decontextualized. Just as a few books on a subject do not represent all books on a subject, thirty or fewer test items don't represent a field of study. A recent international test showing that 42% of U.S. students could not answer why spike heels could cause more damage to floors than ordinary heels (the answer is that more energy is concentrated in a smaller area) was used to lament the lack of scientific knowledge of U.S. students.

Alternative or authentic assessment derives from the belief that assessment should be embedded in classroom work and aligned with classroom methods. For example, group assessment should be used where group problem solving is the norm. Also, alternative assessment encourages the use of a variety of methods so that a richer impression of what students think, believe, and know is shown than that obtained by any single method alone.

Authentic assessment emphasizes (a) assessing complex performance (e.g., reading for the purpose of answering research questions, writing to build knowledge and to influence real audiences, exploring mathematical ideas); and (b) connecting assessment with teaching and learning, with opportunities for students to show understanding of concepts in rich and varied contexts.

Companion
Website

Do you have questions about assessment?

- Assessment in other countries
- How to link local assessment with local standards
- Assessment of creativity
- Validity or nonvalidity of high-stakes tests
- Curriculum-embedded tests

To visit the Center for Research on Evaluation Standards and Student Testing (CRESST), go to *www.prenhall.com/mcneil* and click on the CRESST link.

CHANGES IN ASSESSMENT OF READING COMPREHENSION

Assessment in reading comprehension is becoming less test centered and more student centered with emphasis on observation, use of portfolios, self-assessment or self-reporting, retelling, and free responses. Table 10–1 indicates some of the differences in traditional and modern assessment.

Observations

In the traditional classroom, passive students don't do enough in reading to provide the teachers with something to see. However, if students are constantly producing and receiving discourse, and if the teacher is free to circulate and observe small groups discussing and responding to reading, observational evaluation is possible. Small-group discussions, writing responses to literature, and teacher conferencing give teachers opportunities to observe student progress in reading. Table 10–2 illustrates an evaluation of a student, based on selected dimensions of reading.

Observation of literacy for self-actualization is found in the use of checklists that comprise items such as the following: enjoys reading; shares books; has a reading preference; reads outside school; reads for own purposes; recommends books; learns from books; seeks books outside of class; expresses what has astonished, exhilarated, or dismayed in reading. Of course, discussions, dramatizations, and writings related to the work also provide opportunities for the teacher to observe reading comprehension.

An example of assessing reading comprehension in the content areas is found in the Academic Literacy Course, an alternative to basic skills reading instruction (Greenleaf, Schroenbach, Cziko, & Muefther, 2000). In this course, teachers in the subject fields make the discipline-based reading process visible and help students gain insight into their own reading process by collaborative inquiry about their subject area texts. Table 10–3 includes the dimensions of information sought during instruction.

In the Academic Literacy Course, students converse about what constitutes reading in given subject matters and how they are going about it. Assessment is based on information drawn from discussions, small-group conversations, private written reflections, and logs and letters to the teacher. There is reciprocal

TABLE 10–1 Traditional versus newer assessments of reading comprehension	Old Tests	New Assessments
	Single right answer	Many acceptable answers
	Short passage out of context	Authentic selections
	Discrete subskills of comprehension	Metacognitive strategies
	Literal and limited-inferential questions	Text-implicit and application questions
	No allowance for prior knowledge or purpose for reading	Prior knowledge and purpose for reading are considered in reader's response
	Assess recall of text	Assess learning from text and reading to perform a task

TABLE 10–2 Reading evaluation of a middle-grade student

Criteria	Mary Jones
Valuing	
Aspects prized; how student uses text	Attends mostly to characters, not themes; uses books chiefly for recreational purposes or escape
Critical Thinking	
Questions assumptions and logical inconsistencies; suggests alternative strategies to those presented	Never questions author's statements
Sharing	
Recommends material to others; relates favorite parts; seeks clarification of the text	Initiates conversation with friends about the book
Taking Action	
Seeks other readings on same topic or by same author; writes author; prepares a review for the library or newspaper	No action taken; not interested in dramatizing a scene from the book

teaching in which students learn strategies of questioning, summarizing, clarifying and predicting in varied texts. Moreover, students assess these strategies for themselves as readers.

TABLE 10–3 Dimensions to be evaluated in studying the reading process in content areas

Social	Personal
Investigate relations between literacy and power.	Identify self as a reader.
	Develop reading fluency.
Share book talk.	Develop confidence as a reader.
Discuss reading process, problems, and solutions.	Assess own performance.
	Set goals.
Appreciate different ways of reading.	
Find the classroom "safe"— a place where "it's cool to be confused."	

Cognitive	Knowledge
Get the big picture.	Build schemata.
Break down the big pictures.	Develop content knowledge.
Set purposes for reading.	Develop knowledge of structures in different subject areas.
Adjust process to purpose.	Develop subject-matter knowledge.
Use strategies to enhance comprehension.	

Portfolios

The portfolio contains elaboration of students' work, the "artifacts" of their literacy and learning. The portfolio is increasingly regarded as a valid method for evaluation. In this approach, there is an actual collection of items such as writing samples, observational notes made by the teacher, results of comprehension checks, the student's self-evaluations, and progress notes collaboratively prepared by the student and teacher.

Evidence may be collected independently or collaboratively by the student and teacher (e.g., a student may choose to submit a letter to an author of a favorite book, a semantic map completed before and after reading, a reading log). Of course, the portfolio is easily accessible to both student and teacher and may be used by parents and others.

The range of items is extensive, including written responses to reading, reading logs, writing at various stages of completion, and audio- or videotapes. Teacher and student must be selective about what to look for when evaluating the items to include in a portfolio. For example, will the portfolio be used to assess progress in critical reading, development of interest and desire to read, improvement in summarization strategies, ability to learn from expository material, or skills in using texts to carry out a task? The portfolio can be organized into two layers: (a) the actual evidence and (b) a summary sheet, to facilitate instructional decisions and communication with students and others.

The teacher and student periodically discuss what the items collected reveal about the student's progress in reading comprehension and the next steps to take. At the end of the year, they decide together which pieces will remain in the portfolio for next year and which pieces are ready for the student to take home.

Self-Reporting

Self-reporting is useful in determining both processes of learning and what is learned. Students are better learners when they are able to describe what goes on in their heads when they read. When asked, they can tell where they are in the sequence of reading a book. They can state their purposes for reading and describe the information needed and their plans for getting it. Assessment doesn't focus on how many correct answers students have but on how they behave when they don't know. It also includes noting whether the student is using the strategies of making predictions, seeking clarification, self-questioning, and summarizing in one's own words.

For assessing of depth of comprehension, it is better to ask questions that require linking text relationships that are not explicitly stated rather than to ask questions that demand only recall. Questions that call for inferencing can be asked both during reading (narrow focus) and after reading (wide generalizations). Often the meanings that students construct from a text are more powerful and individual than the test questions aimed at getting a common response. For example, junior high students in 60 classrooms were asked two questions after reading an assignment in social studies: (a) "What did you read that you should remember for a test?" versus (b) "What did you learn that is so important you want to remember it always?" The first question gets at what students think the teacher expects; the second taps meanings that students have created for themselves. Responses to the first question usually consist of specific factual information— answers for questions in trivia contests, such as "Jefferson purchased Louisiana." In contrast, in response to the second question, most students identify generalizations such as "Countries should not find war as an answer to their problems," and the responses are unique to the learner. It is important to note, however, that the results indicate that although students repeatedly face questions of a detailed factual value, they nevertheless concurrently generate significant personal meanings from their reading assignments.

Current emphasis on achievement tests has minimized teacher assessment of the meanings that students generate from their reading. Activity 10–1 can help overcome this dysfunctional consequence of testing and provide valid data about students' ability to comprehend.

■ ─── ■

ACTIVITY 10–1   COMPREHENSION OF ECOLOGICALLY VALID MATERIAL

Many students are labeled poor comprehenders on the basis of their performance on standardized tests of reading comprehension. Although these tests show a high reliability, this reliability comes through following dubious practices. To gain sufficient samples of test structure, content, and difficulty, the test makers offer short selections. Information tested for short selections is usually trivial. Also, to hold context constant across examinees, test makers unfairly discriminate among students on the kind of background knowledge required for making sense out of the selections. In many cases, test items lack ecological validity, which means that the content does not relate to what students experience in their lives in the home, school, and community.

Do the following steps to try to get a better picture of an individual student's ability to comprehend text.

Preparation

1. Consider a student known to you who has been categorized on the basis of a standardized test as a poor reading comprehender. Ask that student to bring a favorite text (book, magazine, almanac) that he or she finds interesting or useful.
2. Read the text; characterize the material as high, middle, or low difficulty; and ask the student to read parts or all of the material.

(continued)

ACTIVITY 10–1 *continued*

Administration of Assessment

Then administer the following assessment:

1. Ask the student, without using the text, to retell, either orally (if student doesn't write well) or in writing, what was read (if material is narrative) or to prepare a summary (if the material is expository).
2. Specify how you will evaluate the retelling or the summary. (If narrative, does the reader include key elements—characters, goals, setting? If expository, what main ideas are present/absent? Are supporting details related to main ideas?)

Interpretation

1. Interpret the results by asking these questions:
   a. Does the learner comprehend better than the test scores would predict? Why?
   b. Does motivation to read, match of topic with personal background, familiarity with material, or some other reason account for the differences?
   c. What do you now believe about the learner's ability to comprehend?
   d. What do the results suggest about what to teach this learner?

Retelling and Responding

Student retelling of stories and giving summaries of what they have read are good ways to gain a picture of what students think is important in their reading. In addition to retelling and summarizing text, other forms for eliciting reader response are open-ended responses, interviews, and "think-alouds." All these types of responses can reveal important aspects of a reader's comprehension: level of engagement, conception of literary characters, integration of text with personal experience, problem solving, interpretation, and explanations of text. Indeed, students may begin with responses relating to their personal engagement and conception of characters, which in turn lead to responses involving integration, interpretation, and judgment.

Numerous categories are used to interpret the reader's responses: inhibition, stock responses, critique; information driven, story driven; normalizing, generalizing; text invoked, reader involved; engagement, disengagement; event oriented, theme oriented; unreflective, reflective on the significance of events and behaviors; and reviewing the text as the author's creation, as well as defining both one's own ideology and the author's. A response to a literature checklist might be used to note whether the student's response focuses on characters, setting, problem, events, solution, theme, application, or personal response. The teacher's goal is not to deny the integrity of each student's response but to broaden the range of each reader's responses.

Figure 10–1 illustrates retelling of the story "The Lion and the Mouse" by a first-grader and a second-grader. The second-grader's response shows a level of

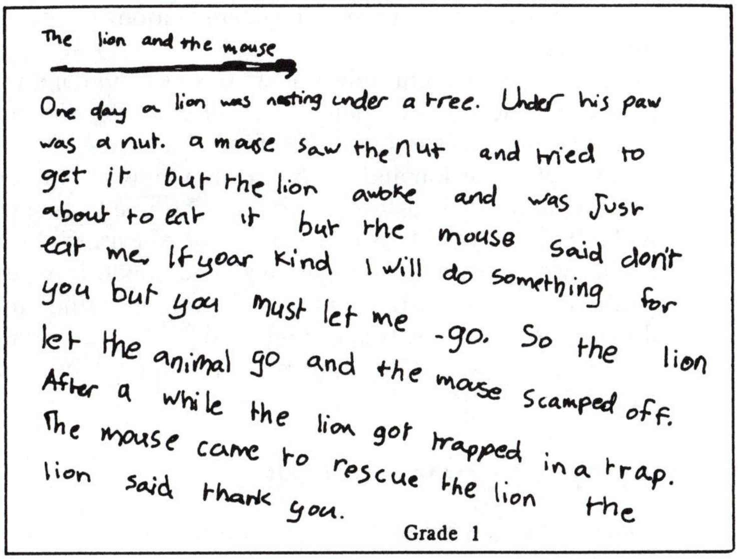

The lion and the mouse

One day a lion was nesting under a tree. Under his paw was a nut. a mouse saw the nut and tried to get it but the lion awoke and was Just about to eat it but the mouse said don't eat me. If your kind I will do something for you but you must let me -go. So the lion let the animal go and the mouse scamped off. After a while the lion got trapped in a trap. The mouse came to rescue the lion the lion said thank you.

Grade 1

The Lion and the Mouse

There once was a Lion awoken by a Mouse. The Lion was just about to reach out his Paw when the mouse said Don't Do That I will Do anything to rePay you back and one Day he did. The lion got cought in a trap and he to mouse heard him and the roar and ran to him and nibbled one rope after another and the Lion was free.

Grade 2

FIGURE 10–1
Samples of student story retellings of "The Lion and the Mouse"

Source: Deakin University Open Campus Program, ECT 401 *Classroom Processes: Task, Pupil, and Teacher*, 1981, pp. 50–53. Copyright © Deakin University, Victoria, Australia. Reprinted by permission.

comprehension that can lead to generalizations about the importance of returning favors.

To learn more about how readers process and comprehend tests, teachers are recommended to ask students to recall what they have read and then interpret the recall protocols in light of both what is in the text and what students recall. Patterns of distortion and omissions may indicate the influence of reader background knowledge. Instead of relying on formal tests of comprehension, teachers will learn more about the comprehension of learners by examining what they do when reading, what they experience, and how this experience is affected by the particular reading assignment. It is important to find out what kinds of meaning different readers construct as they read, and observe what they do with a diversity of materials in many different situations—while reading, prior to reading, and subsequent to reading.

ASSESSING STUDENT COMPOSITIONS

As with other aspects of the humanities, literary writing should not be subject to mechanical evaluation, emphasizing correct responses. Instead, there is need for judgment, incisive criticism, seeing things in context, and allowance for individual responses.

The constructivist teacher is less interested in marking a student's composition by circling all surface errors with red ink or ranking students in their compositions than in having students develop the criteria to use for evaluating their own writing. In her assessment of student writing, Jenkins (1996) emphasizes portfolios as a way to show how students' writing changes and how students develop control of different genres over time. The collaborative portfolio is an especially good way to help children with their writing.

Writing should not be merely to satisfy external demands but to meet personal needs. However, the teaching of composition is more likely to be successful if it allows students to interact with one another about some particular aspect of writing.

For example, to help students learn to write about a personal experience, the teacher might structure, for special attention, topics such as setting and people, developing and resolving conflict, and using dialogue. Students might be asked to write as specifically as possible about faces in a photograph, and they then meet in small groups to share their pictures and what they have written, determining some criteria to apply to their writing before revising it. Or students might pantomime a situation, and the audience then writes several sentences capturing the details of body movements, expressions, and other characteristics of the pantomimers. Students then read what they have written, with peers reinforcing the strongest details. Other activities might consist of writing out dialogues or an extended paper about a personal experience, including brainstorming for ideas, preparing several drafts, trying out each draft, and revising in the light of feedback. Students might discuss samples of their writing and apply particular criteria to them. Then they might apply the same criteria to other pieces of writing, not just judging a piece but generating ideas about how to improve it. Using a promising strategy, students might examine model compositions in small groups with the aid of guided questions and then present their findings in whole-class discussions. The models of writing will be useful not only in helping students evaluate texts but in generating their own texts. Successful revision requires that the criteria be brought to bear on the product to be revised. In all instances, standard usage and typographical conventions are taught in the context of real writing problems.

Teachers expand on their assessments of student writing by sharing their own approach to problems such as relating plot to dialogue and helping students develop characters by asking such questions as "How do your characters stand? What do they carry in their pocket or purse? What happens to their faces and to their positions when they are thinking, bored, or afraid?" (Lamott, 1994).

Rubrics

To clarify what constitutes quality work, students and teachers may develop a rubric or criteria they will use in judging a finished product or project. In addition to clarifying the nature of a contemplated task, rubrics are useful in giving information about how to improve. Learning is enhanced as students discuss what is meant by the different criteria such as often found in conventional rubrics for writing—word choice, organization, and sentence fluency. Activity 10–2 illustrates the importance of criteria in making judgments and the need for additional specifications for general criteria.

The political nature of rubrics should not be overlooked. Consider the following criteria for critical writing:

1. Disrupts the common framework for making sense of the world and ourselves
2. Includes voices usually silenced
3. Includes voices that contradict one another
4. Challenges some stereotypes
5. Confronts one's own prejudices

See Activity 10–3 for additional tips on constructing rubrics.

ACTIVITY 10–2   RECOGNIZING VARIABILITY
IN CRITERIA FOR EVALUATING WRITING

Select two writing samples from a student, and give the samples to four or more readers independently to critique and to assign a letter grade. Compare grades and account for any differences in evaluation results. The four reviewers might then construct a rubric, listing criteria and suggestions that would be most helpful to the students in developing their writing.

■ ── ■

ACTIVITY 10–3   CONSTRUCTING A RUBRIC

Usually, a teacher's time is too valuable to spend on constructing rubrics and portfolios independently of teaching. The real value is the learning that takes place as teacher and students collaborate in developing criteria for evaluating classroom activity.

If you have access to students or if you and your peers would like to experience collaborative rubric construction, select a task such as writing a particular kind of essay, and then attempt to develop a rubric to use in connection with the task. Many ways to proceed are possible:

• Review standards for writing given by external sources.
• Gather sample rubrics that can be adapted.
• Gather samples of writing that illustrates a range of quality.
• Discuss characteristics of work that distinguish good from poor examples.
• Write descriptions for the implied characteristics.

■ ── ■

Using Writing to Assess Understanding in the Content Fields

Because writing is a way to learn, student writing reveals what students are learning—their successes and their difficulties.

In writing about science, students learn the vocabulary, thought processes, and genres necessary for understanding science. Consider that as children write about science, they process the ideas of science, they use the language of science, they learn to think in science, and they prepare themselves to understand their reading of science.

Similarly, in math classes, writing can help students reveal their thinking. During a unit on computation and one on geometry, fifth-grade students completed three types of writing for an uninformed third party. Figure 10–2 illustrates three types of writing for helping students learn and read and understand geometry. It also shows how writing can be used in self-evaluation and for identifying progress in student thinking about concepts in mathematics.

Students' writings and drawings give teachers opportunity to determine the quality of student reasoning about problems. Asking individual students or students in groups to find alternative solutions will reveal much about their thinking and permit assessment of their problem-solving strategies and flexibility. Also, it is useful to see how they would explain their strategies to other students.

ASSSESSMENT IN THE COMMUNITY OF LEARNERS

Assessment and guidance in learning communities depend on establishing a community of discourse where students generate their own questions, assess what they know, and determine what they need to know, engaging in peer assessment and peer teaching. All students are led into new work and unfamiliar

First, students write explanations that describe "How to Do Something." Here Carrie tells President Washington, whose picture is posted in the room, how to multiply with a zero in the multiplier:

$$3764 \times 70 = 368480$$

Mr. Washington I would like to tell you how to do the math problem above. First, you don't multiply the zero, you just write it under the problem in the one place. You do multiply the next number which in this case is a seven (7). You multiply seven (7) and four (4) which is twenty-eight (28). You carry the two (2) and put the eight (8) under the line in the tens place. Next, you multiply...

The second type of writing involves students writing their own definitions, describing something new in their own familiar words.

Assignment: What is a ray?

a ray is a line that goes for ever from one side of its endpoint.

— Emmanuel

a ray is a line that go's one way for ever and the other side stays in place

— Jeff

The third type of writing is "trouble shooting" in which students explain their errors on homework or quizzes.

I missed this problem because I put forty-two down on seven times seven instead of forty -Nine.

— Angela

① I missed it because I used my calculator and it was rong

— Yvonne

I made my mistake by multiplying instead adding

— Tiffany

FIGURE 10-2
Writing to assess mathematical thinking

Source: From "Writing to Learn Math" (pp. 828–833) by Christine Sabray Evans, *Language Arts, 61*(8). Reprinted by permission of the National Council of Teachers of English.

territory. Upon completion of the common work, each student identifies his or her contribution to the effort. Students are taught to monitor their own progress and devise their own remediation, although the progress of each student is the concern of all in the classroom.

Dialogue, debriefing, and planning sessions are opportunities for assessment and for effecting cognitive change as are students' contradictory thoughts and contradictions in the thinking among members of the class. Writing workshops and other occasions offer models by the teacher, visiting experts, and students themselves.

As an example of how teachers can respond to a student's need for alternative conceptions, consider the entrepreneurial curriculum Mini-Society–YESS! in which young children start and conduct their own businesses (Kourilsky, 1996). In this experiential curriculum, problems frequently arise, such as disagreements among students jointly operating a business or problems when partners are facing possible bankruptcy because prices have been set lower than costs. At this time, the teacher may conduct a debriefing with members of the class. Those with the problem first give their views regarding the situation. Then the teacher elicits from everyone possible alternative solutions, with the teacher's introducing concepts from disciplinary knowledge (the concepts of specialization and contracts in the case of problems with a partnership, as well as the concept of pricing analysis in the case of possible bankruptcy). Both of these reoccurring problems in Mini-Society and the concepts that students might use in dealing with these problems are documented in the materials that teachers use in guiding student thinking.

Peer Assessment

Peer assessment involves groups of students with and without the teacher reflecting on their work. Such assessment is a powerful way to improve the classroom experience with everybody learning something. Peer collaboration in evaluation has become a very popular movement. When teachers and students think about their own learning, teachers benefit by better understanding of their own teaching, and students benefit from midcourse corrections. Furthermore, student motivation is greater when they find out that their teacher cares about what they think. Also, after reflecting about what they know and where they are confused, students are more open to learning.

The formative benefits of peer assessment for improving both processes and products is not in doubt. Ways to make teacher and peer assessment helpful in developing competence, autonomy, and relationships have been presented in chapter 3.

A review of 48 studies of student peer assessment found that peer assessments closely resemble teacher assessments when global judgments are made based on well-understood criteria and when students own the criteria (Falchikov & Goldfinch, 2000).

Although group discussion and reports in evaluating work can have a substantive impact on students' learning, the quality makes a difference. Learning occurs as students build on each others' ideas, explain and justify the position, question their own beliefs, and seek information to resolve disagreements.

Assessment as a social activity is fairer. Students from diverse cultures perform better in situations that (a) promote cooperation and (b) encourage students to demonstrate what they know in ways comparable with their backgrounds. However, the more assessment tasks are removed from the classroom experience—as in standardized testing—the wider the achievement gap among students.

Companion Website

> For the latest on evaluation instruments, plans, and reports go to *www.prenhall.com/mcneil* and click on the OERL (Online Evaluation Resource Library) link.

CHANGES IN SUBJECT MATTER AND CHANGES IN ASSESSMENT: THE CASE OF MATH

As indicated in chapter 8, the curriculum in mathematics shifted at different times just as views about the nature of mathematics changed. From being a well-defined field of inquiry that is unchanging and that rests in a reasoning process thought to be infallible, today mathematics is seen as a way of thinking about the external world and constructing meaning based on human experiences. Accordingly, mathematics curriculum has moved away from the teaching of rigid formulas and steps to perform an algorithm and toward a problem-solving view in which students think through real-life problems and figure out what is needed to solve them. Students share their thinking with other students, and the teacher and learn several ways to represent problems and strategies for solving them. Today the elementary school math curriculum offers a range of computational procedures with more emphasis on number sense than on algorithms.

This current shift requires a change in assessment. When mathematics was well defined and its teaching straightforward, the teacher could merely assess the answer to isolated tasks that demanded mechanical mastery of "rules," "methods," and "skills." Now as students engage in real-world tasks and investigations that extend over a period of time, many forms of assessment are used, including interviews, observations, portfolios, student work, student explanations of their thinking in group work, and student participation in assessing aspects of their own mathematical power (Kuhm, Morris, & Gur, 1994). Examples of newer assessments are found in the Balanced Assessment for the Mathematics Curriculum (Balanced Assessment Project Team, 1999). These assessments offer different ways to determine what students know and can do. The assessments involve long and short tasks, basic knowledge, and problem solving; in addition, they encourage students to learn from the assessment.

There are many possibilities for assessment as students carry out their projects. In a unit on rate, for example, in which students use rate as a context for understanding fraction equivalents and for exploring number patterns and testing them for generalizability, one teacher observed students in groups and individually, asking such questions as "Can this student build a rate series? Does she use a model as a referent? Can she explain what terms in the series mean?" The teacher also asked students questions such as these: "How would you explain that to a student who hadn't learned it yet? What are you thinking as you work? How do you know you're right? What does this number stand for?" The teacher did not ask just mechanical questions but probed students' understanding in order to see how students supported their reasoning. Student writings and drawings also give teachers opportunities to determine the quality of student reasoning about problems. As students generate problems for others to do and explain their solutions to one another, they wrestle with terminology, sequences, and logic. In brief, the learning activities are embedded with opportunities for ongoing assessment of student thinking.

It is important to restate that these new assessments reflect the view that both mathematicians and students are creating knowledge—refining, challenging, and modifying older ideas. Hence, the teacher is interested in how students reason about a variety of quantitative and spatial relationships through conjecturing and discussing mathematics. As students solve real-world problems and discuss mathematics in groups, the teacher watches and listens, gaining a more complete picture of student understanding than can be gained from compiling observations from a batch of test papers. Student misconceptions can be noted by listening to student explanations, and then the teacher must decide whether to view the misconception as something that is likely to lead to error or as a road that can lead to new learning. A constructivist teacher is sensitive to errors that occur when learners are extending learned procedures to new situations—for example, trying to apply rules for changing whole numbers to decimal fractions, rules for changing common fraction symbols to decimal symbols, or overgenerating the distinctive property of arithmetic when encountering algebra. Usually the teacher doesn't draw an inference from a single response to a single task but tries to identify the misunderstanding that underlies a number of errors.

In responding to a misunderstanding, the teacher might ask students to look for connections and talk about them. For example, students may be asked to convert symbols, symbolic processes, and their corresponding referents, explaining how the symbolic procedure corresponds to action and a familiar referent. A second-grader given $38 + 6$ might be asked to create and solve a story problem with the same notation.

What is the alternative to telling the student what to do to fix a mistake? Write questions that will ascertain the student's understanding; have students work together to solve a problem, defending and modifying their reasoning; and place more importance on helping the student learn that he or she can independently figure out the difficulty and the solution. Activity 10–4 suggests some other ways to respond to a student's mathematical misunderstanding.

ACTIVITY 10–4   DEALING WITH A STUDENT'S MATHEMATICAL MISCONCEPTION

A student's computations look like this:

41	328	989	66	216
+ 9	+ 917	+ 52	+ 887	+ 13
50	1345	1141	1053	229

What will the student's answers be to these problems?

$$446 \qquad 201$$
$$+ 815 \qquad + 399$$

How will you proceed in dealing with the misconception?

- Ask the student to explain his or her procedures?
- Ask the student to use physical or other representations for the computation?
- Formulate a series of problems so that the student can discover the error?
- Ask the student to rename and regroup numbers, avoiding "carrying"?
- Ask the student to estimate answers by performing a mental calculation?
- Ask the student to monitor how he or she goes about solving the problems?
- Ask the student to give the value of particular digits as they appear in numerals (thousands, hundreds, tens, and ones)?

SUMMARY

There are several trends in assessment from a constructivist view. First is a greater inclusion in the assessment process of students, parents, and others in interpreting and judging the viability of one's thinking. The teacher is not the sole determiner of the rubrics or criteria for judging performance, and the private meanings of the individual student are contested by the learning community.

Second, assessment is for the benefit of the student, not for the gaining of control and compliance from the student.

Third, teachers have many opportunities to assess student learning and to give feedback by listening and observing students as they seek answers to their own questions and pursue their own goals and as they explain and justify their thinking.

Fourth, assessment takes place as students use their thinking in real-life problems and projects as opposed to responding to decontextualized problems of the standardized test.

QUESTIONS FOR DISCUSSION

1. Consider tests that don't focus on learning but serve other purposes:
   a. Gaining control over others
   b. Selecting and sorting students
   What are the characteristics of these tests?
2. The workplace is going to the "team concept" in which "Alpine rules" apply: All make it to the top or no one does. How might this trend influence assessment in the classroom?
3. When you choose a doctor, lawyer, barber, or anyone else in a service profession, why aren't you interested in the person's test scores? What are you interested in knowing about these practitioners? How might your answer suggest needed revision in school assessment?
4. What are the consequences of assessment that
   a. rewards student effort?
   b. recognizes growth in performance?
   c. distributes students on a normal curve?
5. What kind of assessment follows from recognizing that students can express learning achievements in unique ways versus expecting all students to show what they have learned by responding to a common problem with a single procedure for solving the problem?

REFERENCES

Balanced Assessment Project Team. (1999). *Balancing assessment for the mathematics curriculum*. White Plains, NY: Seymour.

Falchikov, N., & Goldfinch, J. (2000). Students peer assessment in higher education: A meta analysis comparing peer and teacher marks. *Review of Educational Research, 70*(3), 287–323.

Greenleaf, C. L., Schroenbach, R., Cziko, C., & Muefther, F. L. (2000, Spring). Apprenticing adolescent readers to academic literacy. *Harvard Educational Review, 71*(1), pp. 79–129.

Jenkins, C. B. (1996). *Inside the writing portfolio: What we need to know to assess children's writing*. Portsmouth, MA: Heinemann.

Kourilsky, M. (1996). *Mini-Society-YESS! Experiencing the real world in the classroom*. Kansas City, MO: Center for Entrepreneurial Leadership.

Kuhm, G., Morris, K., & Gur, V. (1994). *Middle grades mathematics textbook: A benchmark evaluation*. Washington, DC: American Association for the Advancement of Science.

Lamott, A. (1994). *Bird by bird: Some instruction on writing and life*. New York: Pantheon.

National Research Council. (2001). *Knowing what students know—The science and design of educational assessment*. Washington, DC: National Academy Press.

Stake, R. E. (1995). The invalidity of standardized testing for measuring mathematics achievement. In T. A. Romberg (Ed.), *Reform in school mathematics and authentic assessment* (pp. 374–392). Albany: State University of New York Press.

Webb, N. L. (1992). Knowledge of mathematics: A step toward a theory. In D. C. Grouws (Ed.), *Handbook of research in mathematics teaching and learning* (pp. 661–667). New York: Macmillan.

6

Curriculum Materials as Opportunities for Curriculum Development

Technology is getting the attention, but the textbook reigns supreme. New CD-ROMs blaze trails through outer space, time, and the rain forest. Internet material on all subjects proliferate, while electronic mail lets students communicate with experts and distant peers in problem-solving networks. Multimedia systems provide simulations and video explanations related to theoretical principles. However, all is not well.

CD-ROMs on the rain forest may involve playing 14 different computer games built loosely around forest concepts (if you can't beat 'em, join 'em), and they lack the depth and richness of even film clips or the photography in textbooks. Students enjoy visiting those Internet sites that have images but avoid those with text. Just as in the old days when they went to the library, students find it difficult to understand the sources needed for their investigations.

Some teachers are reluctant to give up their role of knowledge provider and would dislike students saying, "She doesn't teach us anymore. She only helps us learn." Like teachers of the past who found it difficult to incorporate radio, films, and TV, some teachers are uncertain how to fit the new materials and technologies to the opportune moment and accommodate them in the time constraints of the classroom.

Obviously, giant strides have been made in using technology for curriculum purposes. Drill and practice have been minimized in new multimedia materials, and there is much more collaboration, simulation, and application to real-world problems. Some teachers see how technology can contribute to students' creativity and personal development and to their problem-solving and design skills. Using technology does not just mean providing students with knowledge and skills for the workplace.

In all this, however, it is the textbook that remains vital. Newspaper accounts of textbook shortages create panic among teachers and politicians. Is it because textbooks contain the official knowledge for preserving the social order, institutions, and power? Are textbooks the real curriculum—the scope and sequence of information that is to be transmitted to particular grade levels? Is it that textbook publishing is big business that must be maintained? Do teachers feel lost without a textbook or a teacher's guide? What do the teachers and students learn from textbooks? Are textbooks necessary for independent learning and supplementing the meager resources that might be available in the home? Are textbooks boring and insulting to students? Would it be better for students at all levels to write their own texts? Why do 9 out of 10 teachers say every child should have use of a textbook, and 7 out of 10 use a textbook weekly and most want *better*, not fewer, books? The chapters to follow should shed light on some of these questions and show how teachers and students mediate materials for their own purpose and understanding.

CHAPTER **11**

SELECTING CURRICULUM MATERIALS: TECHNOLOGY AND TEXTBOOKS

Sara: Isn't the showing of videos a cop-out for a lazy teacher, and why is "textbook teacher" a derogatory expression?

Merl: Just because someone uses a hammer to hit a person on the head, we don't throw away hammers.

Sara and Merl, like most teachers, have different degrees of freedom regarding the selection of curricular materials—computers, videos, textbooks—and how to use them. Although Part 1 presented factors that are impinging on the roles of teachers in curriculum, two forces, which may be contradictory, are influencing teachers' selection and use of materials. The accountability movement leads to prescribed texts and codified knowledge for all learners. At the same time, economic interests are promoting the use of technology in the curriculum that may further student self-directed learning, networking, access to a wide range of cultural knowledge, and perhaps social activism. Business and the government have moved technology into schools, especially computers and their associated devices, in the belief that the information revolution is what is keeping the economy going and that schools must do all they can to prepare students for using technologies as a way to increase their productivity as workers and to maintain national prosperity or at least increase consumer demand for technological products and services. Economists cite the fact that 2% or 3% gains each year in workers' productivity produced in the 1990s (worth billions of dollars and thought to be responsible for full employment and low inflation) occurred because companies increased their investments in computer-based information technologies, including the Internet.

School reformers see technology challenging (a) the organization of schools—more efficient school management (e.g., assessing teachers' performance via electronic portfolios); (b) the role of teachers (e.g., replacing teachers with computer tutoring and individualized assessment of learning); (c) the very concept of schools and curriculum when students pursue on-line their own competency goals without regard for diplomas, degrees, or prescribed courses and home schooling and for-profit groups compete for resources and students.

Within this background, chapter 11 focuses on how teachers can choose technology (both new—computers and associated technologies—and old—textbooks) and serve human values and educational purposes beyond economic interests. A subsequent chapter will describe how teachers adapt curriculum materials to support their visions in practical ways.

CONSIDERATIONS IN CHOOSING AND USING EDUCATIONAL TECHNOLOGY

Kerr (1999) proposes four essential human concerns that technology might address:

1. The acquisition of knowledge as a tool for self-understanding and liberation
2. Self-esteem and a feeling of self-worth
3. Respect for others with different values and characteristics
4. A willingness to participate in the affairs of a democratic world

In his survey of technology in the classroom, Kerr cautions using technology as a toy and an environment that presents the world as simple and controllable. His specific points include these:

- *Spreadsheets*—These may limit assessment of human thoughts and actions.

- *Word processing and desk-top publishing*—This pair may overemphasize details of composition—grammar and layouts—and put presentation over clarity.

- *Databases and hypermedia*—These tools may limit students' specifying a given database software, restricting the kinds of formats of information that can be entered. In addition, quantities of data may be confused with quality, disregarding the work that can be done with it.

- *Hypermedia* (combined video, text, graphic, music, and animation)—such technology may allow the user to follow links among the information, but it might also prespecify the links.

- *Computer and networking*—As students connect locally and around the world, the value and purpose of the links should be considered in advance.

- *Instructional programs and computer-assisted instruction (CAI)*—Many "electronic workbooks" are print materials transferred to the screen and used to limit student responses to the prespecified categories by which information is organized, predigested, and reduced to the elements of concern to an invisible instructor, which might indicate to the student that the world is reducible to such elements.

- *Simulations*—Constraints in working with simulations are subtle but can be overcome by the teacher making sure that students know that simulations are not reality and may not reflect the way the real world works. The variables chosen and their interactions may reflect the value of the designer more than reality. Also, the simulation may end like a game with a score, unlike real life.

- *Multimedia and graphics*—A problem with these approaches is that they convey that the world should be presented as entertaining and exciting. They also limit the amount of other information which the user can access.

Kerr is not opposed to these technologies. He recognizes how students can benefit from them if they are chosen and used to develop individual capabilities in a social context but believes that educational ends should be the criteria for their selection and use.

Teachers have been classified according to their levels of capacity in curriculum development. One scheme proposes the following levels (Silberstein, cited by Ariav, 1991, p. 187):

- *Level 1—Autonomous consumers*—teachers who can use ready-made curriculum materials such as software and textbooks (These teachers know how to assess and select materials and how to adapt materials to particular teaching situations.)

- *Level 2—Consumer developers*—teachers who can develop materials of limited scope to supplement and enrich ready-made materials

- *Level 3—Autonomous developers*—teachers who can plan, design, and develop an entire course of study, often in areas with no or few existing materials

There is no assurance, of course, that a level-3 teacher will perform at that level when working in an unfamiliar subject area and social context.

KNOWLEDGE FOR AUTONOMOUS CONSUMERS

Ball and Feiman-Nemser (1988) found that teacher education programs tend to aim at level 2 or level 3, neglecting level 1 (although the competencies of level 1 may be prerequisite for achieving the higher levels). Many teacher educators promote the idea that good teachers do not use textbooks and guides but instead develop their own materials (units of instruction and courses). In most student teaching experiences in school settings, however, novice teachers use textbooks to teach reading, math, science, social studies, and other subjects. Either their cooperating teacher expects them to use the textbooks, or they resort to the books as a way to deal with the demands of classroom teaching when they do not have the time or expertise to plan in a number of different subject areas for unfamiliar students. Not all student teachers are able to use textbooks effectively. Some follow teachers' guides, mechanically moving through activities without understanding what they are doing. Others are not sure how to adapt the textbooks appropriately.

Ball and Feiman-Nemser recommend that teacher educators consider the contextual constraints and the limits of beginning teachers' knowledge and instead of telling them not to "teach by the book," to help them learn how to teach from textbooks—to use textbooks and guides as instructional scaffolds, as tools for understanding more about a topic and how it is learned. Most textbooks and accompanying teaching manuals show ways to organize content and offer suggestions for helping novices proceed and evaluate their effectiveness. This does not mean that teacher educators must give up preparing teachers for levels 2 and 3. What student teachers learn from textbooks may help them move toward building their own units of study, units that are defensible in terms of subject matter and responsiveness to students.

Indeed, one of the most promising ways for developing teachers is to use replacement units. As the name implies, replacement units replace the textbook. These units suggest investigations and activities related to central questions and usually take 4 to 6 weeks for students to complete. Such units feature examples of student work, classroom dialogue, explanations of key concepts, and illustrations of how other teachers have responded to reoccurring situations.

An appropriate activity for student teachers is to identify the discourse of a textbook—to recognize the central questions that the text purports to answer. Experienced teachers can help them with this task and show them the significance of a topic and how to avoid getting bogged down in details. Student teachers should learn how the central questions have been treated previously in the curriculum and how the responses to these questions as given in the texts will be extended in subsequent study. This activity, of course, is an introduction to "thinking like a curriculum person."

All teachers gain from the practice of analyzing materials and accompanying guides prior to use. This analysis contributes to understanding the subject matter, offers ideas as to how to represent it, and stimulates the teacher to look at content from the learner's perspective. Typically, some of the concepts and procedures introduced in materials will be unclear to the teacher and should be clarified with the assistance of colleagues and other texts or references. New ideas for representing content often may be found in the drawings, illustrations, metaphors, examples, and activities in textbooks.

Viewing the materials from the learner's perspective is especially difficult for teachers who are unfamiliar with the intended student population. When actually using the materials with students, the new teacher needs to find out what in the learners' backgrounds might be useful in making connections to the text and to give opportunities for students to talk about their experiences with the texts. By doing this, the teacher becomes aware of student thoughts and the need for going beyond the text, and the students create new meanings for themselves and the text.

In assessing materials for the purpose of determining their potential meaning and suitability for students, teachers perform three tasks:

1. They evaluate the technical and pedagogical aspects of the materials.
2. They determine the value and assumptions about the subject matter, learners, teacher's role, and educational purposes embedded in the materials.
3. They engage in critical judgments about the material's contribution to justice, equity, and human need.

Each of these is treated in the subsequent sections in this chapter.

APPLYING TECHNICAL AND PEDAGOGICAL STANDARDS

Changes have occurred recently in the basis for judging the difficulty of materials and their value for effective learning. Few teachers today rely on the older practice of applying readability formulas, which take into account the length of sentences and the number of syllables in words but ignore connectors that make text easier to read. Increasingly, teachers attend to both *features in the text* known to affect comprehension—content difficulty, organization of ideas, author's style—

and *characteristics of the learner* that determine the appropriateness of the text for the individual student—learner's background, purpose, and interest. Teachers are more concerned about the match between the material and the learner's background of experience and whether provision can be made for developing the necessary background. Nevertheless, the words of Cronbach (1955) regarding technical and pedagogical criteria are as applicable as ever:

> Does the text create readiness for the concepts and accomplishments to be taught in subsequent grades? Does the text assist the pupil to understand why certain responses are superior to others for given aims, rather than present them as prescriptions? Does the text make provisions for realistic experience, through narration, proposal of supplementary experiences, laboratory experiences and laboratory prescriptions, so that students will be able to connect generalizations to reality? Does the text formulate explicit and transferable generalizations? Are the text explanations readable and comprehensible? Does the text provide for practice in application either by suggesting activities or by posing sensible problems in symbolic form? Do these problems call for the use of generalizations under realistic conditions and require the student to determine which principles to use as well as how to use them? Does the text provide an opportunity to use concepts from many fields of study in examining the same problems? Does the text help the learner recognize the intended outcomes from his work? Does it provide him with means of evaluating this progress along these lines? (pp. 90–91)

Framework for Pedagogical Analysis

The theoretical framework that underlies pedagogical analysis of materials holds that learners generate meaning by integrating old and new information. To be effective, materials must explicitly help learners integrate information. An analysis tool based on this framework has been developed and used effectively by teachers (Educational Development Center, 1990). This instrument requires that teachers consider how well materials provide for three phases of the learning cycle:

1. Getting students ready to learn
2. Engaging students in the learning activity
3. Having students demonstrate competence and extend their knowledge

Consider the following illustration of the criteria used in the different phases, together with samples of the kinds of strengths and weaknesses in science and social studies textbooks identified by teachers using the instrument.

Phase I: Getting Students Ready to Learn

Establishing Focus

Criterion: The material should make clear what is being learned, why it is important, and how it relates to other learning.

Findings: + "The material made explicit the relationship between previously learned concepts and upcoming content."

       − "The material rarely provided prereading activities other than an overview."

Activating Background

Criterion: Textbooks should help students activate their relevant prior knowledge.

Findings: + "Some teacher's editions suggested activities for teachers to use in activating prior knowledge."

− "There was no guidance for assessing and dealing with students' pre- or misconceptions about upcoming information."

Previewing Concepts

Criterion: The materials should separate major themes and concepts from extraneous information.

Findings: + "There were graphic organizers highlighting key concepts and their relationships."

− "There was little guidance for determining the most important information."

Phase II: Engaging Students in the Learning Activities

Active Learning and Connecting Old and New Information

Criterion: The material should help students make the connection between old and new information through active reading techniques.

Findings: + "The teacher's edition provided an extensive repertoire of activities that emphasized active learning."

− "The material promoted passive learning, teacher-directed lecturing, and silent reading."

Study Strategies

Criterion: The material should promote strategies for learning.

Findings: + "The text showed students how to construct their own graphic organizers."

− "The text relied on verbal questioning by the teacher to monitor student progress. There was no guidance in self-monitoring."

Experimental Activity

Criterion: The text should promote experimental hands-on and real-world activities.

Findings: + "The text provided a variety of hands-on learning activities offered to stimulate interest."

− "There was frequent use of hands-on activities, but mostly for reinforcement or follow-up, not to introduce new concepts or to tap prior knowledge."

Cooperative Learning Strategies

Criterion: Texts should encourage cooperative learning strategies at all phases of learning.

Findings: + "Two of the texts fostered group study, team reading, peer teaching, and culminating projects."

− "The text did not provide for small-group learning."

Phase III: Students Demonstrating Competence and Extend Knowledge

Multiple Ways to Demonstrate Mastery

Criterion: Texts should encourage having numerous opportunities for demonstrating success.

Findings: + "Some of the books showed teachers how to encourage various representations of concepts-visual, movement, musical, and other forms of intelligence."

− "Acceptable student responses were linked to single 'correct answers' and verbal and symbolic representations."

Acknowledging Diversity in Students' Strengths and Interests

Criterion: Texts should provide a variety of activities for students to demonstrate their learning.

Findings: + "There were suggestions for using role play, debates, experiments, and demonstrations as alternative ways to evaluate student learning."

− "There was little direction for using postinstructional activities."

Extending/Applying Learning

Criterion: Texts should offer approaches to apply learning in the classroom, in other educational settings, and in relevant nonschool situations.

Findings: + "The teacher's edition provided a range of activities that would relate to the local community and encourage home involvement."

– "Enrichment activities were geared to the most successful students only."

Activity 11–1 is an opportunity for you to analyze content of a textbook, software, activity booklets, or other instructional materials.

ACTIVITY 11–1   ANALYZING CURRICULUM MATERIAL FROM THE PERSPECTIVE OF A THEORY OF LEARNING

1. Select a familiar text, video, or CD-ROM (together with accompanying teacher's guide, activities, skills, test questions, or other supplementary material) or one that you might be expected to use.
2. Using the criteria developed by the Education Development Center that focus on the learning cycle (described in this chapter), analyze the strengths and weaknesses of the material in terms of the framework provided.
3. In the interest of saving time, you may decide to sample particular parts of the material.

EMBEDDED VALUES AND ASSUMPTIONS ABOUT SUBJECT MATTER, LEARNERS, TEACHERS, AND EDUCATIONAL PURPOSES

Most educational materials are efforts to shape the minds of teachers and students. The enduring effect on individuals makes critical analysis of materials a high priority for teachers.

Major Questions Texts Address

Evaluating texts requires one to recognize the major discourse, question, or issue that the text purports to address. A mathematics textbook, for example, is likely to have for its statement or implied question "What does it mean to learn mathematics?" The answers given in the text, which must be inferred from its content, may be conceptual understanding, proficiency in doing textbook problems using specified algorithms, practical application of math in everyday life, or something else.

Heather Hill, for example, analyzed a math series popular with conservatives, SAXON MATH, comparing the materials with math standards. Although she noted few differences between SAXON goals and the goals of the standards, there were great disconnects between content emphasis and pedagogy, with the standards calling for problem solving and constructive math and SAXON MATH supporting traditional teaching methods (Hill, 2001).

This same question can be raised for texts in all subject areas, and the ranges in answers given can be significant. What it means to learn art may be answered by texts that highlight art appreciation or production or expression. Some art texts may imply that art education means finding only beauty in the environment and not learning to perceive the ugly.

One may infer from particular textbooks in science that science education means developing intellectual power, or gaining familiarity with scientific information, or learning to bring a scientific perspective to social and personal problems. In answering the question "What does it mean to learn science?" some science textbooks imply that it means getting students to see science as a non-controversial field, while other textbooks imply a different answer by featuring the conflicts that exist within the scientific community and drawing attention to the controversies that rage over the social consequences arising from scientific and technological policies.

Textbook answers to the central question of what it means to study history and social studies can be found by examining the book's approach to current social problems (featured or ignored), history (simple or multiple interpretations), and stance on citizenship (passive or active).

English and language arts texts differ in their contribution to the issue of what it means to be literate. Some texts imply that it means learning basic skills and language conventions; others, that it is familiarity with the literature that unites the culture and the ability to communicate in writing; and still others, that it means making alternative interpretations and that texts, reading, and writing are for one's own purposes.

Values and Unstated Assumptions

Writers of texts promote their own values. Examination of texts in economics shows that most are biased in promoting economic freedom, private property, decentralization of government, competition, and the use of extrinsic incentives as values. The people preparing new social studies texts tend to value national identity and religion and prize the nation's unity over its diversity, except as that diversity contributes to common outlooks.

In contrasting old and new texts in math and science, one will note a change from an idealistic philosophy to a philosophy of pragmatism. Older texts assumed that a given structure or reality to the world existed and could be discovered through objective and logical methods of science and mathematics. A corollary was that the textbooks should transmit those aspects of this knowledge, particularly those favored by government. Writers of the newer science and math texts are more likely to assume that knowledge is created (not discovered) and that this knowledge reflects the values and experiences of given communities of scholars. Accordingly, some new math and science textbooks attempt to help teachers establish a classroom community that reflects the values, methods, questions, and ways of communicating (special terms as symbols) of the larger scientific and mathematical communities. Students are expected to construct knowledge as they confront problem situations, speculating and making predictions, trying their own solutions, and explaining and justifying them. Problem solving in the newer books does not involve the stereotypical textbook problems ready-made for students but problems that arise from students as they attempt to achieve their goals in the classroom. Knowledge is created as students convince their peers that their solutions are valid as supported by evidence and logic.

Assumptions about the teachers' and students' roles that underlie materials based on the constructivist perspective are in the direction of intellectual autonomy. Both teachers and students are obliged to resolve their problems for themselves, and they are not required to use any particular solution method. An undifferentiated conception of ability operates. Students are regarded as showing high ability whenever they persist in solving personally challenging problems. The teacher's role is one of framing problems and facilitating solution processes; students are expected to explain their solution methods to one another and to respect one another's efforts.

An Analysis of Art and Music Texts

May, Lantz, and Rohr (1990) have illustrated how text analysis can reveal the partisan interests served by texts, calling attention to serious omissions. In one of their analyses—that of an elementary text series in art—they found that the texts focused primarily on design elements rather than on developing the understanding that art has personal meaning to the creator. Because of the series' emphasis on art products and how they are made and used, the investigators concluded that the series presents art as a "commodity." It was clear that these texts perpetuated the myth that art means independently making a product, without regard to how the social influence or context bears on the question of beauty.

In another of May et al.'s analyses (1990)—that of a music text series—the investigators isolated patterns and themes from frequency counts, conceptual mapping, and charted content that was emphasized, underrepresented, or omitted. Among their findings were those showing that the texts presented *how* people engage in musical activities rather than *why*. Most of the musical material was historical rather than contemporary. There was an absence of controversial issues presented in and by music. The music text series avoided multiple interpretations, controversy, and the possibility of critical student discussions. The texts implied that students were incapable of understanding their own social situations or understanding different cultural contexts.

CRITICAL JUDGMENTS ABOUT EQUITY, JUSTICE, AND CONTRIBUTIONS TO HUMAN NEED

Texts, as well as other aspects of curriculum and instructional practice, can be subjected to critical analysis. In addition to the suggestions for conducting critical inquiry as given in chapter 6, many teachers wish to use the following strategy in their critical analysis of materials:

1. Show historical and political connections to the text.
2. Identify what group the material rewards and who it deprives.
3. Interpret the metaphors, images, and arguments that are present in the text.
4. Consider the different potential meanings likely to be confronted by the readers or viewers.

Historical Connections

In their attempts to uncover the historical origins of certain aspects of a text—content, format, methodology—teachers consider the social circumstances that gave rise to the features. Should they find that the same social circumstances do not exist today, then the appropriateness of the features for the present can be questioned, with a view to effecting change. For example, one can examine foreign-language texts to see the extent to which they reflect the influence of such historical needs as (a) the need for social stratification based on classical culture and mental discipline obtained through the study of literature and grammar; (b) military needs for oral competencies in a foreign language met through audiolingual procedures; or (c) the need for social integration and face-to-face communication in a second language, resulting in a natural approach involving contextual cues and genuine dialogues.

Political Connections

Wider political influence from the left on text materials became apparent with the civil rights movement of the 1960s and the increased political pressure on publishers of textbooks from groups concerned about social and personal values. Publishers have responded to controversial issues such as those concerning sex roles, religion, parent–child relations, health (AIDS and abortion), evolution, ecology, population growth, and the problems emanating from these issues in one of these three ways:

1. Avoided the issue
2. Emphasized alternative views in an attempt at balance
3. Took a firm position on the issue

State legislatures and boards of education, under pressure from minority communities and those concerned about the inclusion of women in nontraditional roles, have set policies requiring schools to use only books that fairly represent minorities and women in their content. Most states require that all textbooks pass a "legal compliance" screen before they can be considered for adoption. It should be noted, however, that many textbooks that pass the legal requirement for better representation of members of minority groups and women are faulted by minorities for their superficiality, for "tinkering," or for basically depicting of women, African Americans, Asian Americans, and Hispanic Americans in photographs and other visuals but without discussion of their real roles in history or present-day society.

May, et al. (1990) note in their textbook evaluations that ethnic or gender "representativeness" was cosmetic. Despite the introduction of diverse culture and historical contexts, the series they examined were found to be lopsided toward white, male, and Western culture. In the art textbook series, objects were stripped of their culture and historical context in the interest of analyzing the elements of design inherent in the objects. In the music textbook series, females were underrepresented and misrepresented in terms of composers, conductors, and lyrical content (e.g., women were noted for singing lullabies or as the object of men's lyrics). Although the illustrations of students were diverse by gender and culture, even incorporating a youngster with physical disabilities, these pictures were unrelated to the text (May et al., 1990).

Potential political messages of texts are recognized by those who are sensitive to the overt and implied meanings. In the late 1990s, educational authorities in Mexico faced a political crisis over a newly issued social studies text series. Much of the criticism of the series was in response to changes in the historical treatment designed to support then President Carlos Salinas's relations with the United States and his policies affecting land ownership and use. Gone from the new texts were the traditional stories such as the "Niños Heroes," cadets who died in the defense of the Castle of Chapultepec during the American invasion of Mexico in 1842. Also, the new text no longer said that the United States "took" one-third of the Mexican territory but reports only that the United States augmented its territory by 2 million square kilometers. Critics also saw a connection between the modernization plans of Salinas and the text treatment of history. Porfirio Díaz, the 19th-century Mexican dictator, was no longer portrayed as one who protected the land-owning aristocrats and enslaved the Indians. Instead, the texts praised President Díaz for his role in attracting foreign investment and promoting economic development.

In view of these and other changes in historical interpretation, many teachers in Mexico rebelled over using the official textbooks. The powerful National Union of Educational Workers, for example, asked all teachers not to restrict their teaching to the use of the new text but use their own "baggage" and alternative sources. The union also prepared its own supplementary materials.

The political importance of textbooks is shown in reports from the Russian prime minister expressing his displeasure at textbooks approved by the Education Ministry in 2001 because they paint a mostly glum picture of Russia's difficulties. He wants more emphasis on the kind of people the books are to prepare—those who can act on the value of a democratic society.

More significant, however, has been the Korean protests and threatened trade blockages against Japan over new Japanese textbooks that failed to account for treatment of Koreans by Japanese soldiers during World War II. The textbook has always been a key tool in the National interest, but as the Korean-Japanese issue illustrates, globalization and information as a commodity may cast textbooks in the direction of service to larger communities than the nation-state.

Censorship and Pressures to Include Certain Content

In the United States, advisory groups have examined textbooks for their treatment of evolution, environmental issues, religion, and ethical issues in science. Liberals have detected conservative bias and conservatives found liberal bias. Different groups have worked to censor textbooks believed to conflict with their views on religion, lifestyles, and morality.

People for the American Way, a Washington-based organization opposed to censorship, reported that attempts to censor school texts surged by 50% across the nation and that the censors were successful 40% of the time. Most frequently censored are literature texts such as *Of Mice and Men, Catcher in the Rye, The Color Purple, The Adventures of Huckleberry Finn*, and *The Grapes of Wrath*. It is noteworthy how few titles of the thousands published in the academic fields are censored. However, one can interpret this finding as evidence that censors have been effective in getting publishers to suppress controversial issues. Indeed, some teachers prefer not to use texts that are likely to be controversial.

Several points should be made regarding the use of political criteria, censorship, and its flip side—the addition of content in response to pressure from special interests:

1. *Finding bias in a textbook is not necessarily a cause for rejection of the book.* The overall merits of the textbook should be taken into account, and teachers might regard a serious omission or a questionable interpretation as an opportunity for disabusing students of the impression that a text is an absolute authority. Students can learn to question the text, to see what is missing and what needs clarifying, as well as to think about the adequacy of the content in treating the problem it purports to address. Teachers can help students see human motives in texts and learn how to separate the truth from the half-truth. Of course, the teacher and students will supplement the information and views of the biased text.

2. *Teachers have both the moral and legal authority to resist censorship.* The fundamental First Amendment principle of nonsuppression of ideas protects the teacher. The U.S. Constitution does not permit the official suppression of ideas. However, materials used in the public school must be educationally suitable; the decision to accept or reject material must not be on the basis of ideas expressed but on whether the material fosters or hinders the intellectual, emotional, and social development of students.

3. *Although particular groups have been successful in getting publishers to include information of importance to their causes*—environmentalists (rain forests), industrialists (capitalism), scientists (molecular structure), AIDS activists (AIDS),

cultural literacists (Greek mythology), and many others—inclusion of more material does not ensure that the added content will be treated in depth. In her study of American textbooks, Tyson-Bernstein (1988) concludes that the addition of topics for political reasons results in superficial treatment and the absence of the integrating concepts necessary for building student understanding. The best teacher responses to the plethora of controversial topics in textbooks are (a) to select fewer topics from the textbook to study and to relate the selected topics to a common theme, problem area, or discourse and (b) to go to other sources for additional information on the selected topics.

Activity 11–2 describes how to question a text by locating its subtexts.

ACTIVITY 11–2   FINDING SUBTEXTS IN TEXTBOOKS

Whether selecting textbooks or teaching students to question the text, teachers attend to the subtext—hidden meanings and messages that serve the author's intentions and polemics. Wineberg (1991), studying the effects of subtext, presented an excerpt from an American history textbook to eight historians and eight high school students. All were asked to verbalize their thoughts as they read the excerpt and to rank its trustworthiness as a historical source along with seven other sources, including an eyewitness account, newspaper articles, and historical fiction.

Directions

Read the following excerpt and determine the hidden meaning that the writer wants the reader to carry away. Also, evaluate the historical soundness and trustworthiness of the excerpt.

> In April 1775, General Gage, the military governor of Massachusetts, sent out a body of troops to take possession of military stores at Concord, a short distance from Boston. At Lexington, a handful of "embattled farmers," who had been tipped off by Paul Revere, barred the way. The "rebels" were ordered to disperse. They stood their ground. The English fired a volley of shots that killed eight patriots. It was not long before the swift-riding Paul Revere spread the news of this new atrocity to the neighboring colonies. The patriots of all of New England, although still a handful, were now ready to fight the English. Even in faraway North Carolina, patriots organized to resist them. (Steinberg, 1963)

ACTIVITY 11–2 *continued*

Responses of Historians and Students

You may wish to compare your reading with those of the historians and students in Wineberg's study. You probably identified the subtext as aggrandizing the heroism and resolve of the people who began the Revolutionary War on the American side and the justice of their cause. That was the subtext or latent meaning that eight historians constructed from the excerpt. They also ranked the excerpt last of the eight sources in trustworthiness. The reasons for the lack of trust centered on these points: neither the British nor the American sides ever portrayed the Minutemen as "standing their ground" or "barring the way"; the textbook author labeled the encounter at Lexington as an "atrocity" that started events, setting off associations with other "atrocities" (the Holocaust, My Lai, Cambodia); the description of the colonists went from "embattled farmers," to "rebels," to patriots—which was not in quotation marks, possibly because the author regarded them as real patriots and not rebels in a negative sense; the author appealed to the underdog by drawing a David-and-Goliath contrast ("embattled farmers versus the troops of King George"); and the text hedged on who fired the first shot, together with an implied causal relationship between the statements "The rebels stood their ground" and the "English fired a volley of shots."

The students, on the other hand, rated the passage as the most trustworthy of the eight documents. They thought the excerpt was "just reporting the facts"—the rebels were ordered to disperse and they stood their ground—straight information and a neutral account of the events at Lexington Green. Wineberg points out that although the students have strong factual knowledge of the American Revolution, they did not see the subtexts in what they read. Before students can see subtexts, they must believe they exist.

Metaphors in Critical Analysis

Metaphors and the use of analogies in the critical analysis of textbooks sometimes reveal what is not readily apparent in the textbooks and suggest new ways for helping students gain access to their content. For example, the metaphor of the machine presents an analogy between the characteristics of some textbooks and a world-view in which reality is composed of self-contained units that can be brought into relation with each other. The components are integrated and arranged in sequential order. Textbooks that present a continuum of skills and concepts and that assume a taxonomic or hierarchical ordering of content are similar to machines. Critical analyses of the learning tasks and how to sequence them have little validity; the whole is greater than the sum of its parts, and there is no optimum order for acquiring skills or concepts. The failure to account for human agencies in learning is a central criticism of programs modeled after machines.

The "story" as a metaphor is currently popular as a way of analyzing or approaching texts. A story or narrative is said to be the "natural" way to acquire meaning (Bruner, 1986). The elements of situations, characters, intentions, problems, resolutions, themes, lessons learned by the characters, and lessons generated by the readers are effective in integrating knowledge. The story metaphor carries the connotation that the presentation is but one version of something and leaves open the possibility of other accounts from different perspectives.

Viewing texts as "modern poetry" offers an analogy that is useful in suggesting what teachers must do in helping students relate to textbooks. Such poetry is highly condensed, a complex puzzle with many clues and missing pieces. Readers must infer meaning from the elements that are omitted. To the extent that textbooks resemble modern poetry, teachers should prepare students for understanding the texts. Chapter 12 deals in detail with the ways teachers mediate and adapt the text for better learning and for different goals. However, at this point, consider four problems confronted by students in understanding texts:

1. Vocabulary with which students need to become familiar, including both the denotative and connotative meanings of words in the text
2. The need to overcome the disparity between the author and student frames of reference (Teachers must mediate the mismatch between the students' world-views and those of the textbook.)
3. The need to understand the syntax of the textbook (including the particular organizational patterns and symbols used in books about different subject matters)
4. incompleteness of text

Just as the reader of modern poetry is expected to assemble the meaning of a poem in a unique way, so readers of textbooks have to be taught to find what in the text is personally significant.

THE POLITICS OF MATERIALS SELECTION

Teachers and political authorities have made their selections of curriculum materials a contested arena. Teacher unions, for example, are demanding more control of the materials used in classrooms.

Textbook Adoption

The selection of textbooks occurs at several levels. In 23 states, state boards of education list textbooks that local districts can purchase with state funds. In other states, local school boards approve books that can be used. Board adoption is for the purposes of control and focus. The state board of education in California, for instance, approves only textbooks that match the state curriculum framework and policy. Textbook selection functions as a way to support state curriculum standards and pedagogical reforms. Selection from among the different books on the approved list is usually a decision for individual schools.

Increasingly, representatives of teachers and parents participate on committees that review and recommend textbooks to the state and local boards. However, committees making recommendations often are expected to apply criteria specified by the board. Also, there is a trend to grant teachers in given schools waivers so they can obtain textbooks not on the approved list, if they show that a special student population or program requires something different.

At the elementary school level, teachers usually select, at regular intervals, a textbook series in a single content area from among the approved texts. Secondary school teachers typically make departmental decisions regarding the textbooks that will be used in the particular departments. Members of committees reviewing textbooks for possible adoption at state and local levels have been criticized for the superficiality of their reviews.

The criteria sheets are faulted for listing too many factors and failing to give more weight to the more important factors. The instruments used by such committees average 70 items (Comas, cited in Tyson-Bernstein, 1988, p. 69). Most host committees must attest that recommended texts meet legal standards; that is, they are free of partisan content and provide equal opportunity, support current scholarship, and can be adapted to a range of learning needs. Recommendations for better reviews call for making more time available for conducting the review, discussing the major issues in the curriculum under consideration and the overarching principles that subsume the details of the content, and selecting teaching strategies appropriate to content goals.

Teachers have more influence in making recommendations for textbook adoption at the local level than in statewide adoptions. The local committee is usually made up of experienced and inexperienced teachers who represent a variety of student populations and teaching conditions. Representative members of the community, parents, and, in some cases, students, serve on adoption committees, sharing their expertise and perspectives. A broadly chosen committee is necessary for defending choices in textbooks in the event those chosen are attacked by special interests.

The adoption process at the local level begins with a review of the subject matter and grade-level expectations for which the books are to be considered. Analysis of the existing curriculum ties textbooks to existing curriculum goals rather than permitting the textbooks to define the curriculum. Developing criteria for selection of books to be placed on an adoption list is a major task. The criteria presented in the first section of this chapter are recommended candidates. (See Activity 11–3 for a sample review instrument for math texts.) Other factors may

---

ACTIVITY 11–3   MODIFYING AN INSTRUMENT
FOR SELECTING A TEXTBOOK SERIES

The instrument "Rating Mathematics Texts" in Figure 11–1 was recently used by a textbook committee in evaluating mathematics texts.

1. What are the views of mathematics implied in this instrument?
2. What principles of learning are held by the authors of this instrument?
3. What would you delete or add to the instrument?

RATING MATHEMATICS TEXTBOOKS

How to Use the Rating Form

1. As a group, rank the sections I–V of the rating form in order of priority. Give a weight to each of the five sections by percentage, making sure the percentage total is 100.

2. Individuals next rate all applicable items within a section on a scale of 1–5, the lowest rating being 1 and the highest 5.

3. Total the rankings for each section.

4. Divide the total for each section by the number of items rated, and multiply the result by the assigned percentage for that section to obtain the section rating.

5. Total the section ratings for the text's final rating.

Note: Evaluate student text and teachers' manual, if available, as a unit.

Title _____

Publisher _____

Copyright Date _____

Evaluator's Name _____   Final Score [_____]

Section I—Content

_____
% weight   Section Rating
                                                                    [_____]

1. Problem solving and problem-solving strategies are placed throughout the book.   _____

2. Realistic and everyday situations are reflected in the problems.   _____

3. Mental arithmetic and techniques for estimating and checking the reasonableness of results are developed.   _____

4. Computation skills are developed with whole numbers, decimals, fractions, and percentages without overemphasizing complicated computations.   _____

5. Geometric shapes, concepts, and properties are presented, and geometry is used in solving problems.   _____

6. Techniques for measuring and the basic concepts of measurement (unit, instrument, accuracy) are developed through activities involving distance, area, capacity, weight, time, temperature, and angles.   _____

7. Skills for constructing, reading, and interpreting tables, charts, and graphs are developed.   _____

8. Key concepts of statistics and probability are developed, giving opportunity for data collection, organization, and analysis, as well as the exploration of chance.   _____

9. The concepts of variable and the use of algebraic expressions in solving problems are developed.   _____

FIGURE 11–1
Rating mathematics textbooks

10. Exercises and investigations relate mathematics to science, art, and social studies. _____

11. Other _____ _____

_____

_____

Section II—Content Explication

_____
% weight

Section Rating
[   ]

1. Lessons often begin with open-ended problem situations that interest and challenge students, require students to formulate math problems, and stimulate creative solutions. _____

2. Some lessons are designed for students to work in small groups throughout the problem-solving process. _____

3. Representations of content are varied—verbally, numerically, graphically, geometrically, or symbolically. _____

4. There are opportunities for students to explore and explain concepts and to defend their thinking. _____

5. Students interact with each other—not just the teacher—in discussions, debates, and projects. _____

6. Other _____ _____

_____

_____

Section III—Student Activities and Assignment

_____
% weight

Section Rating
[   ]

1. A variety of operations and solutions techniques are required. _____

2. Activities require students to decide on the method of calculations to use. _____

3. Activities require students to collect data from the classroom, school, and community. _____

4. There are exercises of varying difficulty for each concept developed. _____

5. There is a balance in exercises between skill reinforcement and applications. _____

6. Other _____ _____

_____

_____

FIGURE 11–1 *continued*

Section IV—Teacher Materials (Guide or Manual)

Section Rating

_____
% weight

1. Procedures for analyzing student misconceptions are suggested.   _____
2. There are illustrations of how to integrate other content areas.   _____
3. There are illustrations of how to question, respond, clarify, and extend student learn-   _____
   ing.
4. There are suggestions for manipulatives, games, and other easy-to-use materials   _____
   that are relevant to desired outcomes.
5. There are suggestions for evaluating student understanding through class discus-   _____
   sions, written and oral explanations, and student work.
6. There are suggestions to the teachers for conducting assessment through student   _____
   portfolios, work samples, self-assessment, and complete work.

Section V—Physical Characteristics

Section Rating

_____
% weight

1. The text is attractive and identifiable as a mathematics text.   _____
2. The print size and type are suitable for the student.   _____
3. The artwork is functional and the layout is appropriate.   _____
4. The index, table of contents, and glossary will facilitate flexibility in using the text.   _____
5. The cover and binding are durable.   _____
6. There is an absence of stereotypes based on race, ethnicity, gender, or disability.   _____

_____   _____ × _____
      Total points   Number of items rated   Weight

Total rating (transfer to Final Score box on first page)

FIGURE 11–1   *continued*

be important to a particular committee—content breadth across subject matter, accuracy of content, depth of treatment, capacity to stimulate students. Fewer than 20 items should be developed, and they should be weighted according to their importance.

When comparing textbooks, committee members may reduce the factors to those on which books may differ. Bad and good examples can be taken from various textbooks to define the criteria and to use as models in making evaluations. Tryout of the evaluation instrument and procedures will reveal the need for clarification and revision, and provide an opportunity for committee members to explain and justify their views. The committee's task of evaluating textbooks can be made easier by dividing the work. Some people are better than others at assessing overall coherence, some at assessing community sensibilities, some at judging academic integrity, and others at predicting the textbook's appeal to students.

Procedures for analyzing and comparing examination copies of textbooks vary. Among the most popular strategies are these:

1. Conducting side-by-side comparisons, in which the same element in all books is compared
2. Analyzing the development of a strand or concept throughout the series
3. Checking to see whether the questions, activities, test items, methodology, and content are consistent in the materials

It is desirable for the committee to arrange for short-term tryouts in which teachers try a sample from the instructional units and report on both the specific criteria and general features. These tryouts should be conducted with a range of teachers and students.

Publishers and their representatives can be helpful to adoption committees, clarifying questions that arise before, during, and after the review.

School-Level Technology and Textbook Decisions

At the school level, formulating policy for a particular school is an opportunity for the staff to engage in curriculum inquiry. For what does the school want to be known: academic achievement, creativity, inquiry, critical thinking, or the cultivation of student interests? When agreement has been reached about the ideals or ethos that the staff envisions for the school, technology and textbooks can be evaluated for their possible contribution to this ethos and to other important goals.

A decision should be made about how the technology and textbooks are to be used: as a classroom set or as common resources to be drawn on whenever a particular class is pursuing an inquiry. The sharing of media and text allows for the selection of multiple textbooks and other materials, increasing the resources available to students. The policy of multiple texts rests on the assumption that no single textbook is adequate for all parts of a subject curriculum or serves all students. The policy of locating textbooks at a particular center (e.g., a math and science center, a language and social science center, a music room) also increases the range of instructional materials available for a particular study. Technology and textbooks allocating content by multiple-age groups in centers can be used by many different classes throughout the school day, in contrast to the placing of books in classroom sets that are typically used only during an instructional period. Of course, other considerations (e.g., the importance of each student having his or her own textbook for homework) should be taken into account.

The school's textbook policy should be made only after reflecting on other ways than textbooks for achieving the school's goals. Trade books, periodicals, teacher-made materials, and films, and, of course, technology offer alternatives to textbooks and are cases in point. The use of other experiences—laboratory, community service, independent investigations—to teach those elements of the curriculum best taught by nontextbook activity should become part of the policy.

School faculties use similar criteria and evaluation procedures to those of textbook adoption committees, as they select texts both from titles on approved lists and from wider sources. In the interest of time constraints, only the most promising of textbooks under consideration need to be fully studied. Individual teachers may look at different textbooks in the same series or teach sample lessons from one of the textbooks. Tryouts allow teachers to find out which aspects of a textbook help them achieve their goals.

The practice of involving students is also recommended. Student rating—having students rate three textbooks dealing with a common topic—is suggested. Both teachers and students gain by seeing different interpretations of a common topic and by considering different reasons for valuing a particular book. Criteria for use in student ratings are usefulness of the text, interest level, the author's intention, and supporting evidence for the ideas presented.

Companion
Website

> For more information on textbooks, go to *www.prenhall.com/mcneil* and click on the TLL link.

SUMMARY

In evaluating technology and other curriculum materials, teachers are asked to look at them as more than tools for improving what they are presently doing and instead rethink what they are trying to achieve with students. What are the purposes of education? Use the answers to this question as criteria for selecting and using materials.

Analysis of technology and other curriculum materials means more than attending to features and upgrades and regarding the materials only as additional resources. Analysis is also more than attending to copyright dates, the attractiveness of texts, the representations, illustrations, and other surface features. New tools of analysis include the following:

1. Pedagogical criteria that put student learning above ease of teaching and that reflect the constructivist view that materials should be designed to encourage student interaction with the text and the creation of meanings, rather than to transmit information to passive learners
2. Critical criteria that direct attention to ideologies implicit in materials, including assumptions regarding knowledge (fixed or fluid), cultural values (dominant or diverse), and authority (text, teacher, or classroom community)
3. The stance taken in regard to the central question with which the text purports to deal (The connection of the material to the economic and political interests in the larger context are part of the analysis.)

Textbook adoption policies by state and local boards of education are viewed as attempts at curriculum control. Through the adoption process, policymakers send their messages about what should be taught. There is more teacher participation in textbook selection committees than in the past, and boards of education are more disposed to grant waivers to schools and teachers to select books not on approved lists in order to meet the needs of special programs and students. The setting of a technology and textbook policy by teachers at the individual school site is an opportunity for curriculum dialogue and justification for decisions about what should be taught and how. Guidelines for effecting the policy have been presented.

QUESTIONS FOR DISCUSSION

1. What changes in curriculum would you like to see technologies bring about?
2. In what circumstances would one seek a textbook characterized by breadth of topics, events, and wide perspective rather than a textbook offering deep treatment of a few topics?
3. There is no evidence that "better" textbooks find their way into classrooms where there are state adoptions as opposed to local choice. How do you account for the failure to find differences?
4. Should teachers have the freedom to choose technologies and textbooks without restriction, or should they have to choose from among titles that are on the board-approved lists? Why or why not?
5. In your classroom, would you rather have 40 copies of the same textbook in a subject area or 40 copies made up of different textbooks in the same area? Why? How would you teach differently under the two conditions?
6. In rank order, list your five most important criteria to use in selecting materials.
7. An appellate division of New York's Supreme Court ruled that a college does not have to allow community members to inspect film materials used in a

controversial sex education class. The court said that showing the materials outside the classroom with no instruction or context would have a chilling effect on academic freedom. If someone wants the material, the person should buy it or take the course. Should such a ruling apply to materials in the elementary and secondary schools?

8. What statement regarding censorship of textbooks should be included as part of an individual school's textbook policy?

REFERENCES

Ariav, T. (1991). Growth in teachers' curriculum knowledge by the process of curriculum analysis. *Journal of Curriculum and Supervision, 1*(3), 185–200.

Ball, D. L., & Feiman-Nemser, S. (1988). Using textbooks and teachers' guides: Dilemmas for beginning teachers and teacher educators. *Curriculum Inquiry, 83*(4), 401–423.

Bruner, J. (1986). *Active minds, possible worlds.* Cambridge, MA: Harvard Education Press.

Cronbach, L. J. (1955). *Text materials in modern education.* Urbana: University of Illinois Press.

Educational Development Center. (1990). *Improving textbook usability.* Conference report, Newton, MA.

Hill, H. (2001). Language arts and the integration of state standards. *AERA, 38*(2), 289–331.

Kerr, S. T.(1999). Visions of sugarplums: The future of technology, education, and the schools. In M. J. Early & K. J. Rebage (Eds.), *Issues in curriculum* (pp. 169–197). Chicago: University of Chicago Press.

May, W., Lantz, T., & Rohr S. (1990, April). *Whose content, context, and culture? Elementary art and music textbooks.* Paper presented at the meetings of American Educational Research Association, Boston, MA.

Tyson-Bernstein, H. (1988). *A conspiracy of good intentions: America's textbook fiasco.* Washington, DC: Council for Basic Education.

Wineberg, S. S. (1991). On the reading of historical texts: Notes on the breach between school and academy. *American Educational Research Journal, 28*(3), 495–519.

CHAPTER **12**

ADAPTING CURRICULUM MATERIALS

Sara: How do you use technology and textbooks?

Merl: As a constructivist, I want my students to use technologies in collaborative activities embedded in meaningful contexts—tools to do something with. As for textbooks, they are an information source, and I teach students how to access them. At other times, the text is something for the students to fight with, making and sharing alternative interpretations and whetting their critical skills.

TECHNOLOGY USE IN THE CLASSROOM

Teachers and students use technology and text materials in very different ways from what the originator of these materials envision.

Although constructivist teachers link technologies to student-generated questions, they are not in the mainstream of educational practice that continues a transmission view of teaching. Cuban (2002) estimates that only 5% of 7th to 12th grade teachers use computers imaginatively (see also Figure 12–1).

In English lessons word processing is the most frequently used technology in which students create written materials, such as stories and newsletters. The employment of e-mail in exchange conversations to complement traditional literacy is growing.

English	60%	Science	50%
Social studies	55%	Math	26%

FIGURE 12–1
Technology use in subject areas
Source: Education Week/Market Data. Retrieval/Harris Interactive Poll of Students and Technology. *Education Week, 35*, 45–48, May 10, 2001.

Some teachers have gone from being autonomous consumers to autonomous developers. For example, three teachers teamed up to design a collaboration between two classes at two schools. *Kids on the Net: Conducting Internal Research in K–8 Classrooms* tells the story of how a teacher and her class carried out a research project (Morton & Cohen, 1998). In their unit "Monsters, Mondrian and Me", pairs of students describe a picture in an e-mail message to partner students in a distant classroom. Their writing has to be clear enough that students in the distant class can re-create the picture and make their own abstract painting and self-portraits without seeing the original. In other stages of the project, students reflect on their writing and how ambiguity leads to different interpretations (Means & Golan, 1998).

Social studies teachers encourage Web browsing and CD-ROM referencing. Gathering information from the Internet is a common teacher-directed use of the computer. A few social studies teachers promote telecommunication exchange projects involving peer–peer collaboration, celebrating differences, and exploring foreign places. (Activity 12–1 explores other ways to use technology to foster collaboration.) Projects, such as the "Odyssey World Trek," feature adult teams exploring a foreign place and the opportunity for United States students to visit the team's Web site and to be challenged to think about issues of wealth and governments and to develop friendships and understanding. The team responds to some of the e-mail from students.

Science teachers use simulation software to help students visualize such concepts as molecular structure or the physics of velocity and acceleration. Teachers enhance their students' studies by projects that link with scientists involved in data collecting expeditions. The JASON Project, for example, provides telepresence connections to the Internet, whereby students communicate with scientists who are exploring coral reefs, rain forests, and other ecological sites.

Math teachers use commercially prepared spreadsheets to strengthen foundational and statistical skills, as well as simulations and games that offer real-life applications of math concepts and skills. Only recently, however, has commercial software been designed from a constructivist view, allowing students to formulate their own questions. For example, TIMA (Tools for Interactive Math Activity) helps children construct their own knowledge of whole numbers and fractions by exploring the concept of a rectangular bar in ways that are not possible with physical manipulation.

Students have little opportunity to use technology in order to express themselves through video and Web art or to use technology in addressing local problems. A review of telecommunications in the classroom supports this generalization (Fabos & Michelle, 1999; see also Figure 12–2). The report faults technology in schools as marginalizing local interests and failing to center on social criticism or to raise troubling questions about social inequities. Indeed, students are not encouraged to be critical of technology itself.

Activity 12–1 suggests ways for teachers to use collaborative activities in connection with online instruction (e.g., e-mail, chat room, bulletin boards, etc.) to enhance communication.

ACTIVITY 12–1   COLLABORATING THROUGH TECHNOLOGY

the ways to encourage collaboration through media.)est fits your situation and try it.

Reviewing and Posting an Article

ِ sked to review a different article and post their contribu- ِ onic forum. The review can be discussed and expanded ِ voicing agreement or disagreement.

Team Question

ِ nd have the team members work together in answering ِ a separate related question to pursue. Later each team ِ e class what it learned. All students are given access to ِ ibmission. Some may be chosen for class discussion.

Simulating the Workplace

The workplace can be a school. Members of a team take different roles (e.g., administrator, custodian, teacher, counselor, etc.). The software might be programmed to introduce variables not under control by the players.

Collaborative Writing

Each student writes a short paper for the class and shares it with peers who will comment on it. The paper is revised and submitted to the teacher and made available to the whole class.

One-Minute Paper

Students are assigned a topic with preparatory reading for the class. The teacher talks on the topic for a few minutes, after which students compose a 1-minute paper (two or three sentences) summarizing the topic.

Technology in schools reflects the economic roles and impact of global business interests:

■ Make English the language of commerce.

■ Have schools prepare workers for the technological work environment.

■ Exclude certain populations from the productive aspects of computers.

■ Avoid local interests and problems.

Research on assignments	98%
Write paper	91%
Do homework	62%
Visualize concept	60%
Practice what is learned	57%
Get help in homework	44%
Keep up with news	43%
Study for tests	39%
Nonschool activities	35%
Take exam	20%
Communicate with classmates about schoolwork	19%
Communicate with teacher about schoolwork	14%
Communicate with students from other towns about schoolwork	7%
Take course with students from other schools	5%

FIGURE 12–2
Student use of technology in schools

Commercial software has moved somewhat from drill-and-practice material toward constructivist models that encourage multiple strategies in problem solving and different representations of knowledge, yet a corporate press to wire the world for profit, including marketing of computers, services and material, has worked against teacher deveopment of curriculum. Teachers are more dependent than ever on technical and managerial support from companies in carrying out exchange through telecommunication (Fabos & Michelle, 1999).

The critical interest in curriculum making with respect to technology is missing. Teachers and students might correct this omission by asking who profits from telecommunication projects and making visible the invisible views of knowledge and placement of individuals by commercial software.

TEXTBOOKS IN THE CLASSROOM

Similar to new technologies, textbooks are curriculum documents that offer content and method and that follow some principles of sequencing. Different textbooks in the same field promote different educational goals and vary in their degree of specificity and prescriptiveness. However, teachers mediate the curriculum of the text in many ways. A teacher's adherence to the textbook depends on the degree to which the teacher views the text as the content authority and whether the teacher has a conviction about what should be taught.

Few teachers expect students to read textbooks in isolation from the classroom discourse. For most teachers, textbooks are instructional tools that must fit the teacher's view of the "correct" way to use the textbook: (a) follow the text, teach the text, and test the student on the text; or (b) use the text as a reference for students to draw on as they pursue their classroom investigations. Teachers are more likely to rely on the textbook as the primary definition of curriculum and single source of information in poverty areas where home and community have no other academic resources and the teacher is unaccustomed to generating knowledge from the local environment.

Using textbooks as inquiry is illustrated in the current practice of discourse synthesis, the process of integrating ideas and information from multiple texts and creating new text. In elementary classrooms, students may be asked to select, organize, and connect information from three or four textbooks related to a topic of importance to the student or groups of students. Studies of how teachers use textbooks show that most teachers do not teach strictly by the book. The teacher's own beliefs and preferences, the context in which teaching occurs, the subject matter and grade level, and the particular students in the class all make a difference in how the curriculum of the textbook is implemented.

Many teachers are making it possible for students to gain an expert's approach to accessing and learning from textbooks by following CORE, an acronym for a strategy with four elements (Chambliss & Calfee, 1998). The approach is ideal for use in reading apprenticeships, such as the Academic Literacy Course described in chapter 10. CORE presumes a community of learners working together to construct their own understandings of text. The first element, *C*, is *connect*, in which the students' background knowledge of a topic is connected to the topic of the text. The teacher elicits students' interests, prior experiences, and thinking about the topic by posing questions likely to generate interest and to give students a chance to bring their own experiences to bear as well as questions aimed at clarifying student thinking: "I don't understand. Can you explain it another way?" "Can you give me an example?" The teacher moves student interests and knowledge to what might be found in the text.

The second element (*O*), *organize*, might begin with constructing a conceptual map of ideas about a topic revealing what students know before reading. During reading, students look for patterns and other ways of adding to their conceptual map: "What is being talked about in the text?" "What questions are being answered?" Small groups may take segments of the text, extracting key facts, recognizing organizational patterns and preparing a list of questions about anything (not) found in the text. The group's findings and questions can be summarized on butcher paper under key headings. Students can then organize the information in various ways—adding and connecting their original cognitive map; making knowledge trees and graphs showing key ideas, facts, and their relations. They may find it helpful to note the organizing patterns of texts in different subject matters, themes, topics, and chronological order. They may note that some texts are organized to show cause and effect, comparisons and contrasts, problems and solutions, questions and answers, generalizations, and supporting evidence. Most students are familiar with a pattern associated with narratives—situation, character, problem, resolving the problem, success or failure, and what the character and the reader has learned.

The third element (*R*), *reflection*, gives students opportunity to review (a) what they have done in reading the text, (b) how they can use the new strategy in reading other texts, and (c) what they already knew and what has changed in their thinking.

Students may say how they will use what they have learned or what new questions they have, leading to (*E*) *extend*, in which students continue their learning of a topic.

CORE is adaptable as a single lesson involving a segment of a text, a chapter related to a unit of instruction or a complete text or multiple texts in a course (Chambliss & Calfee, 1998).

MEDIATING MATH TEXTBOOKS

In her study of textbook use in fifth-grade math classes, Stodolsky (1989) looked at the extent to which teachers followed the topics, materials, and suggestions of textbooks and accompanying teachers' manuals. She confirmed that teachers varied considerably, ranging from close adherence to extreme autonomy from the adopted math textbook. Although what was taught was almost always in the books, most teachers skipped topics and chapters and did not follow the sequence of the text. The least agreement was in the use of suggested activities from the teacher's edition. Most teachers ignored the suggestions for enrichment activities and student-centered group projects in favor of teacher-centered written and oral activities emphasizing mastery of algorithms. Teachers did not expect students to learn independently from math textbooks but rather assigned the problems in the text after instruction by the teacher. Investigation of math instruction at the secondary level also indicates that teachers are more likely to omit topics than to add them, and to make minor deviations (e.g., more drill or graphing) rather than significant changes (e.g., reorganizing the text by commencing with equations).

Widely used math textbooks of the mid-1980s rarely posed real problems. Textbooks of this period seldom gave students opportunities to symbolize, explain, hypothesize, or expand concepts. Instead the texts expected students to recall, reproduce, and iterate (Nicely, 1985). Newer math books include more suggestions for extended problem solving, and teachers like Vera Kerekes in Oakland, California, are using textbooks as the basis for entire math courses in the problem-solving mode (Kerekes, 1990). Instead of discussing functions, for example, students in Kerekes's class plot curves that represent real-life situations. Although the first example comes from the textbook, others come from the daily newspaper and the students' own experiences. Students draw different curves to show relations such as the height of a person as a function of time or income as a function of education. Each new type of function (linear, quadratic, exponential) is introduced by presenting data that students graph and use in inferring relations between variables. Strategies such as guessing, building a model, developing charts, working backward, drawing a picture, and looking for patterns are encouraged.

Increasingly, math teachers are providing activities to provoke different interpretations by students. In their discussions, students give explanations for their proposed solutions to problems. These discussions are believed to further individual construction of knowledge through analysis of conflict about concepts and resolving of contradictions. The discussions are also viewed as opportunities for the teacher to understand the mathematical thinking of the student. In a primary classroom, one child may say that a solution to addition of two-digit numbers is thinking of them as made up of 10s and 1s, while another student believes it best to count 46 ones. The idea is not to combine solution procedures to get a joint solution but to develop explanations that are meaningful to someone else and to make sense of another's attempt at solving the problem.

It takes much time to introduce newer ideas for teaching math, such as actively involving students in solving problems at concrete and abstract levels, using several representations, applying math to novel situations, inventing strategies, and assessing the reasonableness of solutions. Accordingly, teachers who want to promote these constructivist practices must alter their textbooks. There is no way that they can "cover" all the topics in the textbook if they want to "uncover" the child's thinking.

Schimalz (1990) illustrates the textbook modifications that teachers are making in response to a changing pedagogy. She recommends that when planning for the year, teachers teach first the topic in the textbook of which most members of the class are unsure, instead of starting with topic 1 of chapter 1. Next, the teacher makes an outline of topics—quarter by quarter—totally ignoring the preceding topics. A less crowded time line permits topics to be introduced at a slower pace and allows several days for students to engage in physical, verbal, and manipulative activity related to problem solving. Topics that have been skipped can be dealt with in review sequences that take place during the first 5 to 10 minutes of the day.

REPLACEMENT UNITS

A growing trend is for elementary teachers of mathematics to use units that replace what textbooks provide. Replacement units usually feature 5 weeks of instruction and address one main idea, such as multiplication or fractions. The units are models of constructivist teaching and learning. Activities in the unit engage students in thinking, reasoning, creating their own theories, investigating patterns, trying to solve problems, and justifying solutions. Most units offer challenging problem-solving situations for students to investigate, calling on ideas from several strands of mathematics—multiplication, geometry, probability, statistics, patterns, and functions.

Some of the more popular replacement units are *Math by All Means: Areas and Perimeters* (Rectanus, 1997), *Math Excursions* (Burk, Snider, & Symonds, 1992), *Seeing Fractions* (Corwin, Russell, & Tierney, 1991), and *Polyhedraville: An Investigation of Three-Dimensional Geometry* (Beyond Activities Project, 1992). Most of these units have been developed by classroom teachers. Marilyn Burns, author of many replacement units, presents samples of children's work and thinking drawn from her own teaching experiences (Burns, 1996). Similarly, *Math Excursions* (Burk et al., 1992), which offers projects and investigations that relate mathematics to children's lives and integrates other subjects, was prepared by three classroom teachers whose units reflect their search for better ways to manage math instruction. The development of these units involved extensive testing and feedback from children.

AUGMENTING SOCIAL STUDIES TEXTBOOKS

In her investigation of textbook use, Stodolsky (1989) found that social studies teachers often conduct additional activities both related and unrelated to the textbook and its content. Although the topics in the book are taught and usually taught in sequence, distinct and unrelated topics are introduced simultaneously during instruction. Unlike in math, the object of instruction in social studies extends beyond teaching discrete topics in the textbook. Also, the use of multiple sources—films, newspapers, and other texts—is much more common in social studies than in math.

Most social studies teachers use the textbook as the starting point for classroom discourse and activity. Teachers try to relate the text to real problems in the students' lives—to issues and current events. The necessity for this practice is supported by findings regarding inadequacies of social studies textbooks (Beck, McKeown, & Gromoll, 1989):

■ Assuming an unrealistic assessment of the intended learners' backgrounds for understanding the concepts and main points of the content

■ Having unclear content goals for portraying social situations

■ Giving little consideration to the messages students are to come away with

■ Offering inadequate explanations (Major concepts and events often go unexplained, and there is a lack of information that would connect facts, events, and ideas.)

Social studies teachers must decide what are the purposes of the courses for which the text is intended. Is it to be a survey course, or is it to focus in depth on several themes or concepts while ignoring many major events and personalities? Does it attempt to introduce political, economic, and intellectual aspects of society, or does it eliminate some of these areas? Should the teacher supplement the text by introducing state and local matters of importance? Aside from decisions about content, social studies teachers must decide whether the course and materials are to be used for ethical judgments and critical thinking, particularly with respect to the evaluation of evidence and the logical consequences of social actions.

RECONSTRUCTING TEXTS THROUGH READING INSTRUCTION

In his study of literature textbooks, Hillocks (1990) faulted those organized by genre or chronology for not giving students opportunity to develop critical abilities cumulatively. Disparate writers or works are clumped together by literary form or chronology, so that each work is treated as an end in itself, rather than as preparation for reading other works. Because knowledge gained about one writer is unlikely to be applicable to the next, students are unprepared for independent reading of subsequent selections and forced into the role of passive recipients of knowledge about individual writers and works. The students depend on the teacher for explanations of the content.

Hillocks (1990) describes how teachers depart from the "separate works of literature" approach, which textbooks tend to use, to provide students a chance to develop concepts for independently interpreting new works. Concepts—such as personality, the hero, courage, and justice—or genres, conventions, and levels of meaning, are the basis for studying literary selections. One teacher's sequential unit began with satire in cartoons and comic routines that used diatribe and exaggeration to ridicule the satirists' target. Then students used that knowledge to examine simple satires based on irony and to develop the understanding that irony operates through contrast. Later, students were introduced to satiric fables that depended on both exaggeration and irony and required students to interpret symbols in order to identify the targets of the satire and the reasons for the satire. Finally, more complex satiric works (e.g., *Animal Farm*) were introduced, and the students were able to construct meanings of literature for themselves, using their increased knowledge about literature.

If a teacher believes that students should generate meaning from literature and relate it to their lives, the teacher goes beyond introducing the selection itself to teaching students ways of approaching it. For example, in her treatment of literary text, one teacher taught students four things (Gudmundsdottir, 1991):

1. *Translation*—to understand the literal meaning of the selection
2. *Connotation*—to understand the symbols in the selection
3. *Interpretation*—to see how the meanings symbolized reveal the author's purpose and world-view
4. *Appreciation and evaluation*—to see how the literature has meaning for the students' own lives

In similar fashion, Wells (1990) offers five different modes of engaging with the written text:

1. Teachers help young children with the *performance mode* by attending to the alphabetical principle, syntax clues, and other linguistic conventions.
2. In teaching the *functional mode*, teachers introduce materials that will help students achieve some purpose, such as reading an instructional manual for a new product.
3. The *informational mode* is taught as students consult texts to find facts on a matter.
4. The *recreational mode* is featured as students explore a world aesthetically in enjoying the literary experience.
5. In the *epistemic* or *critical mode*, students read a text in order to understand what it *can* mean, giving their alternative interpretations and asking, "Is this text internally consistent? Does it make sense in relation to our own experiences?"

In using basal readers, teachers tend to emphasize the performance mode of engagement with a secondary emphasis on the informational. Although the stories and poems of basal readers may elicit recreational and epistemic modes, teachers frequently ask students to recover the literal meaning of these texts instead. Even with literature-based reading programs, there is more emphasis on literal comprehension and the drawing of inferences predetermined by the text or teacher than on encouraging the use of recreational and epistemic modes.

At all grade levels, teachers who employ reader response approaches in their teaching are likely to offer instruction in all modes of engagement. In primary school, such teachers engage beginners in shared story readings, in which they learn that texts represent a world that can be explored, challenged, and even improved on (epistemic and recreational reading). These teachers find that students are more motivated to master the performance mode of engagement because the students want to read for themselves. The students are willing to acquire the knowledge and strategies necessary for participating in literary discourse when made aware that texts represent an author's contribution or stance on a central discourse or issue and that they themselves have something to offer regarding this discourse, drawing on their own experiences and outlooks.

Reciprocal Teaching

In helping students learn to read for informational purposes, especially when reading in the content fields and when preparing for academic examinations and tests of comprehension, reciprocal teaching is highly successful. In this approach, the teacher models strategies for comprehending textbooks, such as summarizing main ideas from text, making predictions about what will follow after certain passages, generating questions about the text and trying to answer them, and clarifying through rereading any aspect of the text that is not understood. After the teacher models the strategies in reading a passage, students are encouraged to imitate the strategies on a subsequent passage, followed by the teacher modeling again on the next page, and so on. Initially, the teacher must prompt by definition, example, and praise as students attempt to apply the strategies. However, with a few days of experience, students are able to use strategies on new passages. Internalization of these reading strategies is of value in helping students become independent in gaining information from texts.

Reciprocal teaching occurs when teacher and students talk to one another about the meaning of a segment of text, each taking turns in leading the dialogue. The dialogue is structured to feature four strategies:

1. *Generating questions about the content.* Students ask themselves, "What questions might a teacher ask about the passage?" Then they try to answer the questions. One piece of advice is this: "If you are having a hard time thinking of a question, summarize first."
2. *Summarizing the segment.* "Remember, a summary is a short statement in your own words." "It doesn't include details."
3. *Clarifying aspects of the text.* "What doesn't make sense?"
4. *Predicting upcoming content.* Students use cues in the text and prior knowledge to answer the question "What do you think will come next?"

Both teacher and students silently read a sequence or paragraph from the textbook and then the teacher begins to model each of the strategies, indicating what must be clarified by rereading or asking someone what needs clarification, posing a question about the segment and trying to answer it (self-monitoring of comprehension), summarizing the passage, and predicting what will follow. Then the teacher and students silently read the next paragraph, followed by the students attempting to apply the four strategies with the teacher prompting as necessary and encouraging the students. Turn taking continues throughout the session. Initially, the teacher constructs paraphrases and questions for the student to mimic, "A question I would have asked would be . . . ." However, after about four to eight 30-minute sessions, students are capable of assuming the role of dialogue leader.

Often students are expected to gain particular understandings from textbooks. They are asked to study the text and obtain content knowledge on which they will be tested. This type of reading differs from reading for pleasure, or for fulfilling one's own purposes, or for creating new interpretations of text. Reciprocal teaching is a highly successful technique for helping students increase their ability to acquire knowledge from textbooks in many subject areas and learn a set of strategies that are useful in independent learning from textbooks. Indeed, it is not

ACTIVITY 12–2   IMPROVING ABILITY
TO LEARN FROM RECIPROCAL TEACHING

Demonstrate for yourself the effectiveness of reciprocal teaching by conducting the following experiment:

1. Create a pretest and posttest by generating questions about two selections from a textbook, preparing 10 questions for each selection. Five of these questions should be factual questions whose answers are directly stated in the text, and the other five should require an inference to be drawn from information in the text. Both selections should be unfamiliar to the student(s).
2. Ask the student(s) to read one of the selections and then answer the questions for that selection. Review the answers and record the number of literal questions and the number of inferential questions that were answered.
3. Conduct reciprocal teaching of the four strategies (as described in this chapter) for at least three 30-minute sessions.
4. Ask the student(s) to read the second unfamiliar selection and answer the accompanying test questions that serve as the posttest.
5. Score the posttests and compare the pretest and posttest scores, noting both the total score and separate scores for literal and inferential comprehension.

unusual for students to improve their comprehension of texts by 60 % or more after being taught the strategies through reciprocal teaching (Palincsar & Brown, 1984).

Although reciprocal teaching leads to dramatic improvement in student comprehension of text, it is important that students know they can get the same excellent results when they apply the strategies in reading other textbooks (see Activity 12–2 for some ways to determine the effectiveness of reciprocal teaching). The technique can be adapted to group instruction and peer-assisted learning.

CLARIFYING SCIENCE TEXTBOOKS

The textbook is the dominant instructional resource for the teaching of science at all levels. Books are used more often than hands-on science in the lower grades or than laboratory or field-based science learning in the upper grades. Presentations and demonstrations are still the typical way to clarify the text. Science textbooks at the elementary level present science primarily as a body of knowledge and only secondarily as a process for creating new knowledge. Topics and concepts are highlighted, and information, facts, and processes are introduced within topics.

Science textbooks at the secondary school level have been criticized for their encyclopedic coverage of topical material and heavy concentration of technical vocabulary. Furthermore, the content of these books is structured into unconnected areas of biology, chemistry, and physics. Without effort by teachers, students are unlikely to consider the social implications of science and technology or to think about the implications of these fields for their individual lives.

Some teachers introduce topics beyond those in the textbooks as electives or digressions. Such topics as oceanography and ecology may be introduced because of the teacher's interest or local influences. Teachers with higher knowledge of science ask about material not in the textbook and require students to synthesize material, while teachers with less knowledge tend to use questions that require recall of information found in the text. Without teachers' supplementing textbooks by introducing hands-on activities, projects, serious questions about the Earth's environment, and the like, the science curriculum is likely to be disconnected from real life. The textbooks themselves tend to reinforce students' conceptions of science as a fixed body of knowledge rather than an active process of inquiry into the nature of the world.

The assumption that ideas in science must be constructed by learners, not transmitted, has implications for textbook use. Teachers are now more aware of students' extant knowledge and how it conflicts with scientific frameworks. Accordingly, instead of having students read about Newton's laws, photosynthesis, molecular theory, and planetary movements, teachers first find out what students think about the phenomena to which these scientific theories relate. By taking account of students' naive conceptions, the teacher can anticipate some of the difficulties students will encounter with texts. Just by clarifying the usefulness of naive conceptions in everyday life—the sun rises and sets—and contrasting them with the nature of scientific explanations, students are better prepared to learn the latter.

Even better is an inquiry approach that challenges and builds a background of experience before reading. The inquiry begins with a focus on a problem and students pursue answers to unexplained phenomena. At the same time, they try to use evidence and logic in justifying their procedures and answers before their peers.

Consider the lesson one science teacher presented prior to reading the text. Knowing that the text would present the concept that air expands when heated and contracts when cooled, the teacher distributed materials containing a clear plastic tube, tube cap, clay, candles, matches, rulers, and some plasticene clay. Students were to examine the materials and place the open end of the capped tube over a burning candle standing in a tray of water. The students observed the water rising in the tube and then addressed the problem focus: "Why did the water rise in the tube?"

The naive explanation that water rose to replace the oxygen being used up was found to be incomplete as students found they could create a rise ranging from 35% to 50% of the volume of the tube by manipulating variables in the system, including the addition of more candles. Also, students viewed a film loop of three mice in a sealed jar that contained a burning candle. When, contrary to their predictions, the mice did not die when the burning candle went out, students inferred that oxygen remained in the jar. Then students predicted what would happen if the cap on one of the plastic tubes was replaced with a balloon and the tube placed over two or three candles set in clay anchored to form an airtight seal. The students watched as the balloon first filled with air and then contracted to the point of being sucked into the tube.

Another experiment followed, in which a small amount of liquid detergent was placed around the perimeter of the candles prior to lowering the tube. Students then speculated about the resulting bubbles, which formed on the surface of the water outside the tube and how these bubbles related to the water rise inside the tube. At this point, students were asked to explain how all the activities were related, leading to the concept that air expands when heated and contracts when cooled.

Opportunities for students to use the new concept were presented, such as predicting what would happen in such situations as placing a hard-boiled egg on top of a milk bottle containing a burning towel, opening and reopening a refrigerator door, and submerging a hot can of duplicating fluid that has steam rising from its open lid in an aquarium of cold water after replacing its cap. Only after these experiments did students turn to their textbooks to compare their observations and conclusions with the text's corresponding photos and explanations (Dantorio & Beisenherz, 1990). Activity 12–3 describes how textbooks can be adapted to specific classroom interests.

Companion
Website

For a review of technology and textbooks, go to *www.prenhall.com/mcneil* and click on the TLL(2) link.

ACTIVITY 12–3   ADAPTING THE TEXTBOOK

There are many reasons for adapting a textbook: to make the text more accessible to students, to bring different interpretations of the topics and issues addressed by the author, to better serve the local community, and to bend the text to the larger goals and purposes of the course or class.

The two processes in adapting textbooks are (a) analyzing the textbook, capturing the strengths of the material, and identifying aspects that should be mediated; or (b) deleting, substituting, adding, and reorganizing the text itself and using framing questions and activities by which students construct their own meaning from the text.

In this activity, you are asked to adapt a textbook of interest to you. You will first analyze the textbook and teacher's guide or a chapter in a textbook, if available, and then state how you will adapt this textbook in light of the analysis. Your analysis should indicate the need for adaptation and provide support for your decisions regarding the textbook and its use. You may wish to prepare your own analytical scheme or adjust the scheme suggested in this activity as necessary to make it more appropriate for a given subject matter or grade level.

Textbook Analysis

1. Consequences and stance. Compare your own purposes and goals for the course or class with the stated and implied purposes of the author of the textbook. Clues to the author's intentions may be found in the preface, introductions to the chapters, teaching and learning suggestions, problem exercises, and presentations of content. Of course, you must be clear about the purposes or major questions, problems, or concepts that are central to your course or class before identifying conceptual discrepancies. Identify the major organizational themes of concepts that bring coherence to the textbook, and reveal the author's stance and possible contributions to the discourse of the class. What is the author's approach to the subject matter? Are the treatments of topics oversimplified, incomplete, or inaccurate? What is missing?

2. Pedagogy. What are the author's assumptions about teaching and learning? What does the textbook imply about the role of the student? Does it assume active or passive learners? Are students expected to construct knowledge from information in the text or reproduce this information? Are students expected to follow the text or to discuss and evaluate it?

Is the textbook prepared as "teacher-proof" material in which question and procedures are scripted and the text is the authority for what is to be learned? Or does the textbook imply that the teacher is the intellectual authority who may construe the content for multiple purposes?

ACTIVITY 12–3   *continued*

Or does the textbook lend itself to shared authority, whereby teacher and students reorganize the book in developing their own meanings from the text and in using the content for their own purposes?

3. Situational relevance. Consider the textbook from the viewpoint of your own students and community. What is the appeal of the book for your students? How well does it match their background of experience? Does it draw on the experiences of these students? Will students have success with this textbook? Under what conditions?

To what extent are the textbook's topics, issues, and concepts relevant to the local situation? Do they serve high-priority community needs? Do they conflict with local tradition and forms of knowledge? How might the community be used both in the development of the concepts and in their application?

4. Practicality. How practical is the textbook? Consider such issues as the depth of treatment versus coverage and the time available. Does the textbook support learning in other content areas or fragment the program? What supplementary materials, if any, are required? What other sources would be more effective and efficient than the textbook in attaining class goals?

Adaptation

After completing your analysis, indicate how you will respond to the discrepancies between the text and your own class goals and purposes. What topics and activities in the text will you feature? What will you eliminate? How will you prepare students for dealing with the text? How will you find out what students already know and believe about the subject matter of the text? How will you introduce the key questions, issues, problems, or discourse of the textbook and show the connection to the discourse of the classroom? What elaborations will be necessary in clarifying the text? What alternative interpretations must be introduced to balance the author's views, to preclude overgeneralizations and to provide inquiry? How are students expected to apply the content of the text? Is there any way students can use the textbook in contributing to life in the local community?

SUMMARY

In contrast to using technology as a new bottle for old wine (e.g., worksheets on a monitor), technology can enhance learning by giving students new tools for achieving their purposes, new ways for seeing the familiar and making the invisible visible. The critical function of curriculum can also be advanced when students examine how economic and other interests detract from educational goals and learn to discern the kinds of knowledge offered by technology—what it says to them about who they are, how they should behave, and what they should value.

Similarly, in their use of textbooks, teachers and students range from those who follow scripted lessons to those who deemphasize textbook learning and instead reconstitute the text. Although much of classroom work is built about the text or based on it, what the teacher decides to emphasize or embellish makes a difference in what students learn. At the same time, the different background knowledge of students and the way students interact with the text produces new meanings and interpretations.

Of course, the nature of the subject field influences the kinds of adaptations that take place. Newer trends in adaptations, such as the replacement unit in mathematics, were presented. Teachers who foster many modes for engaging with texts and establishing a climate for discussion are more likely to succeed in introducing students to a world not immediately obvious and in helping them understand their own thinking and feelings.

QUESTIONS FOR DISCUSSION

1. Contrast the ways technologies are used by teachers with a *transmission* view of learning—whereby students are expected to receive information—with the ways technologies are used by teachers with a *constructivist* view—which encourages students to construe concepts as they interact with teacher and peers.
2. How would you use technology in the interests of the students?
3. What is behind the push for technology in the classroom? How can this pressure be channeled in the interest of education?
4. Consider a textbook with which you are familiar. How would you adapt the book for use with limited English speakers?
5. Where would you place intellectual authority in your classroom: with the text, with you, or with students and teacher as a community of discourse?
6. How do you feel about having students rewrite aspects of their textbooks for their peers, summarizing the key ideas and giving their own interpretations?

REFERENCES

Beck, I. L., McKeown, M. G., & Gromoll, E. W. (1989). Learning from social studies texts. *Cognition and Instruction, 2*(2), 99–158.

Beyond Activities Project. (1992). *Polyhedraville: An investigation of three-dimensional geometry.* Chico: California State University.

Burk, D., Snider, A., & Symonds, P. (1992). *Math excursions: Project based mathematics for second graders.* Portsmouth, NH: Heinemann.

Burns, M. (1996). *Problem solving lessons: Grades 1–6.* Sausalito, CA: Math Solutions.

Chambliss, M. J., & Calfee, R. C. (1998). *Textbooks for learning: Nurturing children's minds.* Malden, MA: Blackwell.

Corwin, R., Russell, S. J., & Tierney, C. (1991). *Seeing fractions: A unit for the upper elementary grades.* Sacramento, CA: Department of Education.

Cuban, L. (2002). *Oversold and underdeveloped: Reforming schools through technology, 1980–2000.* Cambridge, MA: Harvard University Press.

Dantorio, M., & Beisenherz, P. C. (1990). Don't just demonstrate—Motivate. *The Science Teacher, 57*(2), 27–29.

Fabos, B., & Michelle, M. D. (1999, Fall). Telecommunication in the classroom. *Review of Educational Research, 69*(2), 217–261.

Gudmundsdottir, S. G. (1991). Ways of seeing are ways of knowing: The pedagogical content knowledge of an expert English teacher. *Journal of Curriculum Studies, 25*(5), 409–421.

Hillocks, G., Jr. (1990). Literary texts in classrooms. In P. W. Jackson & S. Harouteman-Gordon (Eds.), *Eighty-ninth yearbook of the National Society for the Study of Education: Part 1. From Socrates to software: The teacher as text and the text as teacher* (p. 180). Chicago: National Society for the Study of Education.

Kerekes, V. (1990). A problem-solving approach to teaching second-year algebra. *Mathematics Teacher, 8*(6), 431–432.

Means, B., & Golan, S. (1998). *Transforming teaching and learning with multimedia technologies.* San Jose, CA: Joint Venture Silicon Valley Network.

Morton, M. J., & Cohen, A. L. (1998). *Kids on the Net: Conducting Internet research in K–8 classrooms.* Portsmouth, NH: Heineman.

Nicely, R., Jr. (1985). Higher order thinking in mathematics textbooks. *Educational Leadership, 42*, 26–30.

Palincsar, A. M., & Brown, A. (1984). Reciprocal teaching of comprehension. *Cognition and Instruction, 1*(2), 117–175.

Rectanus, C. (1997). *Math by all means: Areas and perimeters.* Sausalito, CA: Math Solutions.

Schimalz, R. (1990). The mathematics textbook: How can it serve the standards? *Arithmetic Teacher, 38*(1), 14–16.

Stodolsky, S. (1989). Is teaching really by the book? In P. W. Jackson & S. Harouteman-Gordon (Eds.), *Eighty-ninth yearbook of the National Society for the Study of Education: Part 1. From Socrates to software: The teacher as text and the text as teacher* (p. 180). Chicago: National Society for the Study of Education.

Wells, G. (1990). Talk about text: Where literacy is learned and taught. *Curriculum Inquiry, 20*(4), 369–405.

Author Index

Subject Index

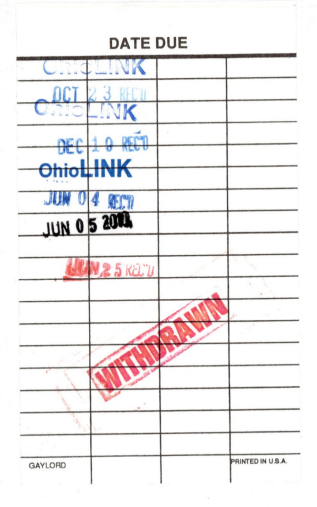